TREND IN WOMEN STUDIES

ENCYCLOPAEDIA OF WOMEN SOCIETY AND CULTURE SERIES-1

Trend in Women Studies

RAJ PRUTHI
&
BELA RANI SHARMA

ANMOL PUBLICATIONS PVT LTD
New Delhi-110 002

ANMOL PUBLICATIONS PVT LTD
4374/4B, Ansari Road, Daryaganj
New Delhi-110 002

Trend in Women Studies

First Edition 1995
Reprint : 1997
ISBN 81-7488-082-8

PRINTED IN INDIA

Published by J.L. Kumar for Anmol Publications Pvt. Ltd., New Delhi and Printed at Tarun Offset Printers, Maujpur, Delhi-53, Phone : 2260794

Acknowledgement

Some good work has been published on the otherwise neglected area of gender studies in the recent past. While compiling the present series we have collated relevant information to answer some of the present day queries pertaining to women studies. In doing so many distinguished contributors have earned our gratitude and we are deeply indebted to them.

Prof. Sheik Ali, Prof. G.C. Pande, Prof. M.N. Das, Prof. Romila Thapar, Prof. Aparna Basu, Prof. Vina Majumdar, Prof. Suvra Jaiswal, Prof. Leela Dubey, Prof. Devaki Jain, Prof. Sardamani have constantly inspired us. We are obliged to them.

Dr. (Mrs.) S. Pruthi, Dr. M. Lakshman and Dr. Neelam Khurana have facilitated the preparation of this series and we are sincerely grateful to them too.

Last but not the least, we are thankful to Shri J.L. Kumar without whose help and cooperation this series would not have seen the light of the day.

Editors

Preface

This volume *Trend in Women Studies* is an attempt to collect and collate informations from various sources on different themes so that it could serve as a repository not only to the masses but also to students, researchers, administrators and planners.

For centuries, women in India have been deliberately denied in the name of religion and ancient socio-cultural practices. The role and status of women in society can best be understood within the cultural content by the operations of various historical, political, economic and educational factors moulding the society within the framework of time and space.

Divided in eleven chapters, the book covers various areas related to women society and culture. We are very happy to place this book in the hands of our esteemed readers. Suggestions and comments for improvement of the book will be acknowledged.

Editors

Contents

1

Role of History

It was Cicero who proclaimed that 'the verdict of history is the victory of liberty.' It was more a prophecy, 'a sweet and charming illusion', than a realized experience. In fact, if at all there is any verdict of history, it is ambiguous. Its interpretation depends on the psychological bias of the social philosopher, whether he is an optimist or a pessimist, a humanitarian or a cynic, a lover of freedom or a votary of authority. The integration of related facts, or the interpretation of the course of history, depends on the historian's own prejudices and preferences. The role of history reveals what the investigator wants to read into it. However, one fact stands out clearly that 'progress and deterioration are permanent possibilities of social history' (Schiller) according as human genius or human folly predominates. Even in the case of individual master-minds is seen at times this alteration between buoyant enthusiasm for dynamism and preference for established 'proved wisdom of experience' for instance, in his *The City of God,* St. Augustine effects a retreat from the flaming individualism he exhibits in his earlier writings, *The Confessions*. The fallacious belief that progress is automatic should be exercised. No ideal can survive and progress without concerted and patient human effort. Ours is a continually changing world characterized by a living process of decay and growth. Sublime ideals and realized experiences play an equal part. 'What is' can only be bettered if 'what should be' is constantly in view. The *elan vital* of human progress is the faith in attaining the Perfect State. Perfection may be impossible but is not inconceivable. When dreams vanish, decline surely commences. Centuries after, even today, the struggle for the assertion and defence of human freedom is not at an end—and inevitably so—for the price of liberty is constant vigilance. The *elixir* of human freedom still eludes our grasp. However, there is no denying that against intermittant onslaughts, the ideal of liberty has survived and has progressed far. The same is true of woman's emancipation. The end has not been actually attained but most of the hurdles in the path have been successfully negotiated. Maybe, as Mrs Pollock says, "inspite of much progress towards equality, life remains, and will probably always remain, more difficult for a woman than for a man" (Mrs Dighton Pollock, *Women of Today*; p. 28). If a rational, not an oracular, prophecy may be hazarded, woman will be the last 'serf' to be universally freed and that will mark the crowning achievement of civilization. To suggest, as some overjealous guardians of men's interests do, that already a sort of matriarchate has materialized with the woman lording it over man is a deliberate falsehood. To think that equality of sexes has been secured is an illusion. To argue that such equality is impossible, even if it were laudable, because of biological differences is pseudo-scientific. Contrary to popular opinion, even in U.S.A., an authoritative and recent study reveals, "probably the most important conclusion....is that wives make the major adjustment in marriage" (Burgess and Cottrell, 1939). In great Britain even today equality between the sexes does not really exist. It was but recently, in 1942, that Mr Pethic Lawrence referred to one aspect of this inequality—"women have always asked two things. They have asked for opportunity and recognition and as far as opportunity is concerned it has largely come their way during the present war. When we come to recognition I confess that I do not think we have played quite fairly by them. Recognition in words is very useful and flattering: but I do not think we have altogether had recognition in deeds—deeds meaning, mainly, remuneration. We have a standard in services that has been expressed roughly as a 'two-thirds standard'—that a woman is worth financially about two-thirds of a man. We have to put women as human beings on an equal footing with men in a great many ways in which we do not put them at the present time." The Nazi and Fascist systems of Europe, as in many other aspects of human development, have retarded women's emancipation. 'Alas!

The evil that men do lives after them.' Though these totalitarian regimes have been removed, their ideas are bound to linger on for some time and strenuous effort and much time will have to be expended to undo the mischief they had done in regard to the development of woman's personality. Even in Soviet Russia, there are in recent years disturbing signs regarding the role of woman in society. We are still far away, very far away, from the *nadir* of woman's complete humanization. As Mrs Strachey says, in her introduction to the symposium *Our Freedom and its Results*, "None of the writers say that we can yet judge what it all amounts to; none of them feel that the freedom of women in society is either really achieved or really stable or that there is any clear evidence as to what its results will be when that time comes".

Treatment Accorded to Woman Since the Earliest Times

In the great majority of uncivilized peoples woman's position was far inferior to that of man. Men had proprietary rights of ownership, enjoyment and disposal over women. Religion sometimes acted to modify the despicability of her subordination ; but more often, religious faiths, superstition and the force of social custom acted still further to choke off woman's personality. Ibsen's thesis is that women are captives. His exposure of the dependent-childwife in *Nora Helmer* is something revolutionary. A fundamental truth, vital to the health of human civilization, has long been forgotten—that without the complete 'humanization'of woman no society can be truly creative. A study of woman's position in society since the primitive age reveals that all the world over it has been, in some form of other,

"The father gives the command;
The mother joins and approves:
Then children all attentive stand,
And each, obedient, moves".

Though traces of mother-right can still be discerned, the matriarchal family has been mostly pre-historic. The patriarchal family organisation has been almost the universal basis of all civilized races. The laws and conventions of the *Heroic Age* of the *Vedas* in ancient India; the Contracts and other scrappy-but-historical evidence bearing on the codes and customs in Persia, Greece and Rome, of the Semitic, Slav and early Germanic tribes, and of Arabia in Mohammed's time; the accepted rules of personal and social conduct amongst the Babylonians about 2200-1900 B.C. as handed down to us by the *Code of Hammurabi;* the classical literature of the ancient Chinese—all bring out one fact that'where civilization is beginning, the family, in some form or other, is already organized under the rule of the father'. The Indian family itself was based on a typical patriarchate. In the early Asiatic civilizations the lordship of the husband over every other member of the household was untrammelled and marriage was a semi-commercial transaction wherein the bride was either purchased for a price from her parents or guardians, or was given as a gift to please, without ascertaining her wishes; sometimes she was taken away as a captive. The 'captive' form of marriage was the earliest, almost pre-historic; the other two kinds of marriage persisted for a long time and are still widely prevalent in many lands, though in modified and varied forms. The son also was equally at the disposal of the parents. His marriage could be fixed in utter disregard of his own likes and preferences. However, we have on the authority of no less a sociologist than Hobhouse that 'the wife had certain pecuniary guarantees against arbitrary divorce, while, if ill-treated, she might leave her husband' (*Morals in Evolution*,p. 181). In the later Babylonian era, the woman was relatively a free agent, invested with a certain legal personality ;she was not denied the freedom to conduct business and commerce, to dispose of properties and to engage herself in other vocations. In the later years of independent Egyptian history, we learn from Heredotus and Sophecles, Egyptian women were remarkably independent. Polygamy was disallowed; kind treatment of the wife was enjoined on the husband; women were not debarred from even administrative and executive work ; there were even ruling princesses governing their 'Queendoms'—queens like Nitocris, Sebek Ra, Nefert, Hatasu were independent rulers of their realms owing no allegiance to any external authority! Universally, we find that motherhood was held in esteem and,'honour'to mother was an inviolable commandment. Though there was no real equality of the two sexes, in ancient Babylon as well as in Egypt and Assyria, the supreme importance of fertility was symbolized in the worship of Mother Goddess like *Ishtar* of Babilonia,—*Astarte, Phanicia* and *Isis* in Egypt. The concept of *patria potestas* was even more strongly developed in Chinese civilization. The husband was the supreme lord of the household and servilient obedience to man's will and abject surrender to man's whims was woman's privilage! Confucius, the greatest of Chinese philosophers, was himself prejudiced against women. "Women are human" said he, "but are lower than men. It is the law of nature that woman should not be allowed any will of her own." "Ignorance is the best ornament of woman" is an age-old Chinese say. The position of women has deteriorated in China through the ages. Lord Acton's (political) dictum—'all power corrupts: absolute power corrupts absolutely'—is true of all unrestrained authority. Without effective checks and balances, authority is invariably abused. When men were given such supreme sway, they swanked like little Gods and kindness and sympathy towards women were dried up. Even evil was attributed to women. The Chinese prejudice against women is typified in the silly old adage 'disorder does not come from heaven—it is produced by the women'. In the Hebrew Laws, the position of women were despicable. Very few virtues were recognized in women and they were considered as depositories of sin and malice. 'Give me any wickedness except the wickedness of a woman' was the horrible theme of Ecclesiasticus. In *Medea* (Euripides) a Greek woman bewails,

> "Surely, of creatures that have life and wit,
> We women, are of all unhappiest."

Plato was more considerate to women. While stressing woman's duties rather than her rights, he emphasizes that 'as far as the State is concerned there is no difference between the natures of man and woman'. Aristotle best expresses the ancient Greek view when he lays down that a man should rule his slaves as a despot, his children as a king, his wife as a magistrate in a free State — but 'rule' he must! In the age of the ancient Romans, *patria potestas* was highly developed. The Roman tradition was impressed by the Spartan ideals of discipline and obedience, law and order. However, the Roman matron retained her status as 'her husband's companion, counsellor and friend'. In the days of Roman glory, while in social relationships and on the moral side man and woman were equal, legally woman was utterly subject to man. In the twilight years of Roman prestige, in the aristocracy men and women were almost equal: divorce was common : *patria potestas* decayed. The Roman family was throughout monogomist. With the advance of individualism, gradually the Roman wife gained. "Family life gave her a dignity, a social importance which the Greek wife soon lost when she was shut up in the women's apartments and left public life to the Courtesans" (J.Declareuil, *Rome, the Law-giver,*). According to the law of the Lower Empire, marriage could be effected only with the consent of the spouses. Parental consent ceased to be the all-determining factor but was properly a measure of protection. Similarly the 'lordship' of the husband over the wife was transformed into 'protection'. Fidelity became a reciprocal duty. But the law of divorce became more stringent for, under Catholic influence, indissolubility of marriage was becoming widely accepted as desirable. Justinian suppressed divorce by mutual consent though, later. Justin restored it. Relaxation of the traditional codes and the propagation of the Christian faith helped to promote equality of juridical capacity between the sexes. Referring to the growth of individualism among women and the consequent loosening of family bonds, Cicero himself remarked that the guardians had passed under the guardianship of the women ! While it is true that 'morals' deteriorated in the last stages of Roman glory, particularly among the ladies of aristocratic society, it is probable that the picture presented to us is unduly blackened and one-sided. "It is true that a moral change was visible in the last centuries of the Republic; but the moralists and the historians, who are given to noting only what is abnormal, have gravely exaggerated it" (Ibid,). However, this development was confined to the rich only, who were a very small proportion of the population. While the Plebians themselves were, as a class, subordinate, the lot of the women amongst the Plebians was much worse. Class distinctions thus cut across the sex line in society so that the Patrician ladies enjoyed better privileges and social position than the men and women of the lower groups. However, even in the highest class men were superior to women.

The Arabs scandalized women as ' the whips of Satan'. Though Mohammed, the Prophet, with great wisdom, admonished "ye men: ye have rights over your wives and your wives have rights over you" he could not effect substantial reforms. He had to compromise his idealism. According to Mohammed, free divorce was legal: sympathetic and just treatment of women-folk was enjoined on all men as their duty. It is significant that Islamic Law recognizes woman's rights to property and other attributes of women's individuality, though actually in Muslim society the lot of women has not been better than in other communities. "In the Islamic system she occupies a far higher legal position than was accorded to her, even in England, until recent years, and a decidedly higher position than in many continental countries" (Ameer Ali Syed, *The legal Position of Women in Islam*). The founder of Islam entertained very progressive views regarding the position of woman as daughter, wife, mother and individual in society. Later, Abu Hanifa (founder of the great *Hanifa* school of Mussalman Law), as early as in the eighth century of the Christian era, did not preclude woman even from the office of the *Kazi* or judge. Such a right to the exercise of judicial authority is yet to be conceded to woman in even the most advanced countries. Fatima, *Lady of Light,* the Prophet's beloved daughter, followed her father into open assemblies to preach and propagate Islamic faith: in *Kitab-ul-Aghani* high praise is showered on the tambourinist Obaidah who was held in esteem by famous musicians in the reign of the *Caliphs* Mamun and Mutasim: Fazal, the poetess, Shaikha Shudha, the scholar in history, Zainat Ummul-Muwayyid, the lady jurist of renown (1146-I237 A.D.) were some of the talented ladies in the Islamic world. The Prophet ordained: 'heaven is at the feet of the mother'—and the mother was placed on a high pedestal for the offspring to revere and emulate. The primitive Germanic tribes, like the Chinese, treated woman as a perpetual ward under the dominating thumb of the man—of father, husband and son successively.

It is interesting to note that religions invariably give an honoured place to womanhood and ordain reverence to mother. Hinduism enshrines woman as the *Shakti* of *Siva,* His Eternal Half; Islam identifies woman with the *Mystery of Being;* Christianity worships Virgin Mary symbolizing all womanhood. But in effect, whatever was the intention, these have served only to delude the woman into appreciating the shining and jingling of her fetters. For very long, religious practices, engulfed in prejudice, ignorance, and superstition, worked in the reverse way and promoted reaction. The influence of the Church in shaping modern European marriage system was to make the consent of the concerned parties the only necessary condition for a valid marriage. The conquest of the primitive as well as feudal traditions by the Church was gradual and painful. The *Canon Law,* however, does not permit divorce. Even in the later Middle Ages, in Europe, the subjection of woman persisted in its crudest forms. Though woman was redeemed from the position of a drudging slave, a mere chattel to be bandied about without any volition on her part, at best her status was still as 'man's liege subject'—if that could be termed status! Then came the Reformers who defied the view of the 'Roman Church' that marriage was sacrosanct. Reformation sought to break up the Canonical view of marriage. Divorce-right was upheld by the enthusiasts of Reformation under Protestant Luther, among whom was the famous bard Milton himself. The wholesome influence of the Church or of Protestantism should not be over-rated. In fact the Christian view towards sex and woman is coloured by spurious puritanism. Christian ethics generally deplored the sexual instinct. Protestants, despite their Reformation theories, were actually as much shocked as Catholic St Paul himself at adultery or fornication on the part of women. Christianity, unlike other religions, has shown a rather ambivalent attitude towards family life. Any lapse from sexual chastity was condemned by the 'moralists' as sin. This continual insistence on virtue was instrumental in degrading woman's place in society for it became the most plausible excuse for segregating and subjugating woman on the pretence of protecting her from sin: how else could her virtue be secured? A flattering unction indeed to man's vain soul! "Woman was represented as the door of hell: as the mother of all human ills.....She should be especially ashmed of her dress, for it is the most potent instrument of the demon. Physical beauty was indeed perpetually the theme of ecclesiastical denunciation............Their essentially subordinate position was continually maintained". (W.E.H. Lecky, *History of European Morals,* Vol.II,pp.357-358.) And, as Bertrand Russel succinctly clinches, "Since the moralists were men, woman appeared as the temptress: if they had been women, man would have had this role" (*Marriage and Morals,* p.52).

Not till the close of the I9th century did the position of woman really improve. A fundamental change from the past was consummated with the passing in England of the 'Married Women's Property Acts' of I870 and I882 giving the basis for the modern conception of personal rights. Militant feminism in Great Britain and other countries was the inevitable reaction to long subjection. The recent trends are towards guaranteeing equality of civil and social status, full legal protection, rights to property and its free dispensation. In divorce, the differentiation between man and woman has been nullified. Marriage has become more a contract and less of a sacrament. Either party has an independent legal personality. The idea of proprietary ownership has been replaced by the realization of individual dignity and mutual love. These developments have not reached the 'finale' in any country in actual practice nor is this unmistakable trend uniform in all lands. However this new philosophy is truly 'ethical' while the traditional one has been 'magical' and 'irrational'.

Recognition of Common Humanity

'Woman, the measure of all things' would be a complementary and apt variation of Protagoras humanistic doctrine. Woman's place in society is one of the reliable criteria for assessing social progress. It is possible to correlate emancipation of womanhood and human development. 'Social progress can be measured with precision by the social position of the female sex' (Karl Marx). To attain the best that woman is capable of in the harmonious development of her personality, to properly discharge her functions in society,'to be herself', as it is true of man, woman must be an independent and responsible agent; her individual talents and qualities must have fullest and unhampered scope; she must be free to shape her career and her life, and it is only through such free development that the degree and measure of differentiation in the 'natural' abilities of man and woman can be realized and gauged. Full responsibility, development of individual character and fulfilment of personality are inseparable. Whatever be the theoretical conceptions in ancient, medieval and modern civilization, too long has the mere biological fact of sex blighted and seared woman's life in society. In actual life, personal and social, woman has been obliged to be a mere camp-follower under masculine *dictat*, so that women are newcomers to public life. Even today, in no part of the world are women yet equals of men. This 'Gods-mad-the-world-for-us' arrogance of men still persists. Centuries-old prejudices die hard. In many instances woman herself, through ignorance of the subconscious inhibitions of upbringing or force of habit and custom, accepts a different and unequal status in life.

Since the closing years of the nineteenth century there has been developing a new attitude of recognizing common humanity rather than the biological accident of sexual difference between man and woman. Among the philosophers and prophets of the French Revolution, Condorcet, Holbach, Holdberg were consistent advocates of the educational and citizenship equality of women. The French Revolution itself restored property and inheritance rights to daughters. Mary Astell, Catherine Macaulay, Condorcet and others assailed the educational, social and citizenship disabilities of women in contemporary European society. They demonstrated to a hesitant, superstition-and-tradition-ridden society and to a determined opposition that was actuated by self-interest and ignorant prejudice that it was urgent to remove the civil inequities and social injustices. It is the lesson of history that every righteous cause owes much, for its triumph, to a few crusading pioneers who, with uncommon moral integrity and courage, espouse and propagate it against all odds. Society, on any issue, can be roughly dichotomized into three camps—the few zealots on the one side proclaiming a new idea or faith to an incredulous or suspicious society, braving all inconveniences and sufferings; the majority of the members who hardly pause to ponder over the issues involved but are unconsciously ruled by the prevalent customs which have a long-but-none-too-hoary tradition bolstering them up ;on the other side, there is fanatical and organized opposition from a small group who want to kill the new idealism in the shell itself. When this opposition group wilts and signs of its decay are clearly visible, the common multitude are swayed away from their apathy and hesitancy and are recruited to the new camp. In the movement for the emancipation of women, Mary Wollstonecraft was one such pioneering free spirit out to break away from the ignoble past. In 1792 was published her great book, *Vindication of the Rights of Women.* To sympathetic but timid women of that age her plea appeared no better than the desire of the moth for the moon. Contemporary orthodox English society raised a quizzical eye-brow : first it was astonished and then it snarled. Many considered the writer indecent and even 'immoral'. It did not dawn on them that here was an iconoclast of false idols. She was an impetuous free-thinker who proclaimed that the shameful shackles yoking down woman—yes : all the chains—should be snapped. "The first object of laudable ambition is to obtain a character as a human being regardless of the distinction of sex". She was thus the high-priestess of common humanity and,common humanity is inconceivable without woman's freedom. Theological orthodoxy felt scandalized and put up uncompromising resistance to 'feminism'. John Stuart Mill's *subjection of Women (1869)* was another crusading denunciation of the humilations heaped on womanhood and was an earnest plea for the 'humanization of woman'. Among politicians, Disreali himself favoured women's suffrage. Richard Cobden, David Hume, Jacob Bright and John Stuart Mill were all convinced believers in women's suffrage and they fought for extending the Parliamentary franchise to women. For the first time, in November 1918, the law was passed making women eligible for election to

Parliament, while the Suffrage Movement in Great Britain came to an end only in 1928 with the recognition of complete political equality, in law, of women with men with the enactment of the Representation of the People Bill in the House of Commons by 387 votes cast in favour against a mere 10 votes; and this measure received Royal assent on 2 July 1928. Earlier in 1917, women's franchise had been extended (in part as a recognition of and concession in virtue of their war services), with a higher age limit of 30 years. During this war, again, it was a welcome sign of the change in social attitudes and also a recognition of the efficiency with which women were discharging their wartime duties when Mr.Winston Churchill assured, referring to the conscription of women for war-work under the provisions of the National Service Act of December 1941, that all women so affected 'will have exactly the same rights and safeguards as men subject to compulsory military service.' In U.S.A., in August 1920, an amendment to the Constitution was effected prescribing—'the right of the citizens in the United States to vote shall not be denied or abridged by the U.S. or, by any State on account of sex." The rigidity of the constitutional framework of U.S.A held up the legal emancipation of women for a considerable time. The American Feminist movement began in 1847. In 1848 was held the first Women's Rights Convention. The National Woman's Party was formed in 1913. The Federal Woman Suffrage Amendment became law in 1920. It is interesting to note that, even as late as in 1911, the Liberal Prime Minister of Great Britain, Mr. Asquith, was a determined opponent of the 'Feminist' agitation for the political vote and other privileges.

It was the female industrial workers who, appalled at the inhuman treatment meted out to them and to juvenile labour in the mills and factories after the Industrial Revolution, fought for the rights of women and finally obtained full access to educational and other facilities and also secured the political franchise and the complementary attributes of citizenship. About the year 1850, in Great Britain, the period when Engels published his slashing indictment *Condition of the English Working Class*, the conditions of work in mines and factories were inhuman. It was a common sight to see "women working half-naked in the coal mines ; young children dragging trucks all day in the foul atmosphere of the underground galleries; infants bound to the loom for fifteen hours in the heated air of the cotton mill and kept awake only by the overlooker's lash ; hours of labour for all, old and young, man and woman, limited only by the utmost capabilities of physical endurance." It was this degrading and exhausting drudgery that drove women, at first in sheer desperate helplessness, to rebellion against such horrid conditions of work for themselves and their kids ; then they claimed economic equality and 'human' treatment. In the years after the `French Revolution (political) and the Industrial Revolution (economic) `the street door that had bounded women' was smashed. Women's interests were no longer exclusively `personal'. Woman began to develop impersonal relationships with the larger circle of life around. Till then,

> "She had lived, we'll say,
> A harmless life, she called a virtuous life,
> A quiet life which was not life at all
> (But that, she had not lived enough to know)"
> (Elizabeth Barrett Browning)

Once the fruits of a fuller and freer life were tasted, they were too jealous in safeguarding their newly-attained freedom and extending its scope. Here was an economic cause that encouraged the women's movement in Great Britain. The growth of the ideas of political democracy was another potent influence. Towards the end of the nineteenth century, intellectual and organisational leaders maintained a consistent and determined campaign against the obvious economic and social injustices and absurdities. Bernard Shaw, Sidney Webb and Graham Wallace initiated the Fabian essays in 1889.

Woman's Inferiority Feeling and the Chivalry Complex of Men

A hundred subtle influences make the woman regard herself inferior and exclaim too often—'Oh, I am only a woman!' Inspite of their clamour for latchkeys and liberty, there has been always among women an inward feeling of a naturally inferior position. This, in part, explains the condescending social attitude towards the female and acts as a serious obstacle to the growth of women's employment. Says the Bhagavatgita 'one should uplift oneself' *(Uddharet atman atmanam).* True : it is a spiritual dictum. Its validity to the terrestrial problems and aspirations is no less. Woman's emancipation is finally in woman's hands. If woman's personality is to be vindicated, if human relationships should cease to be awry, if woman is to extricate herself from the mental prison she is in, woman should rid herself of such subconscious inhibitions and should regard herself not as a mere adjunct to someone else's desires and ideas,—a mere appendage to the apronstrings of the 'superior' male,—but as an independent person. Woman's emotions and aspirations have so long been slobbered-over by men that a mute acceptance of her dependent status in society and resignation to her 'ordained' fate have overcome her. It must be noted however that, while it is true therefore that the core of personality is the person's own conception of self, this self-estimate itself is very largely a reflection of what the others think. "Status is a factor in the determination of one's conception of the self and this conception in turn is a determinant in the behaviour of the person". (J.H.S. Bossard and E.S.Boll, *Family situations*,p.64). Without independent economic means the vindication of personality would remain only academic and remote. But, provision of independent economic rights is only the first, no doubt essential, step. Society is something more than a mere economic hive and human beings are not merely mechanical factors of production and consumption. The rights to work, to free thought and expression of opinion and the other inalienable rights of human beings, the privileges of citizenship and active partnership in a common humanity, transcend in importance the need for economic independence. Nor should this be, as Olive Schereiner sums up in her admirable book *Woman and Labour*, merely a cry for rights but should also be a demand for positive opportunities. And, if adequate opportunities are to be available in reality, there should be provided all the necessary facilities for proper training and equipment. "There is no fruit in the garden of knowledge which it is not her own determination to eat." It is essential that woman should overcome her own mental inertia. And,'to be her own woman', as Charlotte Bronte put it, is a 'painful' process.

Throughout the nineteenth century women were toasted as 'the Ladies' and 'the Ladies' were over-obssessed with deceptive notions of modesty, propriety, gentleness and obedient, good behaviour. They were proud to be clinging vine.

For the Victorian, woman was a 'clinging reed', 'a milk-white lamb that bleats for man's protection' (Keats). Woman is neither a chattel deserving of only contemptuous condescension nor an 'uncrowned queen' quite away from the common working humanity. The chivalry complex of men is as wrong as the inferiority complex of women. Segregation is segregation, whether it is in the ivory tower or in the mud-hut. Women are not 'ministering angels' who should not soil their hands with the world's dirty work. 'Noble maternity','purity of women', 'gentleness and modesty' are some of the fool's-gold expressions of this chivalry complex. Superficially, they have a plausible sound. However, this attitude violates commonsense, pampers laziness and demoralizes womanhood. It is a spurious diadem which, in truth, forges fetters for women though it may embellish the metallic polish. In effect, it only serves man's selfish ends. The picturesque plumage of the peacock hides ugly feet. On the other hand, the real chivalry is that of equal, independent, mutually-respecting beings.

Bring the Home Into the Outer World

It is often asked, if women are'let loose' on the world—that is, if they are given votes ; if they hold conferences, write newspaper articles and embroil themselves in the problems of the outer world; if they apply themselves to the study of all the arts and sciences ; if they get elected to representative and responsible places ; if they begein to administer schools and other institutions ; if they work in industrial and other employments ; if they enter the different professions; if they engage themselves in diverse avocations outside of the home; —will not motherhood deteriorate ? This smacks the unsavoury odour of the old theological concern for the virtue and chastity of woman. "Do shrimps make good mothers?" is the cynical and challenging question. A clencher, in reply, would be—. is this world man's close preserve or is this really a human world? In fact, all these developments that emancipate woman raise motherhood to a rational and, therefore, to a nobler plane because then alone can the home really participate in the life of the nation and of the human community itself. The home is then brought into the actual criss-cross current of life. Segregation is, at best, escapist : active and full participation in the eddies of the outer world really stabilizes family life and promotes harmony. "Home is the empire, the throne of woman.... Here she reigns in the legitimate power of all her united charms." It has been stated too often, almost as an inviolable law of nature. Its validity is not denied. But to make it a conclusive argument and justification for excluding woman from all non-home life, from all the activities, interests and problems of the larger world beyond the home, is arrant nonsense. In fact, this biological function of reproduction which is exclusively woman's may be made an argument for giving weighted consideration to woman in other walks of life. Childbirth involves much pain and risk to woman and 'a whim of nature' has allotted the whole of it to woman. In discussing the idea of just relationships between the sexes, the Russian writer Nemilov (1930), in his *The Biological Tragedy of Women,* points to this significant hadicap of women and urges, "it is absolutely necessary to go beyond social equality and seek such patterns of life which might alleviate the tragedy of sex." Of course to evaluate human relationships exclusively in terms of such pleasure-pain calculus is untenable. Woman has not only been caged : she has also been humiliated and scandalized. The Great Buddha himself says that secrecy, and not openness, belongs to woman. The Strindberg thesis is that women are devils : the Barrie thesis is that they are wistful : the Ethel M. Dell thesis is that they are all nurotic masochists yearning for the dominating hand of a master ! Rousseau himself who passionately bewailed 'man was born free but is everywhere in chains' could not visualize freedom and equality for women. "Girls" he wrote, "should be early subjected to restraint. This misfortune, if it is really one, is inseparable from sex"—as if woman was born in chains and should perpetually be in chains!

When biological, natural or traditional values are stressed to the eclipse of reason, enlightenment and logic, hero-worship is fostered and 'a world of hero-worhippers is a world in which women are doomed to subordination' for society takes care to see that the leader is masculine. Tradition that regards woman as a 'mystery' and man as ' an inscrutable power' is a relic of barbarism : in this scientific world it is an anachronism from a dead past. True, woman should be held in due esteem for her maternity : she should be equally, if not more, respected for her common humanity. Is man confined to fatherhood alone? Exclusive stress on maternity and denial of other purposes in life for woman renders in family the place of the husband and the children primary and positive and that of the woman dependent and wholly ancillary. Child-bearing, though it is the biological and primordial function of woman, can never be the sole role of woman in civilized society. George Meredith, almost the last of the Victorian age in Great Britain, always presented in bold outline the inherent conflict between man's customary ascendancy and woman's claims to her own rights, her urge to pursue her ideals, and her aspiration for the possession of her own soul and, when man seeks to impose his own will on woman, 'he is not merely playing the tyrant but is also playing the fool'. 'To be of any value—I must be myself'— let every woman proclaim it : this is not a mere expression of woman's egoism but is the most elementary necessity. 'Woman continues the creative work of God'. Motherhood has been and will continue to be the main channel for the creative energy of womankind. But cannot woman attain superior heights in other creative directions,— in arts, science, philosophy and literature ? The lives and doings of a Sappho, a Marie Curie, a Catherine of Sienna, a Nightingale, are adequate testimony to put the final quietus on any doubts regarding genius in woman. Such women have no doubt been few. In fact, they have been far fewer than amongst men. Why? An important cause is that, for ages, the requisite education, training and freedom necessary to cultivate and develop the innate capacities of women have been denied to them : their creative intellectual work has therefore been stunted and the world is the poorer for that.

In primitive societies, with the ascendancy of *patria potestas*, the subjection of women stemmed from man's desire to secure woman's virtue. Men feared that the purity and genuineness of family descent might be compromised if women were not rigidly confined to the home. Such subjection of the female to the behests of the male was at first physical. Men found it very convenient and so women came to be precluded from mental avocations outside of the family and the biological function became the sole end of woman's existence. This mental enslavement of women reached its worst phase in the Victorian era. "Love as a relation between men and women was ruined by a desire to make sure of the legitimacy of the children. And not only love, but the whole contribution that women can make to civilization has been stunted for the same reason" (Bertrand Russell, *Marriage and Morals,)*. If a few freaks of genius have shot forth, that has happened inspite of all these oppressive handicaps. How can the supreme authority of the father and the emotional satisfaction of the members of the family go together? To the extent *patria potestas* was the basis of family structure, parental affection was not. In fact, it is only with the lessening of *patria potestas* that the real function of the family, the cultivation of mutual love for the promotion of individual personalities, is being intensified. As MacIver says, "In the patriarchal family the adjustment of the partners to one another was imposed, if not otherwise attained, by economic necessity and social pressure. Today the necessity and the pressure have loosened and the family, no longer strongly, if rudely, cemented by extraneous functions, has to surmount in its own strength the psychological tests of its cohension" (*Society—A text-book of Sociology,)*. While obedience, even sexual gratification and the desire for offspring are being devalued, there is an `avvaluation' of the idea of mutual love and respect so that each individual member of the family—father, mother and child—may be enabled to attain the best he or she is capable of. This conception of equalitarian companionship as the basis of marriage and family is recognized and realized, more than in any other country, in the U.S.S.R and Sweden.

What if Women are More Emotional?

It is often pointed out, with a touch of derision, as a weakness in women, that women are more emotional than men. Even if the proposition were true, why should this be considered a drawback or something to be reproached? Or can it be, in any way, the *raison detre* of man's superiority and domination? It is, on the other hand, a quality that ennobles woman. That may perhaps explain why women are more generally lovers of welfare, harmony and peace. To express the idea differently, while men think, women also feel. Feeling leads to positive action to remedy the ills. The contempt for emotion is un-understandable because emotion is an expression of life itself...Are men unemotional? Why do nations then go to war and why do men hurl themselves against one another in a death-dance of destruction? Only, men's emotions seem to be less creative but more destructive. Woman's sentiments may be of a finer type. Emotions are natural instincts : it is futile and undesirable to attempt to eradicate them. Through self-restraint and enlightenment they can be tamed and raised to a higher plane to become truly purposive. Creative imagination, no less than reason itself, has been the basis of civilization. Emotion and creative genius are closely related. The contempt for emotion is nothing but preferring the burrowing mole to the singing lark. Men die 'with a blithe smile on their lips' in crusading causes and in destructive wars. This has been, in fact,'one of the commonest occupations' of men. Is it not an emotional impetus that impels them forward toward Death?

Factors Working for the Emancipation of Woman

Ethical, political, economic forces have all been working to destroy the unjust and unequal relationship between man and woman in society. Psychological influences, sociological and other facts, political doctrines, historical developments, underline all ethical consciousness : they impinge on the evolutionary process and may help or hinder any particular development. While historical facts play an important role, the effects of contemporary social institutions and ideas are no less significant in modifying, restricting or accelerating the pace of social progress. And again, in every age, there are a few free spirits, freaks of genius, who rebel impetuously against all vestiges of unreason, dogma and bondage and who, by precept and more by living their own thoughts, set up unexpected currents in social evolution. Such persons inspire several other otherwise ordinary mortals and enlist them as crusaders in a cause. The thought of mankind has always been ahead, far ahead, of human achievement. The 'prime mover' behind a great revolutionary ideal or change is rarely accidental. Often individual dreamers endowed with uncommon 'visual-mindedness' (sentimental, philosophical, artistic or emotional), which 'the world's cold thumb and finger fail to plumb', have initiated new trends of thought in humanity thus rendering possible greater achievements. As with Plato, in their 'magnificant dreams', for them their ideals themselves are fundamental realities. They keep tyrst with visionary ideals which may never materialize in full. At the same time, they do not float in thin air. They tread on Mother Earth, lead the common humanity by the hand, directing its gaze towards a better way of life and nobler purposes of existence. With single-minded devotion 'they hew the line and let the chips fall where they may' for they have a living faith in the maxim 'from low beginnings we date our winnings.' These and other imponderable factors have all been at work, through the ages, to emancipate woman.

Woman is Growing Conscious of New Values in Life

The family cult — that is, the intimate, mutual relationship between husband and wife, parents and children—has been a strong social bond in the evolution of human civilization and has proved to be the nucleus of social growth. Some loss of independence for each individual member within the family is the price requisite for this. Untrammelled *potestas* of the father was the basis of Chinese, Greek, Roman, Indian and other ancient family life. Male superiority and female subjection are not necessary for the perpetuation of the family institution—they are, on the contrary, severe handicaps in the performance of its true functions and hobble the healthy development of human society. It is a canard to say that with the freedom of woman the family will become extinct. Never in human history has the family, or for that matter any other human institution, been static. It is only inert matter that is not dynamic. A continual process of change is the expression of life itself, though the pace as well as direction of this dynamism vary from time to time, from country to country. Now marriage is considered to be successful only if the spouses mutually benefit and are happy. The mere legal registration of a wedlock, or even the bearing and rearing of children, living together and such other criteria are no longer conclusive. In the ultimate, beyond all material and objective facts, the content of happiness is psychological. With the transformation of economic life from the early simple pastoral pursuits into the mercantile and later into the complex modern industrial system, urban living has become very common : urban living is a highly individualistic type of living and the impact of social, economic and political happenings in the outside world on the family as a unit as well as on each individual mamber of the family is much more real and intense in our generation. Naturally, women also have been reacting to all the developments around them. And, with this educative experience, they have been'discovering' more and more of their own selves. The mental attitudes of the newer and younger generations are themselves different from those of their parents and sires. It is not mere security nor the smug contentment of a leisured and ignorant life limited to a narrow circle that they covet. Woman, no less than man, is after new values and ideas, new purposes in life. A touch of adventure, the disire to trace a new course in life and the wish to be distinctive fan their imagination, kindle their aspirations and brighten their hopes. Modern inventions like electricity, radio, the automobile and the movie have played no mean part in bringing about a fundamental change in the outlook of the rising generations. It may seem rather strange to many but Bertrand Russell, with no disposition whatever towards levity but in all seriousness, attributes the greater degree of social freedom and 'boy-and-girl-affairs' in America to prohibition and automobiles! Ogburn is more convincing when he maintains that, while steam was an enemy of family life by driving women from their home-crafts into large factories, the new industrial power, electricity, has proved to be a blessing to family harmony by lightening domestic work and by bringing work nearer the home. The undue concentration and localization of industry led to many social ills. Decentralization of industrial production into small units is now possible through the use of electricity.

In this quick-changing pattern of social life, all conventions, traditional beliefs and even ideals change in their relative importance and some are discarded as no longer valid. What was accepted as axiomatic a few decades ago may now be thrown to the muck-heap as of no worth. In this kaleidoscopic and complex modern economic and social life wherein competitive ambition for distinction, power, fame, wealth and uniqueness holds supreme sway, who would not raise an amused eye-brow at seemingly platitudinous gibberish? What Diederot calls'the stirring of doubt' is the characteristic of a rationalist outlook. The 'wisdom' of the past is not accepted unless it is found suitable to the changed contemporary social framework. Appeal to tradition no longer carries conviction. this then is the psychological set-up that has been inducing more and more women to challenge, nonchalantly, conventional codes of conduct and strike out their own careers. Reason has thus played a vital part in breaking down woman's subjection : women's education has been much instrumental in furthering this. Social institutions, like economic institutions, must be continuously pruned, readapted and reformed in the light of the changes in human values, needs and perspective : otherwise, in sheer desperation, the disgruntled and the reformers would join together to throw them over-board.

The State organizations have been assuming an increasingly important and extensive share of the responsibilities that have developed so long on individuals and families. In an increasing sector of economic and social life, the State is actively participating. In maternity and child welfare work, medical and health services, provision of educational facilities and employment opportunities, the State has been playing a leading role. This continually increasing interference of the State has lessened the economic functions that have been traditionally borne by the father. Also, the domestic work of house-wives has been made less burden-some and more pleasant and quicker to do. Women thus have now not only better opportunities but also more time at their disposal to do some 'non-home' work. Women take up vocational or professional work either to be economically independent or with a view to augmenting the family's total income resources:nor does society any longer look askance at this half as severely as before. In U.S.A.; in 1940, there were nearly twelve million women at such work and the figure has swelled during the war years.

The Effects of War Time Experiences

In the war period in almost all countries, particularly in countries actually war-torn, women have been drafted into different categories of work and they have discharged their 'unfeminine' duties on farms, in industry, transport and public utility services, war plants and defence works, quite ably. If not doing work is lady-like, then there have been few ladies in war-time England and in the other war-scorched lands. Housewives and mothers, grannies and girls, have all been working even in civil defence and other essential and tiresome services. "This war" wrote Tom Harrison in *The Political Quarterly* (July-September, 1942), is forcing women to notice more closely the wider implications of their environment, beyond the home, and the corner shop and the town-centre. In one sense this war is a painful process of education in citizenship and the inter-relationshisp of near and distant events." Even in slumberous China there is a new awakening among women, "The fighting record of our women does not permit us to believe" writes Madame Sun Yat Sen, "that they will ever again allow themselves to be enslaved either by a national enemy or by social reaction at home" ('Chinese Women's Fight for Freedom'—Asia—August, 1942). Can women be expected to forget all their war-time experiences and ordeals and achievements now that the war is over? Will they suddenly 'flash-black' to their pre-war life? Is such a sudden reversal to the 'normalcy' of 1938 possible in any sphere? Then, how can we expect it in regard to women alone? In Great Britain the problem has assumed such proportions as to necessitate the appointment of a Royal Commission to examine the question in its diverse aspects.

For the war-scorched countries of Europe and Asia, a season of anguish is at hand in economic and social readjustment and rehabilitation. After the last war Klaus Mann wrote "A world war lies between us and us and our fathers, a sort of revolution. The Gods have torn us apart." During and after the last war, many of the moral trappings of the old era fell away. The war that has just ended has been a worse convulsion for the old ideas, old customs and standards of the inter-war period. It was one of the world's greatest social prophets who counselled "when ye shall hear of wars and rumours of wars, be ye not troubled. These are the beginnings of the birth pangs"(Mark). War itself becomes a social institution and has far-reaching effects on society even after it is ended. The face of society itself is transformed in such 'twilight years' of ferment and popular awakening. Such revolutionary periods generate many new influences in society. If the institutional veneers are not flexible and do not readjust themselves to the changes in mental outook, in due course they may be altogether scrapped. What exactly the New Morality will be it is difficult to 'crystal-gaze' : but one thing is certain, it will be different. There is bound to be a swell of individual freedom: but if men and women are not to get intoxicated with it and if the new freedoms is not to prove dangerous it is necessary that rights should be tempered by duties and that freedom be yoked to social restraint.

2

Women and the Social Order

This enthusiastic upsurge for women's rights should not degenerate into anarchist channels challenging the very basic institutions of marriage and the family in social life. Though Bertrand Russell doubts if Patriarchal Family will continue to be important for any length of time in future and visualises the possibility of families consisting of mothers only with perfect equanimity, modern society will continue to be patrilineal (divested of patriarchal authority): marriage and family will have to survive as an integral part of the civilized social structure for, love, children and works are the sources of fertilizing contact between the individual and the rest of the world. The family is the most important primary human group, the womb of the individual and of the State itself. The family is an institution fundamental to human progress—except, perhaps in a state of anarchism: and, anarchism as a normal state of society is inconceivable. Immediately after the Communist revolution in Russia, sexual freedom in society was untrammelled. There was a dangerous confusion between woman's emancipation and break-up of the institution of family itself. It was Launa Charsky, for many years Soviet Commissar for Education, who declared "women will be entirely emancipated.... Our problem is now to do away with the household and to free women from the care of children.... There us no doubt that the terms 'my parents', 'our children', will gradually fall out of usage, being replaced by the conceptions 'old people,' 'adults', 'children', etc...." Realities have forced this initial communist idealogical outburst to retreat towards a better understanding of the real values of the parent-offspring relationship and there is now a definite bias in favour of family stability even in U.S.S.R. It should be realized, therefore, that marriage is neither a religious sacrament nor a mere prosaic contract in the market place. If the family is to serve its true function in the social framework it must be based on the bedrock of willing and enlightened cooperation and mutual respect amongst the members there of and not on an irrational servilliance of the female or of the young.

The Functions of the Family

"There are in general two sorts of forces, one personal and one institutional, which hold people together in wedlock. By the personal I mean those which spring more directly from natural impulses and may be roughly summed up as affoction and common interest in children. The institutional are those that come more from the larger organization of society, such as economic interdependence of husband and wife, or the state of public sentiment, tradition and law" (C. H. Cooley, *Social Organization,*). Many sociologists have attempted to enumerate family functions and to assess their relative importance. Ogbrun, for instance, draws a six-fold pattern—affectional, economic, recreational, religious, educational and protective. Race perpetuation, socialization, regulation of sex and economic activity are listed together by Reed. The dichotomy into biological, economic, emotional cultural functions is Mowrer's. Nimkoff's variation is—social, marital, and filial (a detailed discussion of these three broad categories is given in his *Family,* Ch.ii). Dr. Bernard mentions these functions as pertaining to the family in its role as a 'primary group' — the reproduction of legitimate offspring, protection of the offspring, socialization of these offspring, furnishing of affection and emotional security to family members. `As an institution or complex of institutions,' the family is charged with regulating the relationship between the sexes, between parents and offspring, among siblings and other relationships embraced within the family (Jessie Bernard, *American Family Behaviour,* p. 26). Groves refers to protection and care of the young, regulation of sex, conservation of culture and provision of intimate contacts. A common denominator can be seen underlying these various types of classification. Broadly it may be stated, therefore, that the institution of family is governed by three forces—the satisfaction of the sexual urge, procreation of children, companionship and understanding between the spouses. Of these, religion has invariably stressed, almost to the exclusion of others, the continuation of the human species as the basic function of marriage and family life. Since earliest times, from the proverbial Adam-and-Eve days, the sexual impulse has been a primary influence. While religion, in the East as well as in the West, has always sought to imprint on the human mind the profound conviction of the importance and dignity of chastity, 'puritanism' has always been obsessed with sexophobia. Catholic St. Paul in his *First Epistle to the Corinthians* condemns fornication as a `deadly sin' and prescribes marriage itself, `by permission and not of commandment,'as a regrettable concession to human weakness, so that adultery and fornication may be prevented. "It is good for a man not to touch a woman. Nevertheless, to avoid fornication, let every man have his own wife, and every woman have her own husband." Significantly enough, he chooses to be oblivious of the biological function of marriage and family life. Marriage only to prevent sin—what an ideal to set before humanity! The whole system of Christian ethics, Catholic as well as Protestant, is based on the trite dictum `it is better to marry than to burn' which implies a belief in the impurity of sex urge itself. St. Paul's is a noxious view of asceticism which prompts him to deprecate the sex instinct itself. Howevermuch `moralists' may deplore the development, in recent times, the sexual impulse has become more and more important in extra-marital relations and is losing its prime or motivating importance, particularly in western countries, as the sustaining force for the institution of the family.

The desire for children is now perhaps the least important and, in the more enlightened groups in the community, thinking men and women are now actuated by economic and other considerations in limiting the family size. It is not just accidental that wherever the 'totalitarian' infection spread, as in Nazi Germany, Fascist Italy and Shintoist Japan, there was a State drive for larger families and greater numbers. And now in Soviet Russia too ! One fails to understand why 'the brotherhood of the international proletariat' requires for its realization or furtherance more impressive population figures. It is only aggressive State nationalism that clamours for superior numbers. In uncivilized pastoral communities wives and offspring were desired for the labour they provided and for the other economic advantages that accrued in their wake. The very idea seems preposterous now. Parents desire children because, otherwise, there is left an important gap in family happiness. As for children themselves, without a strong family bond, their instinctive and emotional nature becomes lop-sided. The disintegration and liquidation of the family cannot be contemplated with any equanimity. A child that is deprived of the normal 'family gang' environment in its formative years is very much handicapped in life. Parents are almost universally fond of their sons and daughters. The State, on the other hand, takes a live interest in accelerating the rate of population growth because children provide the raw material for political machinations and canon fodder for militarist schemes. And this drive for population increase has become competitive !The perverted ideology of the modern nationalist State can hardly sink lower.

Co-operative Partnership is the True Basis

Be that as it may, it must be realized that the future of the institution of family depends not so much on sex gratification or the desire for children as on the adequacy or otherwise of the facilities available for community of living and thought between husband and wife and it is this urge for mutual companionship that is playing an increasing part in bringing together men and women into families. It is only when man and woman 'tone' into each other that there is happiness in a family. The most important explanation for divorce lies in a lack of this companionship. Though proof of adultery is legally necessary for granting a divorce decree, adultery has been proved to be not a major cause of divorce. Marriage refers to mating by public social sanction and subject to systematic social control. As such, marriage is human institution and is unknown in the non-human animate world : because reason is the distinguishing attitude of the *Homo Sapiens*. Offspring are the biological consequence of mating. Nimkoff distinguishes between mating and marriage and both from the family. But his thesis that without children a family is inconceivable is no truism that cannot be called into question. 'A childless family' is a fallacy of nomenclature, in his view. A married couple, living together happily for a number of years, he denies them the family status. Obviously the moment a child arrives in the household, even if it be through adoption, the family comes into being. Such a rigid limitation of the family seems to be rather untenable, particularly in view of developments in contemporary society. It is a different thing to argue that through offspring the family is stabilized and that a sterile marriage is more liable to dissolution. If mating, marriage and offspring are the three fundamentals of the family, inspite of the real and very common presence of each one of these three elements, how is it that the family as a social institution is decaying, particularly in the western countries ? Obviously, there must be some other element that is absent in a large measure and which is equally essential to the institution of the family, for no secondary or tertiary factor can be potent enough to be destructive of an institution that is bolstered up by three such primary motives. Without the solemnization of marriage and the institution of the family the sexual-impulse can be gratified and there can be procreation of children also. What distinguishes the family therefore is the bond of common interest and understanding between the husband and the wife and between the parents and the children. Through living together for some time in intimate contact they develop mutual respect, affection and a feeling of oneness. As Westermarck points out'...apart from the purely sexual instinct, conjugal affection may keep man and wife together even after their marriage has fulfilled its original aim (the act of propagation). And conjugal affection has certainly become more durable in proportion as love has been influenced by mental qualities' (*A Short History of Marriage,* p.299). The family is now under a dark cloud. If it is to be securely placed on a firm basis as an institution beneficial and indispensable to human society, the idea must become general that the family is an 'adventure' in active cooperation and not in possession, in emotional understanding and sympathy and not in emotional exploitation.

Divorce and Marriage

Roman Catholic opinion holds marriage indissoluble. But is the Christian Gospel so clear in its denunciation of divorce ? As Dr. Inge, the late Dean of St. Paul's, testified before the 1909 Royal Commission on Divorce, "the doctrine that marriage is absolutely indissoluble cannot, in my opinion, be proved from the New Testament." The Hindu Code denies the right of divorce. To deny a way of escape from impossible, frustrated and unhappy marriages equally for the woman, as for man, is irrational : for such denial would imply a negation of the fundamental truth that marriage is a social institution devised for the happiness of men and women and would render the woman a mere tool for the purposes of the institution itself. Before Christian influence imposed a more rigid view of marriage, a very free divorce code was prevalent in early Roman history and, even till the sixth century of the Christian era divorce by mutual consent persisted in Roman society substantially unaffected. Against the growing interference of the official Church in affairs of matrimony, Emperor Justin `yielded to the prayers of his unhappy subjects, and restored the liberty of divorce by mutual consent' (Gibbon,*The Decline and Fall of the Roman Empire).* But, era long, Ecclesiastical Law asserted itself over Civil Law in the domain of marriage and, in the eighth century, Emperor Leo repealed Justin's legislation. From that time only Ecclesiastical—that is, indissoluble—marriages became legitimate and the idea of divorce was all but repudiated. Since 1100 A.D. Gratian and the other Canonists and Divines made a `mess' of the law of marriage. They swore by eternal fidelity—'whom God hath joined, man shall not put asunder'—forgetting that, at times, man joins those whom God intends to be separate !

Protestantism was a rebellion against some of the 'whims' of 'Romish' Catholicism. However, in Great Britain, for a very long time even the embracing of Protestantism did not dispel the social prejudice against divorce. In his famous treatise, *The Doctrine and Discipline of Divorce,* Milton, in the seventeenth century, had to deplore the rigidity of contemporary marriage laws—"what thing more instituted to the solace and delight of man than marriage ? And yet the misinterpreting of some Scripture...has changed the blessing of matrimony not seldom into a familiar and cohabiting mischief...without refuge or redemption. So ungoverned and so wild a race does superstition run us, from one extreme of abused liberty to the other of unmerciful restraint." More, Milton, Seldon, Grotius and Leyser vehemently controverted the Ecclesiastical standpoint. Pufendorf, Montesquieu, Pothier and Voltaire continued the fight for freer divorce laws in the eighteenth century on the continent. One may recall to mind Seldon's bald but compelling statement : "of all actions of a man's life his marriage does least concern other people : yet, of all actions of our life, it is most meddled with by other people." In Germany the influence of Voltaire, that arch-breaker of idols, was felt and Frederick the Great liberalized the Law of Divorce. Switzerland, Denmark, Norway and Sweden quickly ignored the Ecclesiastical injunctions. But in Great Britain individual social reformers like Milton and agitators like Romilly failed to effect a substantial alteration of marriage laws till the Utilitarians and the Feminists joined forces in a determined drive to 'easy' the conditions of divorce. For the first time divorce was placed within the reach of the masses of the people in England with the passage of the Matrimonial Causes Act of 1857 : it was much extended in 1923.

To conclude from the increasing divorce rate that marriage has become bankrupt reveals little erudition and much prejudiced assumption. Nor is it true to argue, on the basis of the growing sexual relations outside of the family, that the family has become obsolete in fact and continues a hobbled existence only 'as a genuflection to convention, and a convenience to escape social embarrassments and stigma' (V. F. Calverton, *Bankruptcy of Marriage*,). On the other hand, Westermarck maintains, in refutation of this view, that divorce, far from being the enemy of marriage and family, is the saviour of marriage for, he rightly observes, 'however painful it may be, it is after all the remedy for a misfortune and a means of preserving the dignity of marriage by putting an end to unions that are a disgrace to its name' (Westermarck,

Future of Marriage in Western Civilization,) . When matrimony becomes empty husk, is not divorce the only way out in order to make real the concept of marriage as a social institution based on an exalted emotional urge ? True, even in such instances, divorce may be a dreary prospect to contemplate : but it is an inescapable necessity.

Will the Family be Liquidated ?

The 'most essential thesis' of Westermarck is that "if there will be a time when conjugal and parental sentiments have vanished, I think that nothing in the world can save marriage and the family from destruction. " Parental sentiment is not likely to be in future so decisive as it has been throughout the ages. It is uncertain if the parental feeling is a natural instinct. "The pre-maternal drive...has apparently no psychological basis, cannot be demonstrated in animals below man, and its distinction among human societies appears to be determined by the economic and social motives operative in the community. The same is true for the attitudes of the father. In any case, whether they have a psychological basis or not, the functioning of these motives is clearly influenced by cultural patterning and conditioning" (Otto Klineberg, *Social Psychology, p.78)* . As for the conjugal sentiment, it is relevant to the married or family state itself and not before and, as such, is the consequence and not cause. This conjugal sentiment itself is fostered and developed by other factors like sex impulse, desire for one's own offspring on whom parental affection can be bestowed, and the craving for mutual companionship of the sexes. As has been already stressed, the last is becoming the vital influence impinging on the family. If society fails to take due cognizance of this new trend and does not provide adequate opportunities for the promotion of mutual understanding between the spouses, it is not improbable that family as a social institution may wither away. Community of life between husband and wife may itself be the source of friction and unhappiness unless mutual understanding exists. And if such a mutual understanding between the spouses is to grow, it is only possible if each takes an intelligent interest in the aptitudes and work of the partner. This can be effected only through work, recreational and cultural pursuits, intellectual similarity and other common grounds. 'The family', Dr. James Plant says, 'must be considered in terms of what it means or provides to the individuals within it' *(Personality and the Cultural Pattern)* and what it does mean and provide is not the series of disintegrated factors but the whole of the family milieu (Bossard and Boll, *Family Situations,).* The family as a unit of interacting personalities—'each with a history' (E. W.Burgess as amended by John Dollard) is the modern sociological approach to the concept of the family and its problems. While the origin and evolution of the family from its most primitive forms is a very interesting study, while an appraisal of the vicissitudes to which the family, as a social institution, has been subject in response to the changing economic and social environmental set-up is helpful in understanding present-day problems confronting marriage and family, it is the promotion of the personality of each. Individual member in the parental family, the avoidance of family disorganization and the control of fissiparous tendencies that is of vital urgency. Family disorganization mainly arises from maladjustment in marriage which results in unhappiness for the mates. This explains the preoccupation of psycho-analysts with the content of happiness. To understand what is and what ought to be the place of 'the family gang' in the social framework and what should be the conditions and relations obtaining within a family if it is to have the real 'gang' atmosphere, we need to undertake excursions into history, psychology and physiology and even into the juvenile and divorce courts : we need to realize that the expressions 'repression', 'complexes', 'frustration' are not merely the ornamental embellishments of modern psychology but have a real content with intimate bearing on present-day family life and its future. But happiness itself is the least definable of all and varies with the generally prevalent social values. The manner of adjustment between the husband and the wife differs according to the basic demands made on marriage and family life—whether 'fertility' is accorded weighted premium or whether greater stress is laid on the institutional functions of the family in the promotion of human personality. What is required is 'education for family life', a type of education that is realistically related to individual urges and social needs and is directly useful as a preparation for adult life. Even in U.S.A, as a recent authoritative study reveals, "probably the most important conclusion....is that educators as well as their parents had almost completely ignored the evident need of women to have preparation for the certain inevitabilities of life." The manner in which individual personality is moulded through the family depends on the values chosen in a society. 'The family as the threshold of Democracy' was the title for a discussion in U.S.A. at the 1940 White House Conference on Children in a Democracy. On the other hand, the Nazis held that 'the sickening cry for women's emancipation and independence' contributed to the effiminacy of German legislation under the Weimar Republic. Let us, every one of us, have a candid inward peep. When women demand equal opportunities and responsibilities, why do we 'gang up', openly or covertly, against such 'revolutionary' changes in the existing pattern of society? The more tactful among us disguise this opposition in the garb of intellectual honesty and reason. But, whether we admit it or not, pride, sense of power and prestige, and the possessive instinct impel us into opposition. This opposition is sheer senile stupidity and arises out of a distorted sense of values.

Woman under the Fascist Code

The progress of the movement for woman's emancipation and freedom has been neither uniform nor uninterrupted. The world moves monotonously between progress and reaction and forces of growth and decay always work side by side. In every cause there are certain definite periods of setback. The entrenchment of Fascism in Italy and the Hitler regime in Germany retarded the progress of European and world civilization. In fact, today, after the Nazi blight has been rooted out, the legacy of war seems to be so stinky as to threaten the survival of western culture. Under the Nazi regime of totalitarian dictatorship, as every other aspect of life was rendered subservient to the demands of the impersonal 'Total State' and the Race Myth, just as the individual citizen's independent personality was not recognized apart from the all-enveloping will of the State, so the rearing of children for the glorification of the State and for the perpetuation of the pure Aryan Germanic Race was made the exclusive function of women in Germany. "Marriage must not exhaust itself in the idea of comradeship : it must be more a unity from the midst of which new life emerges-the child-that is called upon to continue the noble line of ancestors of German blood." Under the National Socialist code, 'marriage and motherhood' was the goal of every woman. The wife and the mother were discouraged from all professional and other non-home interests and were to be confined to a private life within the family. The Nazis saddled on themselves the mission of bowdlerizing the German Race and, to subserve their Race Myth, hierarchical organization of the State and 'leader' principle, they flashed back to the discarded medieval cant about woman's subordination and her 'appointed' role....Fascist States "have done their best to order women back into domesticity and subservience and have reversed the historic fact of liberation and equality. They have in the course of this policy....tried to push into the background the liberating influence of Reason, and to do so they have glorified an ideal of woman that might be labelled as provincial, lower middle class, and even pre-industrial. She is fit and eager to bear children year in and year out, to cook and clean for them, but is not to aspire to educate, to guide, to discuss with them, to be their mental equal." (Charlotte Luetkens, *Women and a New Society*)

The fallacy of Race has proved to be 'man's most dangerous myth': for the recognition of a ruling race based on supposedly superior culture is the logical extension of any rigid race differentiation. Peace can never be real or lasting unless it is founded on a common conviction in the solidarity of all humankind born out of the recognition of the organic and mental equality of all peoples. As Ernest Renan wisely remarks:'Ethnic facts, though they constitute the main problem in the early stages of history gradually lose their momentum in proportion to the progress of civilization.' The Race Myth was not an original innovation of the Nazis: it was already in existence before they came to power and they found it a handy tool for their political machinations. The arrogance of race superiority has long been an Anglo-Saxon trait. Rudyard Kipling equated Freedom and England in his couplet:

What stands if Freedom fail?
Who dies if England live?

The Nazis made 'race' their ideological basis. Dr. Lothar Tirala, a leading exponent of the Nazi 'race science' said, "the voice of blood and race operate down to the last refinements of thought and exercises a dicisive influence on the direction of thought." The arch Nazi distorter of truth, miscalled 'philosopher'—why? the Devil alone knows,—Alfred Rosenberg laid down the Nazi laws of heredity when he theorized: "A Nation is constituted by the predominance of a definite character formed by its blood, also by language, geographical environment and the sense of a united political destiny. These last constituents are not, however, definite: the decisive element in a nation is blood." This is merely an adaptation from the racial doctrines of the eighteenth and nineteenth centuries when transmission of hereditary traits was believed to be through blood and when biologists and scientists were yet unaware of 'genes.' Modern science has conclusively disproved this 'blood' theory and has established that it is the 'genes' in the Chromosomes of the germ cells (spermatozoa in males and the ova of the females) that are the transmitters of features or qualities to the offspring. As such, the race ideology based on blood relationship may be anything—it is not scientific. The 'Nordic race' myth is an engineered offshoot of the 'Aryan fallacy.' It may be epitomized thus: just as family members are kins, nationalities have a common blood tie: the Nordic blood connection is the supreme of all bestowing qualities of initiative, leadership and inventive genius: the purity of the Aryan Nordic stock must therefore be preserved. This 'master-race' mysticism has been draped in pseudo-scientific robes. The scientific approach lies in an appeal to facts and, 'facts are sacred, comment is free'. Facts prove that any clear dichotomy of humanity into distinct races such as superior and inferior population groups is anything but scientific. "The violent racialism to be found in Europe today is a symptom of Europe's exaggerated nationalism......The cure for the racial mythology, with its accompanying self-exaltation and persecution which now besets Europe, is a reorientation of the nationalist ideal......Science and scientific spirit are in duty bound to point out the biological realities of the ethnic situation and to refuse to lend sanction to the racial absurdities and the racial horrors perpetrated in the name of science.....Racialism is a myth and a dangerous myth" (Julian Huxley, Carr-Saunders and A.C. Haddon, *We Europeans*). Of course in any positive population policy, eugenic considerations are important. But *eugenics* is entirely different from *racism.* The term eugenics (eu=good, gen=race or stock) was first used by Sir Francis Galton to mean 'the science that deals with all influences that improve the inborn qualities of the race; also with those that develop them to the utmost advantage'. Eugenics, it must be noted, has nothing to do with the 'Iron Law of Nature' propounded by Nazi race maniacs nor has eugenic hygiene any similarity to the dogma that race superiority and purity must be maintained. Dr. G.M.Morant, Britain's foremost physical anthropologist living, in his address to the Royal Anthropological Institute at its centenary meeting, put the final quietus on race differentiation when he observed, "The idea that a race is a group of people separated from all others on account of the distinctive ancestry of its members is implied whenever a race lable is used—but, in fact, we have no knowledge of the existence of such population today or in any past time" ('The Future of Physical Anthropology'—*Man*—XLIV-I944). Similar authoritative, scientific evidence can be easily culled from different sources to knock the bottom out of the doctrines of race superiority. As Eric Mahler observes, "Historical evidence proves beyond doubt that the exact opposite of what the so-called race theory pretends is true. Any decisive advance in human evolution has been accomplished not by breeds that are pure either mentally or physically, not by any cultural inbreeding, but by an intermixture, by mutual impregnation of different stocks and cultures" (*Man, the Measure*). Something seems to be basically wrong with the German mind. A young German philosopher, long before World War I—to be exact, in I908—in a treatise, *Sex and Character,* stated, "There is no real dignity in women....Gentlemanliness does not exist among Jews. Women and Jews....have no intrinsic standards of value (and have) nothing in their souls by which to judge the worthiness of any particular object." It is hardly necessary to point out to the close parallelism between these hideous ideas and distorted philosophies that later permeated the Nazi Movement. The Aryan man has, on the other hand a 'transcendental standard' and only Aryan men (neither non-Aryans nor women) can share 'higher metaphysical life.'

'Virtue' was sought to be vigorously enforced in Fascist Italy and Nazi Germany by the State from above, presumably because 'immorality' was the exclusive prerogative of the State! Even unmarried girls were to be permitted to enter only occupations considered 'natural' to woman. Traditionally certain emotions, feelings and qualities are attributed as 'native' to women—and, invariably, it is men that have addressed themselves to such a dichotomy between the instinctive attributes of man and woman. Under the totalitarian systems of government, it was women's proud privilege to be 'bearers of fighters and labourers'! Is it not presumptuous to seek to prescribe rigidly the 'nature' of woman and what she should and should not be allowed to do? As John Stuart Mill long back argued; "One thing we may be certain of—that what is contrary-to women's nature to do, they will never be made to do by simply giving their nature free play. The anxiety of mankind to interfere in behalf of nature, for fear lest nature should not succeed in effecting its purpose, is an altogether unnecessary solicitude. What women by nature cannot do, it is quite superfluous to forbid them from doing." The Fascists thought otherwise! In fact, the ideas of individual freedom and choice were the worst anathema to them. The Fascist system of government was based primarily on the osciffication of personal rights and the suppression of free thought. In the words of Dr. Frick, one-time Nazi Minister of Internal Affairs: "The mother should be able to devote herself entirely to her children and the family: and the wife to her husband: and the unmarried girl shall only be allowed in those occupations which correspond to the female nature. For the rest, of course, all occupations shall be the preserve of the husband." There was thus a nauseating and dangerous backward glance in the Nazi conception of family life and woman's place in the social framework. This 'kitchen-maid culture' of Nazi Aryanism was of course quite consistent with their recurring themes of *Blut, Boden and Volk* (Race, Land and People). The National Socialist literature is typified by rebellion—rebellion not against tradition and convention but against the forward outlook, against individualism, against intellectualism, against reason itself. However, though the Nazis perverted it to serve their own evil ends, one thing should be stressed: the family is not a mere mechanical relationship but a vital organic unit; the woman is not just a cog in the social machine but is the nerve centre, the heart, of the family organism. But if this ideal is to be attained, freedom of woman is the essential pre-requisite. While the tendency in U.S.A. (the land of the 'Dollar Princesses'!) and other Western countries has been lately to think over—much in terms of distinct, almost mechanical, human particles with no bonds connecting them with the past and segregated from one another by individualistic attitudes, in the totalitarian systems the stress on organic wholes has been overdone, dangerously overdone. Unless truth is muzzled, totalitarianism is doomed. *Leher-freiheit,* the right to pursue truth with single-minded devotion to objectivity, untrammelled by any ulterior considerations, was claimed by the German universities in the nineteenth century. In fact, "in the wonderful adventure of the human spirit, the universities of Germany took and almost maintained the lead...." (*Religion, Science and Society in the Modern World,* Lindsay,).....

> "Learning dawned, its light arose,
> Thus the Truth assailed its foes."
> (Mendelssohn at Leipzig, in I840).

"Yet in the very country where the freedom of scientific thought had been so triumphant, the German universities made almost no resistance to the forces that attacked that ideal...(and)....Germany gave up one of her greatest glories with hardly a protest" (Ibid,). Universities were soon converted into partisan voices of the German nation: they ceased their search for scientific truth and became subservient to whosoever happened to be in political power: education became a medium of propaganda for the governmental authority: learning was prostituted to subserve despicable political ends: German professors began to `heil' the `kitchen-maids-culture': German scientists were groomed and harnessed to destructive purposes. The ideal Nazi woman, according to a pronouncement by Feder in 1926, was to be `maid and servant'. According to the Nazi women leader Diehl Guida, woman was to rule by service and be `a servant, queen and mother'. In the Fascist scheme, there was always an under-current thought that woman's domain was strictly confined to the tiny world of the family. "The man upholds the nation while the woman upholds the family" was their text. `Reproduction,'`womanly work,'`the home' constituted the three-planked platform of the Fascists for their women. However, it may be observed that the actual position of women in Germany or Italy could not be regimented exactly on this ideological pattern: it altered with the economic rythms. The Nazi theory was to some extent defeated by the economic forces of capitalism and the demands of militarist preparation. It was found impossible to rigidly confine women to the triple interests of *kinder, kuche, kirche.* For instance in 1936, thirty-one per cent of the employed Germans were women, which was a higher proportion than in Great Britain or in France or even in U.S.A. Economic realities defeated Nazi ideology but the ideology itself was stinking.

Women in Soviet Russia

And now, to U.S.S.R. and its women. The heritage of the common masses of Russian women was one of degradation and suppression. However, in the 'ritzy' Moscovite aristocracy, many women indulged in an orgy of extravagance and sexual licence. On the other hand, long before the eclipse of Czarist Russia, there were other women who had taken active part in social and political revolutionary movements. Finally, under Lenin's inspiring leadership, the agonized Russian workers and peasants rose in revolt against Czarism and all the evils it symbolized: then ensued 'the ten days that shook the world.' Czarism was overtaken by the nemisis of its own creation and the Communist U.S.S.R. was established. As our own India today and the Colonies of the British, French and Dutch Empires, in 1917 Russia was rich in natural resources and was densely populated but woefully lacked skilled labour, technological development and the State itself was apathetic to the economic progress of the common men and woman. In I932, Stalin urged, "we are hundred years behind the advanced countries. We must make good this distance in ten years. Either we do it or they crush us." The magnitude and the character of the change can best be realized if we recollect that the U.S.S.R. first appeared on the world's map in I917, that till I923 the U.S.S.R. was met by open hostility from all other leading countries of the world today, with the U.S.A. and Great Britain, she stands supreme as one of the three leading industrial and military powers of the world. True, there have been grave lapses: but, before judging the U.S.S.R. on that score, should we not bear in mind that the tempo of their change has been terrific, that since I917 they have had to be in great hurry, that the U.S.S.R. has been trying to cram into one generation political, economic and cultural changes and growth that Great Britain had taken over two hundred years to accomplish and U.S.A. over a century? Since I917, the State in U.S.S.R. has been a great 'liberating agent,' a 'hinderer of hindrances' to social well-being. Their conception of freedom is essentially economic, that is, freedom from want. Through grim work and sacrifice they have attained that end more than the others. The colour bar is entirely absent in the U.S.S.R. They have admirably solved the problem of the minorities. It was an Irishman, Dr. E.J. Dillon, who wrote as early as in I929, "their way of dealing with home rule and the nationalities is a masterpiece of ingenuity and elegance. None of the able statesman of today in other lands has attempted to vie with them in their methods for satisfying the claims of minorities." What is most important of all, the common people, men as well as women, have a sense of continuous participation in public administration through social work.

In the last three decades, Russia has been catapulted from medievalism to the twentieth century at an unprecedented speed and the radical transformation in the status of women is one of the remarkable achievements to the credit of the Soviet Administration. Lenin declared: 'No nation can be free when half the population is enslaved in the kitchen.' Article I22 of the New Constitution reads: 'Women in U.S.S.R. are accorded equal rights with men in all spheres of economic, state, cultural, social and political life. The exercise of these rights by women is ensured by affording women equally with men the right to work, payment for work, rest, and leisure, social insurance, and education and by State protection of the interests of mother and child.' Article I37 reads: "Women have the right to elect and be elected on equal terms with men." More than two-thirds of the able-bodied women of working age are employed outside of the home on a salary or wage basis. In I926, only 40 per cent of the women had exercised the vote while by I934 more than 90 per cent voted. It is true that the franchise in Soviet Russia, where there is the one-party system and that one party rules the State, has not the same significance that the political vote has in democratic countries. However, what is relevant in this context is the fact that in the election of the Soviet, in the management of the collective farms and the factories, women have the same voice as men. Though, in every sphere, actually recorded statistical figures do not reveal a state of absolute equality of women and men, there is an unmistakable approximation to cultural and social equality between the sexes. Legal and constitutional rights apply to all citizens alike. Urbanization and rapid industrialization have furthered this equalization process considerably. Collectivisation of farming has liberated the women and the young from the age-old authority of the manager of the household. In Czarist Russia, the wife and the children were used by the Russian peasant as his farm capital. Today, even in the Moslem East, women have come into their own in economic and administrative activities. A community of interest is thus particularly seen between the Soviet State and the womenfolk of U.S.S.R. A net-work of public services, covering different aspects of individual and collective life, enmeshes the Russian mother and the child so that by assuming many of the cares and responsibilities of the parents, the State greatly facilitates the participation of women in industrial, economic and social life. Creches for babies in factories and on collective farms: equal pay for women for equal work: leave on full pay before and after child-birth and free medical treatment: equal access to higher education, scientific as well as technical, based on the sole test of efficiency in the lower grades: are some of the more important reforms effected by the Soviets which have been instrumental in bringing women into their own. Though family life has become somewhat unstable because of this sudden spurt in opportunities for equal participation in national life, the family—even in the U.S.S.R.—remains the primary form of social organization. The guarantee of collective security against different individual risks has hastened the process of emancipation of women. This fundamental remoulding and re-ordering of human relations in Soviet Russia is symbolized in the irreconcilable contrast between an old Russian adage,'a hen is not a bird; nor a woman, a human being' and Lenin's clarion call to the womanhood of Soviet Russia in his famous dictum—'Every cook must learn to rule the State.' It is ridiculous to talk jeeringly of 'the dictatorship of women supplanting the dictatorship of the proletariat' as some unsympathetic impressionist critics have done. Whatever the blunders and excesses Soviet Russia may have committed in the early years of its revolutionary zeal in other respects, whatever be the sinister truth about the censorship beyond the 'iron curtain' across Europe from the Baltic down to the Black Sea, whatever political and diplomatic machinations Stalinist Russia may be accused of in recent years in her competitive powerpolicies with Great Britain and the United States on the European and Asiatic chessboards, the achievements of U.S.S.R. in emancipating its womenfolk are to be admired and emulated, particularly when one recollects the grim truth that as late as in 1917 Russian women were as ignorant and oppressed as women in China or India or in any other backward country. In 1935, over 60 per cent of all able-bodied women of working age were employed, contrasting with about 40 per cent in U.S.A.; 33 per cent of all employed persons were women (in 1936) contrasting with 31 per cent in Germany and 24 per cent in U.S.A. (in 1940). Almost from scratch, in the brief span of less than three decades, the Soviets have erected an economic and cultural system whose achievements appear almost incredible to those who have not actually witnessed them in the U.S.S.R. There are about two hundred delegates in the Supreme Soviet—the apex body in the governmental hierarchy. In 1937-38, taking the national economy as a whole, over 35 per cent of the total number of workers were females, with public health services and education topping the list of occupations, with about 75 and 60 per cent respectively. Nearly 45 per cent of the students in the higher educational institutions were women. The State care for the mother and the child surpasses that in any other country in the world. Prior to the war, over three hundred thousand mothers received direct State aid and, what is more significant, in the six years between 1935 and 1941 State expenditure on maternity and child-welfare services more than doubled. As early as in 1935, according to an estimate by Kingsbury and Fairchild of U.S.A., ninety-eight per cent of Moscow babies were born in hospitals. While in 1917-18 two-thirds of the entire population were illiterate, in 1939 hardly fifteen per cent were illiterate. Classified according to sex, before the Revolution, in 1917, while 50 per cent of the males and only 12 per cent of the females were literate, at the end of 1938 the respective percentages were 87 and 68. The overall achievement of the U.S.S.R. regime is that unnatural cultural differentials have been largely obliterated. Male and female sections, town-folk and rural inhabitants, industrial and agricultural populations, are converging. "The Revolution has been particularly beneficial to the peasants and to the women—most of all to the womenfolk of the countryside" (Steinberg, 'Education and Culture', *Our Soviet Ally*—a symposium). This is a revealing eye-opener for the representative national government in India and to the Indian social reformer, for our inheritance from the past, the oppressive magnitude of our present-day economic and social problems in regard to the rural womanfolk, are similar.

Totalitarianism and Women's Purpose

Women, more than men, in the Totalitarlian States are not required to have brains. Women are by nature individualists and individualism is the enemy of the Total State. With all their advantages and privileges, women in U.S.S.R. too, as in Nazi Germany and Fascist Italy. are sought to be moulded to conform to a set pattern, to subscribe to the interests of the single-party State. And now, since the beginning of the second world war, paradoxically enough, 'children—more children' for the State, has been adopted by the

Soviets also. Why does the Brotherhood of the International Proletariat demand 'teeming millions'? Such a population policy of the State implies that the dignity of the woman is recognised only in the context of, and to the extent it promotes, the interests of the nation's power and glory. To emancipate woman only for the children she bears, to respect, woman only because she is prolific, is an affront to her soul. The flaming idealism of Lenin has been gradually shoved away by the sordid motives of competitive national aggrandizement. It is unfortunate that the only social system that could have veered the world away from aggressive nationalism and selfishness has itself been trapped in the ruck of competitive, narrow, State interests. As Julian Huxley points out, 'the family has been produced by Nature, the nation by Man himself.' The family is an ancient biological institution. Kinship is its emotional stimulus. The modern Nation State is the outgrowth-from certain social, economic, political and environmental conditions and dates from about the Renaissance period in Europe, that is, about 1500 A.D. Group sentiment holds the nation together. This group sentiment is but a projection of kinship into larger human aggregates; but, while kinship has been creative, group sentiment is easily perverted to subserve expansionist patriotism against the ideal of common humanity. This group sentiment, the active consciousness of the oneness of nationality, if it expresses itself in the perfectly legitimate and essential patriotic urge to be free from external domination, serves as a civilizing and creative political force. This was true of the nineteenth century Europe and is now helping to mould the dependent regions of Asia into live and free organic entities out of their age-long torpor and subjection. However, the mythical implications of this group sentiment are many and dangerous and can be easily exploited by unscrupulous political adventurers so that not infrequently a nation becomes 'a society united by a common error as to its origin and a common aversion to its neighbours.' Regimentation to a lifeless pattern imposed from above and de-intellectualism are the very basis of totalitarianism. It was Paul Drucker who once characterized all planners as improvisers. However, thoroughly directed and managed, 'cultural' improvisation by a bureaueratic hierarchy is not really conducive to the harmonious development of human personality. Individuals become pawns and the sanctity of individual personality is not recognized as inviolate. Reflective consciousness is the unique gift that human beings possess and is denied to lesser organisms. In every totalitarian State, capitalist or communist, it is the free exercise of these reflective powers that is sought to be silenced. Even the idea of the Functional State may be over-done to the detriment of the fruitation of individual personality. "The State is not a goal of human activity but only a means. It is not a sociological synthesis but merely a form of sociality" so that all attempts to turn the State into the sole unifying power of society obstruct the path of social progress. "What should be retained from the modern State is its structural value, the progress in means of protection, order and defense, the development of instruments of culture and activity and material data of an evolution evidently useful and worthy of man—above all, the ethical, juridical, political and social conquests made by the State or through the State....what must be rejected is the State's claim to ethicity, the monistic conception of its sociological character, its consequent and absurd totalitarianism—in a word, the coercive political unification of society in the State, and the submerging in the State of human personality" (Luigi Sturgo, *Inner Laws of Society*). In all Fascist countries,'the cult of the cradle' was assigned supreme importance. And today, in U.S.S.R. also, we find fecundity is revered as a worthy 'patriotic' virtue! Why?—because, babies are potential citizens and potential soldiers! Respect for maternity is different: it can exist in its highest form without this deliberate and systematized population cult engineered by the State itself. In the wake of what Cicely Hamilton in her book *Modern Italy* calls 'the cult of the cradle' follows a suspicion that woman's real personality may in reality be stifled. This surely is not the way for ennobling motherhood but only for its debasement.

Women and Work

In all agricultural communities based on domestic and family work and on handicrafts, man and woman work together. Wordsworth in his sonnet ' *Nuns Fret Not* ' writes glowingly of 'maids at the wheel sitting blithe and happy.' Spinning at the cottage doorway and the other leisure-time handicrafts, grinding and husking of corn for payment, work on the agricultural farms in co-operation with their men, are still quite common in every Indian village for women. To eke out a subsistence living, every individual member of the house-hold, including children, must work. The Industrial Revolution, characterized by the displacement of the customary decentralized production in small units by the factory system organized on a capitalist basis, broke up the old family basis in Great Britain and other countries, temporarily throwing women into idleness and destitution by depriving them of their incomeearning avocations in their spare-time: but later, it has assigned to women a definite role to play outside of the home and has become an important influence in building up a new economic foundation for a form of society wherein the equality of sexes can no longer be denied.

The flowering of woman's innate abilities and their full utilization is as beneficient and necessary to commonweal as that of man's. All education should be open to women and men on the same terms. "Let a woman learn in quietness with all subjection: permit not a woman to teach nor to have dominion over a man, but to be in quietness" (*Verse from Timothy—ii*). It is interesting to note that Frederick, the Great, of Germany selected this couplet as the text at the thanksgiving service he ordered to be arranged to commemorate the victory of the Prussian arms against the forces of Empress Maria Theresa! It is not such learning that woman should have. She should be free to pursue any subject of study on completely equal terms with man and to make what use she thinks fit of the knowledge she acquires. The mere granting of the political vote to women or any other forms of legal equality would be of little purpose. If there is to be no gap between legislation and reality, positive opportunities to actively and freely participate in public life must be provided to women. It must be realized that the start is in no way the same between the two sexes. Woman has weighty initial handicaps. "There can be no freedom of contract where there is no equality of status" (Wendell Holmes). One is reminded of Anatole France's jibe at the impartiality and greatness of justice, in *La Revolte des Anges,* that the millionaire and the starving pauper are punished equally for the same offence—for stealing a loaf of bread! Particularly in professions it is not such spurious equality between the sexes that is desired. As John Stuart Mill in his epochal essay, *The Subjection of Women* (1869), stated: "With regard to the fitness of women not only to participate in elections but themselves to hold office or practise professions involving important public responsibilities—I have already observed that this consideration is not essential to the practical question in dispute; since any woman who succeeds in an open profession proves by that very fact that she is qualified for it. And in the case of public offices, if the political system of the country is such as to exclude unfit men, it will equally exclude unfit women..... As long as therefore it is acknowledged that even a few women may be fit for these duties, the laws which shut the doors on these exceptions cannot be justified by any opinion which can be held respecting the capacities of women in general." If it is argued that higher education 'defeminises' women, may it not be countered, with an equal measure of validity, that higher education pares down the impulse to fatherhood? The truth is that neither consequence ensues to any noticeable extent and any generalization in this regard is fatuous. There is an axiomatic relationship between professional education and professional opportunities. Barrier to woman's higher education keep women away from professional fields. So that, unless facilities are thrown quite open to women to train and equip themselves with the requisite knowledge and experience, women will be largely precluded from entering the more important professions though there are no legal obstacles in their path. In fact, taking cognizance of the special disabilities weighing on women at present, they must be given even favoured treatment in the matter of education. Marriage and motherhood can be combined with professional or other employment. As doctors, teachers, social workers, women can bring feminine gifts for the amelioration of human suffering and promotion of common welfare. It is noteworthy that in Great Britain a woman, Miss Ellen Wilkinson, has been Minister of Education. Welfare administration, work connected with medical and health services, management of educational institutions, the imparting and supervision of elementary vocational guidance—these and other duties women can discharge with exceptional ability. Infant and child-welfare work and nursing are intimately related to motherhood. As Professions, these are complementary to the medical field. Motherhood and service to others in ailment are `natural' to womanliness. As such, nursing and the medical profession are well-suited to woman's aptitudes. There have been in Great Britain medical women like Elizabeth Garett Anderson or Dr. Ida Mann, the recently appointed Reader in opthalmology in the `conservative' medical school at the Oxford University, who `have become good doctors, despite the fact that they are women'. Secretarial work, journalism, the stage and even business and commerce, the woman may enter. Even in a highly advanced country like Great Britain women have been effectively shut out from executive offices of business and commercial houses though there have been exceptions like Miss Nettlefold, Viscountess Rhondda, Miss Haslett and the single woman stockbroker (!) Miss Gordon Holmes. In 1931, out of a total number of 21,054,000 occupied persons in Great Britain, 6,265,000 or 29.8 per cent were females. This percentage had hardly improved since 1911. Most of the women workers were segregated and concentrated into particular occupations of which personal service alone absorbed 30.7 per cent of all occupied females. Subsequently women could be found entering in noticeable numbers in trades and professions previously monopolized by males (cf. Mark Abrams, *The Condition* of the British people, 1911-1945, pp. 56-59). Women can, with advantage take to architecture. In architecture one has to see shapes, as one appreciates melody, in a sensual experience. Architecture is concerned with structure, accommodation and appearance: it resembles painting and sculpture: but it is design in spaces. An aesthetic outlook is indispensable to be a successful architect. And, sense of charm, orderliness, beauty is innate in woman more than in man. Architecture is a visual art in which, to be successful, a sense of pattern is indispensable. It is therefore a profession wherein, given adequate facilities and the requisite training and apprenticeship, women can fit in pre-eminently well. It is thus difficult to rationalize the exclusion of women from most of the professional fields. Work is as natural to woman as to man and the majesty of life is in work.'

Biological, economic, and political considerations are all vitally important. But beyond all these is 'culture' that ultimately counts. What is this 'culture' we so much talk about? Murdock epitomizes much valuable material on this subject when he analyzes culture as being learned, inculcated, social, ideational, gratifying, adaptative and integrative. Much cant has been said and written about culture and what men and nations have understood by it has most often depended on the blinkers through which they have chosen to have its perspective. Dynamically, we may say, "culture is the total, miscellaneous aggregate of the products of human activity and invention which are transmitted and communicated to other human beings and succeeding generations thereof" (J.K. Folsom, *The Family and Democratic Society,* pp. 46-47) so that, if an analogy may be offered, if the human community can be visualized as a musical instrument, culture corresponds to the piece of music or tune played upon it. How can woman, then, participate in and contribute to the cultural development of a community or of a nation or of the human species unless she is absolutely free to drink deep at the springs of art, science, philosophy and literature? Unless women have equal rights and opportunities to become doctors, educationists, writers, artists, teachers and scientists, how can they become scions of culture? As for woman's capacity to engage in these diverse activities, John Stuart mill, having demonstrated the absurdity of prescribing certain types of work as 'natural'to woman, goes so far as to say: "if anything conclusive could be inferred from experience, it would be that the things which women are not allowed to do are the very ones for which they are peculiarly qualified." On the need for the economic independence of women, apart from the characteristically Shavian touch of superior cynicism, there is much sound commonsense and wisdom in Bernard Shaw's profession of faith: "I believe that any society which desires to found itself on a high standard of integrity of character in its units, should organize itself in such a fashion as to make it possible for all men and women to maintain themselves in reasonable comfort by their industry without selling their affection or convictions" (Preface, *Plays Pleasant and Unpleasant).*

Work and Home

It is best to so arrange woman's professional or other work as to supplement, and not supplant, home responsibilities. Electricity helps to bring work to the home; an extreme degree of decentralization in production is rendered possible through the use of electricity as motive power. The much-advertised economies of large-scale production concentrated in a few gigantic plants have now become less sure from the viewpoint of social costs; and electricity helps to solve the problem by making it possible to take work to the home and has thus proved itself to be a friend of the modern family. Experience in recent years in U.S.A. and other western countries has shown, in certain extreme cases of complete negligence of family ideal some disadvantages ensue: a sterile home environment for the children results because children are left at home without the companionship and watchful guidance of their parents: a falling birthrate is said to be another consequence. Strenuous and over-crowded professional work may in fact hamper the development of personality instead of facilitating it. Recent statistical studies in Great Britain and U.S.A. reveal that in many cases woman's professional work outside of the home has been actuated by the desire to improve the family's standard of living rather than by woman's ideas of independence. The disabilities that are becoming evident in the wake of the wholesale full-time employment of women in these and other countries are leading to a hange in the outlook of thinking men and women. It is necessary to be clear on this point because there seems to be an apparent conflict between woman's employment in any sphere of work and her maternal responsibilities in the family. What is stressed is that every woman should have the unrestrained right to enter any occupation she likes provided she has the requisite training for the same, on the same terms as are applicable to men. All educational and other facilities for this must be provided. At the same time, the general education imparted in society must be designed to promote her sense of responsibilities to the family and to stress the fact that, beyond the conception of equal rights and the desire for economic independence which are essential, there is the supreme idea of realizing her true self. Education is not merely training for shaping the next generation on the present ideals of individuals and social life but, more, for new ideas and knowledge which is free, free to accept or reject authority. As Kant observed, "Children ought to be educated, not for the present but for a possibly improved condition of man in the future." "It has been said that the schools must follow-not lead. This statement is based on a false view of education. We educate for the future — beyond ourselves." (H.G. Stead, *Full Stature-Education and Tomorrow*, p. 135) and educators must always seek to realize their true function:

> "We are the workers of a new dawn,
> ...Men who look forward and not back.

In the household as well as in the wider community, each woman must be conscious of her independent personality with a will of her own. Woman herself will keep aloof from such kinds of work as are likely to militate against the development of her personality. The chief concern about the family seems to be not so much how strong it may be as an economic unit as how well it performs its functions for the harmonious development of the personalities of its individual members. It is, above all, the individual personality of the father, the mother and the child that is of the highest importance. For this to be promoted in full, the family should be a democratic unit in a democratic society : society should guarantee to every individual member a basic irreducible modicum of economic security and well-being. Here is one of the borderlands of different social sciences. The place of woman in society and the future of the institution of family is essentially a sociological problem; at the same time important economic and political influences impinge on it.

3

Woman and Literature

Mere geet,
mere saian!
tusan lai gae gae geet...
utthan tarangan sagaron ae paun vangun.

My songs, My Beloved!
Songs sung for you...
The waves rise like wind from the ocean

I shall now focus on the works of a modern writer-Bhai Vir Singh (1872-1957). His writings clearly do not belong in the category of sacred scriptures. Nonetheless, they illumine a later age with insights derived from the holy writ. This is a big leap in time, but the intervening period proffers little creative or philosophical writing of any significance. The turmoil which overtook the Sikhs after the passing away of Guru Gobind Singh in 1708 at once brought the dominance of heroism and restrained the profusion of learning. Guru Gobind Singh's own epoch was anything but quiet;yet he had striven to preserve and enrich the literary tradition bequeathed to him by his spiritual predecessors. The elements of disturbance were to rule the day when he was no longer on the scene. It is for this reason that we encounter very little philosophical or scriptural exposition for most of the eighteenth century.

One new genre of Sikh writing which developed during this period was the *rahitnama* series. The *rahitnamas* (from *rahit*, "conduct," and *nama*, "manual") were codes regulating Sikh practice and custom. They came to be composed in the name of Sikhs who had been close to Guru Gobind Singh and were meant to carry the authority of the Guru himself. They were terse, apophthegmatic, and hortatory in style. Here, the necessity and immediacy of the announcement took precedence over the spiritual and metaphysical nuances of early Sikh writings. Austerity overrode imagination. The moral stipulations for a community under siege could not but be mundane and direct.

Some historical works also emerged during this period. The first among them was *Gurbitas Chhevin Patshahi* (AD 1718), which is an account of the life of the sixth Guru, Guru Hargobind. That was followed by Koer Singh's *Gurbitas Patshahi* to (AD 1751), the life story of the tenth Guru; Kesar Singh Chhibar's *Bansavatinama* (AD 1769), a genealogical account of the Gurus and their families; Sarup Das Bhalla's *Mahima Prakash* (AD 1776), lives of the ten Gurus; and Sukkha Singh's *Gurbitas Dasvin Patshahi* (AD 1797), a biography of Guru Gobind Singh. All these books are in verse, with flashes of poetic imagination and embellishment, but metaphysical or philosophical speculation seldom belong to this class or writing. There is hardly any other work worthy of mention falling within this period.

The more settled period of Sikh rule followed in the Punjab from 1799 to 1849, but these years also failed to produce any important speculative writing. History continued to dominate the world of Sikh writing. Two important works of this period were Ratan Singh Bhangu's *Pracin Panth Prakash* (AD 1841), a versified account of the history of the Sikhs from the time of Guru Nanak to the third quarter of the eighteenth century, and Bhai Santokh Singh's *magnum opus, Sri Gur Pratap Suraj Granth* (AD 1843). This work consisted of the lives of the ten Gurus and of Guru Gobind Singh's disciple, Banda Singh Bahadur. It was in verse and abounded in a wealth of detail and poetic imagery. Another important work of this period was again historical,'*Umdat-ut-Tawarikh*, written in Persian by Sohan Lal Suri. He was the court diarist of the Sikh sovereign, Ranjit Singh, and hisbook was a comprehensive story of the Sikhs in five volumes. It included the lives of the ten Gurus, the early struggles of the Sikhs during the eighteenth century, and biographies of the Sikh rulers, Maharaja Ranjit Singh, Maharaja Kharak Singh, Nau Nihal Singh, Maharaja Sher Singh, and Maharaja Daleep Singh. It ended with the annexation of the Punjab to the British Indian dominions.

Some theological writing appeared during this period in the form of commentaries on the scriptural texts. These works displayed an intellectual disposition that was predominantly Hindu. Rather than accepting the straightforward meaning of the text, they proffered an esoteric interpretation. Two such schools of Sikh scriptural interpretation then were Udasi and Nirmala schools, and scholars within these traditions were essentially reared in classical Indian exegesis. They amplified Sikh thought through classical Hindu texts. The works of Anandghana and Bhai Santokh Singh - representatives of the Udasi and Nirmala schools respectively - have been carefully researched by Nripinder Singh. His study shows that the Udasi and Nirmala exegesis of Sikh scripture was saturated with Upanisadic and Puranic learning. The style and content of their speculations brought about a reincubation of Hindu ideology in Sikh thinking. For instance, an eminent scholar of that period, Anandghana, commenting upon a line from Guru Nanak's *Japu* - *"Guru isaru Guru gorakhu barma Guru parbati mai"* - construes him to be a follower of the six Hindu deities. Anandghana explains that Guru Nanak in this verse acknowledges Isar (Siva), Gorakh (Visnu), Barma (Brahma), Parbati (Parvati), Ma (Laxmi), and I (Sarasvati) as his Gurus. It is ironic that Anandghana would provide such an explanation for the fifth stanza of the *Tapu* which opens with a ringing statement of the unicity of the Infinite. The Sikh vision of the Transcendent began to get eclipsed by the Hindu *Zeitgeist*.

The Punjab was the last of the Indian provinces to succumb to British Rule. It was also the last to be exposed to western ideas and western education, but when it experienced this modern influence, the Punjab was quick to respond and interact. The first Christian center was established in 1834 at Ludhiana across the Sikh border. This was under the sspices of the Western Foreign Missionary Society of Philadelphia. After the occupation of the Punjab by the British, missionary activity was extended to cover the newly acquired territory, and it received government patronage. The Christian enterprise also penetrated into spheres of social welfare such as education and medical care. After the famous Wood's Despatch of 1854, the government's policy was directed towards opening schools and colleges and encouraging private initiative by the grant-in-aid system. The effect was twofold. The mutual contact of the two cultural streams encouraged some western scholars to devote themselves to the study of Indian thought and to discover its richness; on the other hand, it initiated among the Indians a new process of literary, social, and cultural resurgence. Christian missionary activity led to a fresh appraisal by the people of their own religious traditions. Three powerful movements of reform and renewal arose in the three major traditions of India - Brahmo Samaj in Hinduism, Aligarh in Islam, and Singh Sabha in Sikhism. The Brahmo Samaj founded by Rammohun Roy in Bengal in 1828 comprised western-educated intellectuals who wished to create a synthesis of enlightened Hinduism and European liberalism. Founded by Sir Sayyid Ahmad Khan, Aligarh initially began aa a secondary school patterned after European models in 1875 in India and soon established itself as an influential modernizing movement in Islam.

In Sikhism, the religious doctrines and practices had suffered considerable retrogression during the century preceding the rise of the Singh Sabha movement. With the establishment of Maharaja Ranjit Singh's rule in the Punjab and the elaboration of pomp and ceremony at the royal court, formal ritual and ceremonial were also ushered into the Sikh faith. Brahmanic rites discarded by the Gurus entered into the Sikh way of life. The loss of political power following the annexation of the Sikh kingdom to British India encouraged conversion to the faith of the new rulers and, oftentimes as a response to that phenomenon, reversion to ceremonial Hinduism. Conversions by Christian missionaries particularly added to the gravity of the identity crisis. The Sikhs, roughly estimated to be about 10 million in Maharaja Ranjit Singh's Punjab, dwindled to a mere 1, 141, 848 in the census made in the Punjab in 1868. The Sikhs articulated their apprehensions with a sense of helplessness.

An English newspaper writes that the Christian faith is making rapid progress and makes the prophecy that within the next twenty-five years, one-third of the Majha area will be Christian. The Malwa area will follow suit. Just as we do not see any Buddhists in the country except in images, in the same fashion the Sikhs, who are now, here and there, visible in turbans and their religious forms like wrist-bangles and swords, will be seen only in pictures and museums. Their own sons and grandsons turning Christians and clad in coats and trousers and sporting toadstool-like caps will go to see them in the museums and say in their pidgin Punjabi : "Look, that is the picture of a Sikh - the tribe that inhabited this country once upon a time."

It was in the face of such a tragic situation that the Singh Sabha arose. It issued from the deliberations of leading Sikhs of the time such as Thakur Singh Sandhanwalia, Baba Sir Khem Singh Bedi, and Kanwar Bikrama Singh of Kapurthala, who met in Amritsar in 1873. Less than a year old at that time, Bhai Vir Singh eventually became its most ardent exponent and eloquent spokesman. According to Harbans Singh, Bhai Vir Singh's central aim was the furtherance of the Singh Sabha enlightenment: "He was able to comprehend the significance of the Sikh traditions so accurately and interpreted them to his generation so powerfully that Sikhism experienced a much-needed revival."

The Singh Sabha aimed at recapturing the original message of the Gurus and recovering and reestablishing Sikh identity. While it looked to the past to revive the original purity of belief, it also looked to the future with a view to leading the community into the modern age. Bhai Vir Singh possessed this dual vision of a past and a future and concretized it through his writings. The sourcre of his inspiration was the Sikh faith, and the resurrection of the message of Guru Nanak was the singular principle of his leterary creation. He made simple Punjabi the medium of his writing. Since the time of Guru Gobind Singh, two hundred years before this, Punjabi had been neglected as a leterary language by the Sikhs. Through his study of Sikh scripture, Bhai Vir Singh had acquired a deep respect for the Punjabi language. His versatile genius modernized the language and gave a new life to it as a literary medium. He marks the beginning of a renaissance in Sikh culture. His revival of the popular tongue found literary expression in a wide variety of genres, some of which had never before been attempted in Punjabi. His literary production is voluminous, and includes eight collections of poetry, four novels, a play, five biolgaphies, and nine texts that he meticulously annotated and commented upon. Throughout his literary career, he kept up with his journalism and his tractarian writing. Late in his career, he devoted several years unsparingly to the monoumental project of writing a formal commentary on the Guru Granth, which was published posthumously in seven large volumes. Bhai Vir Singh's exegesis of the *Japu* in 178 pages is a telling illustration of his erudite scholarship. The verses are analyzed in great depth; allusions and symbols are explained; a glossary of terms is provided; individual words are traced etymologically; extensive references to preceding commentators are included. He also revised the *Guru Granth Kosh*, a dictionary of the Guru Granth which explains important terms and allusions in great detail. It provides valuable information on the musical notation adopted for the Guru Granth as well. In Bhai Vir Singh's works we have an authentic renaissance of the spiritual legacy of the Sikh faith. As an interpreter of the Sikh metaphysical and philosophical thought, he served as an outstanding model for his own and later generations. It is with his writings, especially his poetry and the novel, that we shall continue the exploration of our theme.

The female principle dominates Bhai Vir Singh's creative vision. When he felt that Guru Nanak's vision of the Transcendent was becoming blurred amongst the Sikhs as a result of the challenge from Hindu and Christian ideals and valres, he created female rolemodels for his people like Sundari, Rani Raj Kaur, Satvant Kaur, Subhagji, and Sushil Kaur. These women were paradigms of moral strength, spirituality, boldness, and keen insight for the Sikh psyche, which was now at a low ebb. Through them Bhai Vir Singh wanted to remind his people of the revelation of the One mediated through Guru Nanak and of its implication for society, that is, the oneness of humanity. All of his major novels — *Sundari, Bijay Singh, Satvant Kaur* and *Baba Naudh Singh* — have a female character at the core, be it Sundari or Sushil Kaur, Satvant Kaur or Subhagji. He handles these characters with the utmost delicacy and esteem, and projects through them his cherished worldview.

In his poetry also, Bhai Vir Singh identifies himself with the woman character: it may be the widow Rani Raj Kaur, who is imbued with an intense spiritual longing, or it may be the beautiful maiden in the prime of her youth who asks the fundamental existential question *"Jivan Ki Hai?* — What is Life?" The identification of the poet with the female and the creation of female protagonists as the paradigms of morality, courage, spirituality, and philosophical quest manifest not only the tenderness of Bhai Vir Singh's poetic perception but also his, that is to say, the Sikh, worldview in which women enjoy great esteem. These characters are not abstractions of an "eternal feminine." Each is a living and breathing individual. They are not fairyland characters, but human beings of flesh and blood. Each in her own and separate way is a model worthy of emulation by women as well as by men. The young maiden who weaves painful and lyrical songs in the anthology entitled *Mere Saian Jio (O, My Beloved),* the maiden who seeks to comprehend the meaning of life in the composition *"Jivan Ki Hai?* (What is Life?)" from the anthology *Lahiran de Har (Garlands of Waves),* Sundari, whose name provides the title for the first novel in the Punjabi language, and Rani Raj Kaur, who ascends from tribulation to beatitude in the epic *Rana Surat Singh* — will be the focus of my study. The individual roles of these four women elucidate the Sikh vision of the Transcendent from the romantic, existential, ethical, and aystical perspectives.

Mere Saian Jio (O, My Beloved) is an anthology of short poems that Bhai Vir Singh brought out at the end of his poetic career. This form of the short poem was an innovation in Punjabi literature and became popular instantly. While ushering new and quicker lyric tunes and measures into Punjabi prosody, the short poem introduced new words and images as well. *Trel Tupke* was Bhai Vir Singh's first collection of poems, to be followed at quick intervals by *Lehran de Har, Bijlian de Har, Preet Veena,* and *Kant Maheli.* An anthology of songs in praise of the Sikh Gurus was published in 1933 under the title *Kambdi Kalai(The Trembling Wrist0,* and *Mere Saian Jio* itself wås his last collection of verse. The dominant strand underlying this prodigious output was his use of poetic strategy to evoke, elucidate, and expand the Sikh scriptural message. Poetically Bhai Vir Singh grasped the Guru Granth, making it diaphanous and alive for his readers. He is, to use Emerson's analogy from "The Poet," a glass through which later generations can see the Guru Granth in all its richness.

Mere Saian Jio

Mere Saian Jio was published in 1957, when Bhai Vir Singh was eighty-one years old. But this last specimen of his poetry, in Harbans Singh's words, "had the same morning-dew's distilled beauty, the same deeply-felt longing of the heart and the same sensitive energy of expression as his precious Rubaiyats or haunting Kashmir poems written in the beginning of the century."

The basic Sikh philosophical concept is elaborated by the heroine of *Mere Saian Jio.* In ardently addressing her Beloved, she is but substantiating the opening statement of the Guru Granth: *Ikk Oan Kar.* The existence, the Being of the Beloved, is affirmed in her very salutation:

Mere geet
mere saian!
tusan lai gae gae geet...
utthan tarangan sagaron ae paun vangun,
chhir paea mera cup gala, boldi bulbul vangun,
han bal-gale dian thibakdian thibakdian

tusan - mere saian Jio - di
hazuri vic!
My songs,
My Beloved!
Songs sung for you...
The waves rise like wind from the ocean;
My silent voice has now burse! forth like the nightingale
singing;
Like from a child's throat
May the tremors reach forth.
To your presence,
O, my Beloved!

There are the opening lines of the poem and provide a personal witness to the is-ness (*Kar*) of the Beloved. The expression is imaginative. The woman's silent voice (*cup gala*) now rings like the nightingale's song. The vibrations gushing forth from her heart have been compared to the gusty wind from the ocean on the one hand, and to the tiny tremors in a baby's throat on the other. But where are these sound waves heading towards? "Tusan—*mere saian jio—di hazuri vic!*—To your presence, O, my Beloved!" is the answer. The presence of the Beloved is thus acknowledged and celebrated. The destination may be far—the gusty wind indicates that—but it certainly exists. The woman needs no ontological, cosmological, moral, or teleological proofs: she knows, she feels, and therefore yearns for the presence (*hazuri*) of her Beloved. She lyrically asserts the scriptural view that the One is present everywhere, a view we find stated by Guru Nanak, "*jah jah dekha tah tah soi*—in whichever direction I turn my eyes, I see You," and by Guru Arjun, "*Nanak ka patisahu disai jahara*—Visibly present everywhere is the lord of Nanak."

The origin of her longing for the Beloved she traces to the Beloved himself: "You are the One who implanted this sapling—*tuhon butie lai si.*" In this short poem, the woman states that his single glance of benevolence—*ikk nadar*—breathes new life into her; his single beautiful gesture—*ikk naz de gamze*—fills her with fragrance:

> *musk ikk phir maci*
> *magan surati hu ai si...*
>
> An aroma struck the mind again;
> Intoxication overtook consciousness...

The Beloved is thus the one who created her, sustained her, and awakened her. The aroma, a hint from him—the yonder, formless, intangible, yet powerful and aesthetically pleasing—touches her, and she becomes inebriated with longing for him. Interestingly, the sense of fragrance intoxicates her mentally, dissolving the usual dichotomy of body and mind. Clearly, her desire is not only material in nature but also spiritual. It comes from the depths of her very being. This combination of materiality and spirituality underscores the message of the Guru Granth: it is the physically attractive woman dressed up in all her finery—with perfumes and jewels—who has the longing for the Divine Groom.

With the vista of the garden as a backdrop, she also makes the philosophical point that the entire unvierse is dependent upon its singular gardener, her Beloved. In the Guru Granth, the totally abstract and metaphysical One is also addressed metaphorically as the gardener: "*ihu jagu vari mera prabh mali sada samale ko nahi khali*—the world is the garden; my lord is its gardener; ever he guards it, leaving none without protection." Through his twentieth-century protagonist, Bhai Vir Singh is paraphrasing the creating and nurturing functions belonging to the Gardener. Through the course of the brief poem, we hear her repeat several times that he is the one who has implanted the sapling (*buti*). For their origin and sustenance, the individual shrub and the garden as a whole depend upon him: "If you forget us even for a moment, how will we remain in bloom or be fragrant?" she asks. The fragrance which the gardener bestows upon the (*buti*) is both her elemental energy and the desire for him; the identity between her *elan vital* and the longing for the Gardener, the Beloved, constitutes the core of the thematic burden of the poem.

Bhai Vir Singh is simultaneously highlighting another element from the Sikh worldview: the feminine dimension of the Transcedent One. The One beyond (*Ikk*) is a Gardener—ever caring and nurturing the world. A harmonious and loving relationship between the Creator and creation is postulated. The Beloved (*Oan*) is transcendent—beyond reach and beyond all categorizations. Nowhere are any contours drawn sketching his form or personality. The metaphor of the Beloved is quickly and skillfully moved into the second person, *tun*. Although in our references (and in translation as well) the specification of gender occurs, in Bhai Vir Singh's composition itself there is scarcely any. *Sajan Jio* is constantly beckoned, grammatically, in the gender-neutral form of the second person—as *tun*, the neuter "you". The Beloved is thus encountered informally, intimately, but without any emphasis upon "Its" form. Therewith, the utter unicity and singularity—the *ikk-ness* of the Sikh ultimate reality-is also projected. In one passage she rhythmically repeats "you, you, you—*tuhin, tuhin tuhin,*" which but echoes the scriptural style of saluting the *Ikk Oan.* Guru Arjun's words *"tun mera pita tun hai mera mata tun mera bandhapu tun mera bhrata*—you are my father, you my mother, you my friend, you my brother," shatter the monopoly of male symbols in depicting the unicity of the Ultimate Being, and they also express the intimate relationship between one and the One. Again, we find that the "I—Thou" encounter put forth by Buber echoes the Sikh communion between the individual and the Divine.

Instead of creating or employing male images, we hear and see the singer of *Mere Saian Jio* trying to visualize the One—the totally abstract and metaphysical Being—in aesthetic terms. A prominent "form" for the Infinite Beloved comes from the aural sphere. It is rendered through the term *rasa* and its variations. These terms form the very title of the poem "Rasa, Rasia Rasal," which ends with the following lines:

vah vah coj tere, mere saian

tere geetan dian tainu vadhaian
tuhon geet, sangeet, te suad
ras, rasia te ap rasal.

Wondrous, wondrous are your sports, my beloved;
Congratulations to you on the beauty of your songs;
The song, the music, and the essential taste are you;
You youerself are the joy, the enjoyer, and the bringer of joy.

These lines are truly untranslatable, and there can be no adequate version. First the maiden expresses her amazement at the marvelous aspect of the Beloved. She then celebrates the richness and beauty of his songs (*geetan*). In line 3 she goes on to identify her Beloved with the song (*geet*), the music (*sangeet*), and the essential taste (*suad*). Finally, she addresses him in a play on the word *rasa*: he is the aesthetic delight (*rasa*), the relisher of aesthetic delight (*rasia*), and the provider of aesthetic delight (*rasal*). The Beloved is therefore all-encompassing: he is not only the aesthetic joy but its savorer and bestower as well. He is the primal cause and ultimate end of joy. His Oneness is repeated over and over again. Again, Bhai Vir Singh is expanding upon scriptural ideas and vocabulary. Song, music, and tasting were, as we saw, very important factors in the creation of the Guru Granth itself. The songs that Nanak sang, the songs of which the holy book is composed, had their genesis in the Divine Beloved. The image of the Transcendent as possessor of *rasa* also has its archetype in the Guru Granth. For, we may recall, our bride addresses her Beloved as "*din daialu pritam manmohanu ati rasa lal sagurau*—compassionate, beneficent, beloved, enticer of the hearts, overflowing with *rasa*, like the *lala* flower." In fact, the passage quoted above from *Mere Saian Jio* echoes much of Guru Nanak's terminology and is evocative of his verse in the Guru Granth: "*ape rasia apu rasu ape ravanhar*. It itself is the relisher of *rasa*, it itself is the essence, it itself is the bestower."

In her perception of the Beloved, Bhai Vir Singh's heroine

also avails herself of the symbol of light. For instance, she exclaims that one ray of the Beloved, from his luminous form (*nuri rup*), enchanted her. The Arabic and Persian, term for light (*nur*) is also used in two other instances to qualify the Transcendent: "Your light pervades the earth and skies"; "I am desirous of the vision of your luminous form." In another verse she implores her transcendent Beloved:

> Bestow your vision upon me,
> Oh radiance of radiance (s).

Here she alludes to him as light of lights or radiance of radiance(s)—*ujjalan de ujjal*—which recalls the preception of Ultimate Reality as *Jyotisam jyoti* and *Nur al-anwar* from the Hindu and Islamic traditions, respectively. In the Guru Granth, as well, "light" in its Sanskrit and Arabic equivalents has been extensively used as a symbol for the Absolute. The following instance in the Guru Granth comes from Guru Nanak himself:

> *jahi jahi dekhan tahu joti tumahari*
> *tera rup keneha!*

> Wheresoever I turn, I see your light;
> What a wondrous form you have!

The concept of light and wonderment at the brilliance of this form is riterated in *Mere Saian Jio*.

The distance fron him—underscoring his transcendence—constitutes the core of the intense experience for Bhai Vir Singh's heroine. He remains an enchanting paradox: he is infinite; he is infinitesimal! In either fashion, he is totally beyond her grasp. In the poem entitled "Nikki God Vic" ("In the Tiny Lap"), she marvels at the allpervasive Beloved playing in the tiny lap of a rose:

> *aj nur de tarke*
> *jadon lai rahi sisaver angraian...*
> *ikk khire gulab di kuli god vic*

tusin khed rahe sao mere saian
kinjh, han kinjh! a gae sao
os nikki god vic?
mere aidhe vadhe visal saian!

At the touch of light (*nur*) today
When the morning was beginning to stir...
In the silky lap of a blossomed rose,
You were playing my Beloved.
How, yes, how
Did you enter that tiny lap?
My great and vast Beloved!

The reader is not to infer that her Beloved was literally playing *in* the silky rose! It would be a gross misunderstanding of the Poet's intent and message to believe that the Beloved was encapsulated in the rose. The maiden is struck with the sight of the rose in full bloom during the glory of the morning. So overpowering is the scene that she imagines the infinite Beloved playing in the little rose. The Transcendent is never enclosed; It is never in the rose as such. That Its infinity and formlessness can never be confined in a finite frame is categorically affirmed in the Guru Granth: *"thapia na jae*—It cannot be molded; It cannot be shaped," says Guru Nanak in the *Japu*.

Similarly, in "Sadke Teri Jadugari De" ("Homage to Your Magic Feats"), she states that he is within her:

mere andar, dhur andar, dhur andar de
kise ohle luke mere pritam!
han,
tumbane o apnian sangeetak tumban nal
jaga dene o tarban taran
andarle dian
gaondian han uh geet

—tusan ji de birhe, tusan ji de milan de tarane-
jo karde han jadugari mere hi utte
meri main bir bir takkadi
rahi jani e kambdi te tharrandi
ah pritam
dissan de ohle luke pritam
kol kol par dur dur,
dur dur par kol kol
sadke teri jadugari de

In me, deep inside, deep inside somewhere
is hidden my Beloved!
Yes,
You strike me with your melodious tunes,
Touching
My inner strings.
They sing songs-
Songs of separation from you, songs of the anticipation,
of union with you.
These do cast magic upon me.
I gaze all around.
Trembling, quivering.

Oh Beloved!
Behind sight hidden Beloved!
Very near (*kol kol*), but far far (*dur dur*)
Far, far (*dur dur*), but near, very near (*kol kol*)
Homage to your miracle!

Paradoxically, closeness to and distance from the Beloved, as well as his infinitesimalness and infinity, are felt deeply by the woman. He is "ure ure par agamo agam—close close, but farther than the farthest." He is so close and so small that he abides in her innermost being. But he is hidden (*ohle*) somewhere. Thus even though he may be very close, very near, he remains inaccessible, totally transcendent. Again, it is clear that he is not enclosed in her; his form is not present within her. Formless, he remains hidden somewhere in her being. Simultaneously, he is infinite and far, far away, and the categories of time and space do not delimit him. In "Dil Saddhar," she proclaims his infinite nature:

> *agamo agam agam he mere tun pyarna.*
>
> Unfathomable amongst the most unfathomable are you, my Love.

Finally, she accepts the utter ineffability: "Tongue, be silent! Trembling and quivering tongue, be silent! Friends! Nothing can here be uttered." The paradox therefore cannot be verbalized. Silence alone can be the only indicator. Having him so close and yet so far, experiencing his infinitesimalness and infinity together is totally overwhelming and defies articulation in human speech.

What we have here is a poetic exposition of the scriptural dialectic of the transcendence and the proximity of the One (*Ikk*). While maintaining the utter unfathomability and infinity of the Ultimate. Reality, the Guru Granth posits Its presence within everyone:

> *tun adi purakhu aparanparu karta*
> *tera paru na paia jai jiu*
> *tun ghat ghat antari sarab nirantari*
> *sabh mahi rahia samai jiu.*
>
> You the Primal Being, you are the Infinite Creator;
> None can fathom you.
> But within each and every being you are
> Equally, constantly ever.

These words of Guru Ram Das (Nanak IV) are reiterated by his successor Guru Arjun (Nanak V): "*tu sabh mahi vartahi api*— you are present within all. In the *Arati,* Guru Nanak exclaims:

"*sabh mahi joti, joti hai soi*—within all is the light and the light is That One." The symbol of the insubstantial and non-material light is used extensively in the Guru Granth to portray the Transcendent One in all of Its manifestations. In another passage, the Guru Granth declares Its infinite nature directly: "*agam agocaru sacu sahibu mera*—unfathomable, ineffable, truth is my lord." The holy book also contains passages expressing the marvel of the dialectic: "*nirgunu api sargunu bhi ohi kala dhari jini sagali mohi*—formless and yet archetypal, it takes on substances that enchant all." This enchantment felt by the fifth Guru finds a precedent in the thought of Guru Nanak: "*sahas tav nain nan nain hahi tohi kau sahas tav murati nana ek tohi...—sahas tav gandh iv calat mohi*—you have a thousand eyes, but without eyes you are; you have a thousand forms, but without form you are...you have a thousand noses, but without a nose you are; I am left thoroughly enchanted." Through the word "thousand" Guru Nanak is describing the One in terms of the entire gamut of comprehension. Additionally, he juxtaposes Its immensity and infinity, and thus delineates. It as beyond all expression and thought. In line with the concept of the *Ikk Oan Kar* as expounded in the Guru Granth, the woman's vision renders a very positive and joyous image of the Transcendent. Yet, it is no image, for the aesthetic delight is devoid of all materiality and substantiality; its intangibility and transcendence can never be formalized into a figure. Pure form is the Beloved—but form realized only in experience. Thus, the marvel of the paradoxical nature of the Metaphysical One, which was expressed in the Guru Granth and in Guru Nanak's encounter with the Divine (as recorded in the *Puratan Janamsakhi*), is recreated with a sense of wonder and joy in Bhai Vir Singh's poetry.

In spite of her expansive imagination and varied idealizations of the Beloved, the heroine of *Mere Saian Jio* retains a remarkable consistency. Whether as light, knowledge, beauty, *rasa* or artist, as innermost or farthest-off, her Beloved is envisioned as formless, transcendent, totally beyond her grasp. Throughout he remains the absolute Source and the acme of beauty, love, and art. In her we thus have a true exponent of *Ikk Oan Kar,* the fundamental Sikh ideal. As noted earlier, even in her most intimate poetry she uses the vocabulary, symbols, and metaphors of the Sikh scriptures. Her very yearning for the Beloved also has its prototype in Guru Nanak's hymn *Barah Mah.* Bhai Vir Singh's work is, in sense, an exposition of the scriptures, but instead of being aridly intellectualized, it uses the medium of romantic poetry. The concept of the Existence of the One Being is not expounded; it is experienced by our heroine at its very deepest.

In presenting through his poetry the central Sikh concepts enshrined in the Guru Granth, Bhai Vir Singh has succeeded remarkably in emulating the mood and idiom of the Sikh scripture. The anthology of poems *Mere Saian Jio* is saturated with the personal pronoun *tun*—encountered in the Guru Granth. The vocabulary, metaphors, and symbols of that text—*agam, mali, rasa, nur*—occur frequently in his own poems. The very title, *Mere Saian Jio,* seems to be both based upon and in turn unfolding the scriptural verse: "*kar kirpa mere sain*—be gracious, my Beloved."

Besides interpreting the fundamental theological concept, Bhai Vir Singh's *Mere Saian Jio* also unfolds the essential epistemological ideal enshrined in the Sikh holy text. The basis of Sikh epistemology is that the *Ikk Oan Kar* is not intellectually apprehended or made the object of reasoning, but felt. The One cannot be objectively proved—it cannot be tested out in mathematical equations; rather, it is subjectively recognized. The *Ikk Oan Kar* is not posited as an impossible goal; rather, it becomes an object of ardent quest, of ardent longing to be undertaken by the self to attain supreme knowledge.

In "Saian Jio di Sian" ("Recognition of the Beloved"), Bhai Vir Singh's protagonist actually refutes those who think that the Metaphysical One is impossible to know. The poem opens with this question:

e kaun han jo akhde han:
"tere saian ji sian nahin hunde?"

Who are they who say:
"Your Beloved cannot be known?"

After posing this question, she directly addresses her Beloved, saying that those who see, hear, smell, touch, and taste discern him. Again, it is a short poem, but of great artistic and philosophical import. The maiden asserts that "those who have eyes discern him from his overflowing beauty (*dhulh dhulh pai rahi sundarta ton*), which is reflected from the scenes around (*nazarian ton*) and upon the eyesight, (*nazarian te*)." She continues in the same lyric style: "Those who have ears know him from his melodious word, which reverberates everywhere....those who drop their fears know him from his sensation-creating touch." His brimming ambrosial drops fall into the mouths of those who, like the *papiha* (a mythical love-bird), longingly sing for him. At some auspicious moment these ambrosial drops provide the taste of his existence (*hond*). It is thus a clear announcement about the certain possibility of the apprehension of the Beloved—of the *Ikk Oan Kar,* the Ultimate Reality.

Her emphasis is upon *sian* or recognition, an immediate and exhaustive recovery, a reseeing. The Beloved is here, there, everywhere. The vast and magnificent panoramas, the dulcet symphony echoing throughout the universe—these are hints of Its ontological presence. But it is the human being who has to apprehend that through her or his five senses. The physical senses are thus a crucial channel. The process is not an arduous one; it does not call for asceticism; it does not call for the stifling of the senses. Knowledge too is not of any new theme, nor a garnering of new abstract or scientific facts. On the contrary, the physical senses have to be sharpened and heightened in order for them to recognize the spaceless and timeless Beloved. It is as if Bhai Vir Singh were illuminating for the reader and hearer the third stages of the *Jape,* the *Saram Khand: "tithai ghariai surati mati mani budhi* — here are sharpened consciousness, wisdom, mind and discrimination." The heightening of the senses means sharpening the perception so that instead of dull and ordinary sensations one experiences deeply the extraordinary. As Bhai Vir Singh's heroine says: *"panjan de rasian ton rasa ucian nun, han, lakha deno ho tusin ap* — those who transcend the ordinary seeing, hearing, smelling, touching, and tasting, yes, you yourself reveal yourself unto them."

The process of recognition (*sian*) which underlies the Sikh envisioning of the Transcendent is further elaborated in the poem entitled "Andarle Nain" ("Inner Eyes"). In this poem the maiden throws light upon the phenomenon of insight, which combines physicai seeing with knowledge and intelligence; *sian* (recognition) by the individual with *lakhana* (revelation or showing) from the Beloved. The poem in its entirety may be translated as follows:

Eye — the human eye
Could not see you,
My Beloved!
Darmness has overtaken
Knowledge (*ilmu*) and intelligence (*aql*).
Yes, the strong light of intellect.
It still cannot see you:
The brilliance is too dazzling.
Do cast a favourable glance (*nazar*),
Do please open the inner eyes,
Which would see you —
Whether it be light, dark or bedazzling,
You, my Beloved! Beloved!
In every place (*har ja*) in every colour (*har rang*)
    in every direcstion (*har su*)
Playing (*karda dhelan*), yet remaining apart (*rahinda asang*).
Handsome, you are the acme of splendor.

It is reiterated that the Beloved is all-pervading. The One is in all space, in every colour, and in all derections. That he is not only in light but also in darkness is an interesting perception by the maiden. And he pervades everything. Yet, paradoxically, he always remains apart (*rahinda asang*) from everything. Again, he is not in anything — he plays within each and every thing, but constantly maintains his distance. The Transcendent always remains transcendent.

In the poem "Bithun Pathar" ("Amorphous Stone") it appears that the maiden even gives up her attempt to envision her Beloved. She seems to accept the sheer impossibility of imaging the Formless and Transcendent One. The Beloved cannot be seen! The maiden emerges as a deeply thoughtful character, constantly making smooth and liquid transitions between art and metaphysics. At the opening of the poem, she describes a stone lying on the wayside, amorphous and shapeless. A sculptor chances upon it and perceives in it the form smothered by the unwanted mass of rock. He takes a chisel in one hand, a hammer in the other. Carving and cutting, he takes off the unwanted mass. "Behold, it turned into handsome form — *suhani tasvir* — that formless piece of stone."

She then compares her own mental state to that of the amorphous stone — in its former shapeless and lifeless condition. Perceiving her Beloved as the artist whose art is full of grace, she wishes that he would chisel away all the unnecessary and extraneous matter, leaving but the imprint of his own picture upon her. She thus asks of her Beloved himself to carve his image upon herself. The chiseling away of the superfluous matter is a symbolic expression of her wish to get rid of material desires and, may be, of her own ego also, so that the intrinsic, essential image, the beautiful picture of the Beloved, alone would remain. The Transcendent's portrait would breathe life into her present condition. The short poem leaves us with two empowering facts: that our very constitution, our *elan vital*, is the Transcendent Reality; and that the female body, the female form, is fully capable of mirroring the Infinite One. *She* is the one made in the image of the Transcendent Creator.

While maintaining her inability to conceive an image of the Beloved and therefore imploring him to imprint his image on her mind, she simultaneously sees him as the supreme artist. "Bithun Pathar" ends with these words:

My Beloved, you are an artist;
Your art is full of grace.
Give me the power to understand this;
Do rip off the surrounding veil of ignorance.

The Beloved, then, is an artist, but one whose art is full of grace — *mehar bharpur*. Loving and nurturing aspects of the singular formless Artist are clearly identified.

The image of God as artist is well—known. But in our maiden's articulation, the emphasis is on his grace. Human knowledge and intelligence are deficient; the physical eye is precluded from discerning It. But a favourable glance (*nazar*) from the Other would open the inner eye and thus provide insight into the Divine Reality. It is, then, the inner eye which perceives the omnipresent Being. This is the fourth stage of spiritual ascension as delineated by Guru Nanak in the *Japu - Karam Khand*, the Realm of Grace. Gace (*nadari*),i.e. his glance (*nazar*) of favour, is what the maiden seeks. Touched by his grace, her inner eye would encounter the bedazzling brilliance. The merging of eyesight with insight brings about this juncture where human effort is touched by divine grace. It is also the moment of revelation.

Central to Sikh epistemology is the vision of the Ikk Oan as a perennial movement. As originally experienced by Guru Nanak and as illustrated by the heroine of *Mere Saian Jio*, it remains the objective, the goal for every man and woman. The longing for the vision of the Beloved, a mystic consummation between one and the One, is the domanant motif of this anthology of poems; yet the longing remains sheer longing. the finale of *Mere Saian Jio*, is the poem called "Nam Piala" ("The Cup of Nam or Word"):

The cup of the beautiful Word
Is overflowing, O friends.
Who will have a sip of it?
Keep watching, O friends.

She whose own cup of longing is brimming,
She alone will receive the cup of nectar...

The poem recalls the historical moment portrayed in the *Puratan Janamsakhi* — the moment of Guru Nanak's mystic experience some five hundred years earlier. That is when he received the ambrosial cup of the Divine Name and was launched on his mission. Bhai Vir Singh's interpretation of that event thorugh the medium of twentieth century Punjabi poetry acknowledges that primal moment in Sikh history and projects its application towards the present and future. In "Nam Piala," the heroine is addressing her female friends. The future of society depends upon them and their male counterparts. Interestingly, the female (*sakhi*) is the generic term, inclusive of men. Their mission will get launched with the drinking of the ambrosial Word. But who gets to have a sip of it? Who savors it? Paradoxically, it is the individual whose cup brims (*dhulh dhulh pai riha hovai*) with longing (*saddhar*) who stands to gain! For the emptier the inside, the stronger the urge; and, hence, the greater the chance of receiving the divine nectar. Bachelard's prayer for "hunger" is implicit here.

Thus, we see the solitary maiden and we hear her. She weaves garlands of songs and waves. Naomi Goldenberg, modern feminist writer, observes that the image of a woman weaving is a positive one:

A woman who weaves is concentrating on changing natural materials into something useful for civilized life. She is skilled at a craft, which she has studied to the point of its becoming second nature. When she weaves, she uses this skill to bring something she alone can visualize psychically — like the shape of a basket or the design in a tapestry — into a material form which everyone else can see and use in their world.

The image of weaving portrays, we could add, the woman's meditative and reflective proclivities. Bhai Vir Singh's maiden weaving garlands of songs and waves is certainly highly skilled in her art, for her words are so natural and intrinsically so powerful. the garlands — "like the shape of a basket or the design in a tapestry" - are visualized psychically by her and presented to the reader.

What is finally woven by the maiden are polarities, polarities such as proximity and distance, infinitesimal and infinite, human and divine, male and female, past and future, empty and full. The heroine of *Mere Saian Jio* weaves garlands of songs for her Beloved, who, though close by, remains constantly far away. The *Ikk Oan is* felt intimately by her — within her very self. Yet That One , transcendent, remains ever transcendent. Through the maiden's songs one realizes that distance and proximity in the Sikh tradition do not violate each other; instead of being mutually exclusive they enhance each other. The Unfathomable Infinite Beloved is "seen" by her in the dew-prop shimmering on the silky lap of a rose at the break of dawn. The shimmering minuscule droplet presents the indescribable vastness. Human language explodes and participates in the communication with the Divine, for how else would there be garlands of waves? Fearlessly, the maiden expresses the emotion of love delineated in the Guru Granth and in spite of the chasm that lies between them she weaves together the human and divine realms.

Bhai Vir Singh's heroine has the power, the skill, and the sensitivity to work on this cosmic loom. Like the bride figure in the Guru Granth, she restates the primacy of the feminine consciousness in the search for the Transcendent One. Through her, the curcial moment in Sikh history — the experience of the "Primal Paradox" by Guru Nanak — is thrust into the future. And the emptier the cup of longing for a vision of the *Ikk Oan,* the fuller will be the experience of union.

4

The Christian Missions and Women's Studies

Despite the continuity of conversion as the ultimate goal, the institutions which the AMM designed for Indian women can be divided between those which fit into a larger Indian context, and which had the potential to be reorganized under indigenous control; and those which were aimed so exclusively at conversion that non-Christians were not interested in their future. Institutions in the first category received government financial assistance at sometime during their development; those in the second were privately supported either directly by ABCFM or WBM funds, or by independent charitable contributions. Unfortunately for the historian, the gradual process of transfer or dissolution is not, in most cases, as clear as one might wish. The ABCFM books are officially sealed after 1929 to protect the privacy of persons still living, as a result of which the record the section "Work for Women." And as "work for women" they shared several important characteristics. They received little or no financial support from the ABCFM. They were mainly the result of the efforts of one, two, or sometimes three women, who considered them their special duty, and without whose support they weakened and sometimes died. They were quided only by a loose collection of ideals, which often conflicted with social realities, and which circumstances assured would seldom be consciously and systematically developed.

First it is necessary to set the stage: the place of missions in educational development in India as a whole, and the place of women's education in this larger setting. This will give us the background with which to look more specifically at the institutions of the AMM.

I. The Development of Public Education in British India and Its Relationship to Missions and Government

The interrelationship between education, missionaries and the government in British India is notable for its complexity. In this Section I shall discuss briefly the historical development of these relationships, simplifying but, I hope, not unduly distorting them. This topic has been fully researched and discussed in several other works, the best being that by Syed Nurullah and J. P. Naik. In my discsussion I shall rely heavily on their comprehensive treatment, to which I refer the interested reader.

There were to be a series of ongoing conflicts over the future and purpose of education in British India between the three groups most involved in its development, and it is useful to keep them in mind while discussing specific historcal shifts. The most important question was who was to control the development of Western-style educational systems: a governmental bureaucracy, Christian missionaries, or autochthanous elites? A second question concerned the object of education for India: was it to spread knowledge of Western literature and science, and perhaps religion, or was it to preserve ancient Eastern scholarship? The third concerned the medium of instruction: was it to tbe English, ancient Sanskrit, or the modern vernaculars? A fourth question concerned methodology: given monetary restraints, was it better to educate a few to the highest levels and rely on what was called 'downward filtration' eventually to spread education to the masses; or was it better to design educational policies to reach minimum levels of literacy across society before supporting higher education? Each of these questions was to surface again and again in educational debates in the nineteenth century, and while answers were sometimes temporarily agreed upon, many continued into the twentieth.

Despite royal patronage of scholarship and the arts, education in pre-British India was mainly a private matter, initiated by individuals or family groups and aimed at the preservation of ancient Sanskrit learning. In the eighteenth and early nineteenth century, as the Company was consolidating its control over South Asia, with few exceptions formal education was the province of an elite, male group. By the late eighteenth century, Missions in Bengal had established local schools for boys and were in some outstanding instances fostering Oriental learning with their patronage.

Until 1813, the relationship between missionaries and the British East India Company was antagonistic. It was company policy to refrain, as far as possible, from interferring in the internal affairs of South Asia and the Directors felt that missionary activity could do little but stir up trouble. Due to pressure from evangelical Christians in England, however, when the Company Charter came up for renewal in 1813, missionaries were granted permission to enter India. Offering primary education to children was one of the surest ways to provide continuous contact with young Indians, and from that time on, through the nineteenth and into the twentieth century, missionaries became involved in all levels of South Asian education.

The practical result of the Woods Dispatch was the rapid Westernization of Indian education. Indigenous institutions were neglected by officials and for several decades there were few remnants of this alternate system. While there were some government schools in major cities directly administered by municipalities, most education was in the hands of private agencies through the medium of the grants-in-aid system. The private agencies best prepared to apply for those funds were mission groups like the AMM, especially in the first two or three decades after the 1859 implementation of the Woods' suggestions.

> Under the system of state aid, inaugurated by the Dispatch of 1854, by which large sums of money were devoted by the government to the assistanace of private efforts in education, the missionaries were able to develop that side of their work at a comparatively small expense. Government supervision and partial control tended to make their work

> better systematized [than it had been prior to 1859] and excepting the distinctly Christian instruction, the *two systems of state and missionary education tended to become more and more like* each other.

The congenial relationship between government and mossions was not to last. By the 1880's and 1890's competition for funds was increasing between schools managed by the Education Department, those run by missionaries, and a small but growing sector of Indian educators from social reform groups. It was largely due to the complaints of disgruntled missionaries that government appointed an Education Commission in 1880 to inquire into all aspects of public instruction. Missionary groups felt that the ideals of the Woods' Dispatch had been ignored and that it was unfairly administered by the Education Department. Despite explicit instructions to the contrary, missionaries said too much money was expended on higher education and as a consequence government colleges in Calcutta, Madras and Bombay were flourishing, while primary education was neglected. This complaint was really an indirect dispute over control, since government colleges were not under missionary auspices. Furthermore, missions felt that government regulations were strangling their primary and secondary schools, making them too secular and irreligious.

The Hunter Commission's Report of 1882 was the result of an eight-month tour by its members resulting in 222 recommendations. The Report recognized the gap between the intent and the results of the Woods' Dispatch, and reaffirmed the priority of mass education over higher education. Several other missionary complaints were also recognized as valid. While on the one hand the Commission recognized the government's debt to mission workers, on the other it did not trust mission motives. The Report stated:

> Those who assist the state by managing...[schools] should have great influence in determining all questions of general educational policy... The Director of Public Instruction should be guided as much by the views of those interested in aided education as by those of Departmental officers.

While those who managed scholls in 1882 were most frequently mission groups, the Commission implicitly recognized that this was a temporary state of affairs.

> Missionary institutions hold an intermediate position between those managed by the Department and those managed by the people themselves. On the one hand, they are the outcome of private effort, but on the other they are not strictly local; nor will encouragement to them directly foster those habits of self-reliance and combination of purposes of public utility, which is one of the objects of the grants-in-aid system to develop....It must not be forgotten that the private effort which it is mainly intended to evoke is that of the people themselves. Natives of India must constitute the most important of all agencies.... Other agencies may hold a prominant place for a time, and may always find some places in a system in which great variety is on every ground desirable.

It is indicative of slipping missionary influence that the Commission's Report was not exactly what the missionaries might have wanted. It reaffirmed government's commitment to the diversity of mass education by saying that government scholarship holders could attend non-government schools, but it also introduced a conscience clause stating that a child could refuse religious instruction when offered along with regular classes. It affirmed that grants-in-aid in the past had been biased towards established institutions, usually missionary, by being determined on the basis of successful government examinations. It recommended that this bias be overcome by taking into account other circumstances, such as location and local initiative, when evaluating and renewing grants.

The Hunter Commission's recommendations were to be implemented by the Provincial Governments, resulting in a swing away from mission control. By the turn of the century, Indian private enterprise was rapidly developing into the most important agency for the spread of Westernstyle education. In turn, British officials felt that the quality of education had deteriorated since 1880, and a split developed among educationalists over the quality issue. At a conference of Directors of Public Instruction called by Lord Curzon in 1901, British officials recommended that the government curtail expansion in favour of controlling and upgrading existing institutions. Many enlightend Indians still supported the earlier Report, and advocated further emphasis on private enterprise, expansion, and a laissez-faire attitude on the part of government. The conflict between these two factions resulted in an almost complete victory for the official line: control expansion and improve quality though stricter regulations. The principles which had been declared in 1854, and reaffirmed in 1882, calling for a viriety of educational opportunities and applauding the diversity which the mission and independent schools represented, were no longer in vogue. The twentieth century trend away from private and toward public education was begnning, and in the process missionaries lost most of the power which they had formerly had over state decision making.

In the years between 1901 and 1921, when the Department of Education was turned over to Indian Ministries, many of the same issues over control and purpose continued, now in an atmosphere of increasing unrest. By the time Indian Ministries gained control over the Department of Education in 1921, and Provincial Autonomy was granted in 1937, world economic depression and ideological conflicts combined to ensure that their first efforts would be plagued by failure. In the meantime, mission groups were feeling the same economic pressures and ideological shifts, and retrenchment was the order of the day. The Lindsay Commission on Christian Higher Education issued a report in 1932, which observed a "quality of psychological inrtia" in mission education, and recognized that the pioneering days of mission schools were over in India. In many cities mission schools had lost their priority and were only second best when compared with Municipal and Government schools. Indian political independence and control over educational systems was drawing nearer, and subsequently the Christian mission school was to play a smaller part, catering mainly to a poor, often dependent, Christian community, not to the larger Indian population.

II. The Development of Women's Education in British India

Keeping in mind the chronological framework presented in the last section, it is important here to review the place of women in the educational systems of British India. It is generally agreed that in the early 1800's when the AMM and other mission groups were settling into their locations, Hindu and Muslim women had little opportunity for anything but household education. Nurullah, for one, says of the 1820's,

> ...it may be concluded that barring an extremely small number of women who received some rudimentary educaion either at home or in schools, general or specific, almost the whole of the female population of the country was deprived of formal education.

AMM Reports illustrate Indian resistance to female education by repeating the story of a Brahmin gentleman who scoffed to a mission worker that one might as well teach donkeys as women. Despite the distasteful superiority assumed by this story, it epitomizes early Indian attitudes towards female education. The religious texts upon which such a learned Brahmin based his statement predated the Christian era, and had been reinforced by centuries of social traditions. A review of the gradual evolution of women's role in Hindu religious texts, and the later addition of *purdah* by the Muslims, is not within the scope of this thesis. It is, however, important for sevaral reasons to note Indian resistance to wemen's education. One is to recognize that the Company was right in its early perception that women's education was a controversial question. The second is to emphasize the religious as well as social basis of Muslim and Hindu resistance to it. The idea of formal educaion for women was an alien idea, one which was disruptive of Indian norms. Formal female education was begun, not in response to indigenous demands, but on the initiative of Christian missionaries looking for converts.

Furthermore, it did not have the enthusiastic support of most of the British Governmental establishment. As late as 1850, it was the official view that formal education for Indian females would be a natural result of educating Indian men, and was a controversial subject best eschewed by the company. If missionaries were important to the mid-century development of schools for men, they were even more vital to the introduction and maintenance of those systems for women. Typically, the first school for Indian girls in the Bombay Presidency was opened by the AMM in Bombay city in 1824, and the first in the *mofussil* was opened in Ahmadnagar in 1832. In 1853 a report from Bombay was given in Parliamentary Committee to the effect that no girls had yet attended a government school.

> Although a letter was published two years ago by one of the secretaries to the Government of India to the effect that where any portion of the natives desired female education, the government institutions were to embrace females, I do not think as yet a singly female has come under the Government system of Education in Western India.

The Company's avoidance of the subject of state support for female education ended with the Dispatch of 1854. The Dispatch intended schools for girls to be among those eligible for the new formal grants-in-aid progaramme and included the following words of encouragement.

> The importance of female education in India cannot be overrated; and we have observed with pleasure the evidence which is now afforded to an increased desire on the part of many of the natives of India to give a good education to their daughters. By this means a far greater proportional impulse is imparted to the educational and moral tone of the people than by the education of men. We have already observed that schools for females are included among those to which grants-in-aid may be given; and we cannot refrain from expressing our cordial sympathy with the efforts which are being made in this direction. Our Governor-General in Council has declared, in a communication to the Government of Bengal, that the Government ought to give

to the native female education in India its frank and cordial support; and in this we heartily concur.

The newly created Departments of Education were instructed to pay special attention to girls' schools. Between the time of the Dispatch and the Commission of 1882, small gains were made in primary education for women. These could hardly be attributed only to the verbal support offered by the government, however, since by this time Indian Social Reform movements had made the issue of women's education one of national political importance. While the average parent continued to be against women's education, urban liberals felt it could do no harm, and perhaps some good, if girls learned to read and write.

The 1880 census of Ahmadnagar District illustrates the gains made in the direction of female education; 871 women were recorded as literate or under instruction, out of a total female population of 369,497. The census further illustrates what may contemporary observers noted; Christian women were far more likely to have access to formal schooling than non-Christian women.

TABLE 4.1

Literacy Rates Among Women: Ahmadnagar District, 1881

	Population	*Literate or Under Instruction*	*Percent*
Hindus	348,043	419	.001
Muslims	19,489	48	.002
Christians	1,965	404	20.000
Total	369,497	871	.002

The District Gazeteer also shows the importance of private agencies' involvement in educational development. Although unfortunately it is not detailed enough to make as many comparisons as one might like, the figures for the city of Ahmadnagar show that approximately 30% of all pupils in daily attendance were enrolled in non-government schools. There were twelve government schools in the city, three of which were for girls. Of the eight privately operated schools, four were designed especially for girls. In other words, private agencies, mainly the AMM, were responsible for more than doubling the number of schools for girls in the city.

As we saw in the last section, the Educational Commission's Report of 1882 was ambivalent about the role of mission schools; on the one hand, they recognized the important contribution of mission, yet on the other they issued fair warning that this was a temporary situation. Part of this ambivalence stemmed from the Commission's realization that female education was especially dependent upon private enterprise. On the subject of aid to girls' schools the Commission said,

> ....female education is still in an extremely backward condition.... The sympathies of the people do not yet run sufficiently in this direction to induce local bodies to devote to female education any of the funds at their disposal. Hence we think it expedient to recommend that public funds of all kinds—local, municipal, and provincial— should be chargeable in an equitable proportion for the support of girls' schools as well as boys' schools; and that the former, being in an earlier stage of development, should receive even something more than what might appear to be strictly impartial share of encouragement. Public opinion in this matter connot yet be accepted as the standard of what ought to be done.

The commission went on to say that due to dependence on religious agencies, the kind of education offered to girls often included some Christian teaching, but that was unavoidable for the time being.

> The Principle of religious neutrality prevents aid from being given for religious teaching as such, but we see no reason why such secular teaching as is actually given, if only incidentally, in schools intended mainly for religious teaching, should not be *pro tanto* rewarded. If a girl, in learning to

> read a religious book, acquires the power of reading the vernacular, it is at least something accomplished, and may serve as a basis for something more. There are so many obstacles to the progress of female education that we think the conditions on which aid is granted to it should be made as easy as possible.

It added that while indigenous control of women's education was a goal to strive for.

> It may perhaps be found that Municipal and Local Boards are not in all cases prepared to undertake the management of girls' schools; to force it upon unwilling persons would not be likely to lead to satisfactory results.

In the meantime, the Report suggested facilitating women's education by offering scholarships, supporting boarding institutions, and encouraging normal classes wherever possible. It also referred to what was to become an important issue later on, the fact that "it ought not to be taken for granted that the instruction which is suitable for a boy must necessarily be good for an Indian girl."

None of the Commission's recommendations on women's education, however, contained any mention of specific financing schemes, or explicit amounts to be expended for women's schools. It in no way represented a radical departure from past positions and it did not suggest either rapid expansion of girls' schools or mention the possibility of compulsory education for girls at any level.

> On the whole, therefore, it may be said that the Indian Education Commission did nothing more than recommend slight alterations in lines of policies which had already been developed.... For these and other reasons, education of women did not expand very rapidly between 1882-1902 although most of the recommendations of the Commission were accepted by the provincial Governments.

III. Industrial Training

If all of the girls and women who came into contact with the Mission could not, or would not, conform to the attainments of cultured women, what was to be done with the rest? Actually, after the famine and plague, this meant by far the majority of girls under the Mission's charge. If they were unequal to the literary and academic standards to which the Girls' School aspired, for what were they to be trained? This group included most girls resident in Alice House, almost all of those in the Chapin Home, and a goodly number admitted as boarders to the Girls' School. A variety of plans and projects were proposed to meet their needs, none of them very successful; mainly, I submit, for two reasons: one, the Mission as a whole, and women missionaries in particular, could not see beyond their own narrow experience and dreams; and two, because of the pressures of time and money, many decisions were made by the Mission after the fact, with only a vague understanding of future consequences. This was especially true for plans concerning women, which were circumscribed by the ambivalent position of women in the Mission.

Industrial training," which to the AMM meant almost any training other than literary, was always a controversial subject in the Mission community. This was true about training designed for men as well as for women. It is significant that the two men most convinced of its necessity and involved in male industrial training, were seen as outsiders in Ahmadnagar's close circle of mission families. Neither James Smith or D.C. Churchill were ordained ministers. Churchill was hired mainly on the insistence of Smith, who felt that he could only inadequately teach industrial arts. He insisted that a trained person was necessary.

> The assumption that any intelligent missionary is qualified to conduct industrial work is probably responsible for most of the failures one finds in such work.

The Mission never did commit itself to industrial training on the scale both Churchill and Smith recommended. Like medical work, potentially much money could be spent on it, but few conversions were likely to result.

> The Industrial work of the Mission has always been a source of great anxiety to the Mission. Technical Education is the most expensive, and for certain classes of people the most valuable. The Board has never contributed to the support of this work in this mission, with the exception of the salary of the missionary in charge.

Although a rug factory set up by the AMM was regarded as a model for other mission, industrial training as a concept was always on the fringes of mission activities. To make a success of such an experiment would have required a far broader understanding of economic development, and this, for a variety of reasons, the AMM did not have. On the issue of industrial training, Churchill was one of the Mission's harshest critics. Discussing lace making by women as an "illustration of the unsoundness of some of our attempts, "Churchill wrote that it was,

> ....a fair representative of other industry taught in this country especially among phi- lanthropic bodies, where art and excellence of product, as viewed from the European point of view, is maintained as the high idea.

He proposed that instead,

> ....we try to make the quality of our product correspond to the taste of the Indians rather than to our own.

Disillusioned with the Mission's inability to attain the ideals he saw working successfully at centers like the Tuskegee Institute in Alabama, he returned to the U.S., saying that industrial training was "nothing more or less than a bait to help the mission fish for men."

Practical training of any sort for women was a concept which came belatedly to the Mission's attention. Sewing and needlework had always been taught, but only because it was assumed to be part of every woman's life.

> Sewing had been taught...to women ever since missionaries came to India, especially to women who became Christians, it being a female adjunct to Christianity in all lands.

But it was not until the 1880's and 1890's that the self-support issue became an urgent one. As Katie Fairbank wrote in 1903,

> Plain sewing has always been taught all girls in all mission stations, and some sorts of fancy work in the high schools, so that girls on leaving school were able to make their own clothes and those of their families. Qualified women also became Bible readers, but there was no special demand for industries to make women self-supporting before the famine of 1877.

In an article called "Industrial Training for women" written in 1901, Anstice Abbot illustrates the sort of short-sightedness Churchill warned against. Abbott attempted to come to terms with the complex needs of Indian women, but her essay is a classic example of cultural naivete.

> Where Christianity and civilization have not touched the women of India, the womanly industries are but few.... A few women and these mostly Mohamadan, can sew and embroider in silks and wools. As a rule, the women of the higher classes have no proper industry. The cooking done, there is nothing for the day but worship, sleep and gossip...A good caste woman knows nothing but cooking and if she is well-to-do she is spared even that knowledge.

She recognized that lower caste and poor women always had to work hard to survive, but for this sort of work she had little admiration. She also knew from experience that as a result of the famine many formerly comfortable women suddenly had to provide for their own support. She suggested that there was a new need, which mission training centres potentially could fulfill.

> If industries were provided suitable for high caste women and the women could learn to them and what an honourable life of self-support would mean to them, there would be an army of women besieging the gates. The need of work for women is undoubted.

But faced with the question she posed for herself, "for what purpose are women being taught, and aimed?" And again; "the question then is, what industries will best meet the need? Abbott was forced back upon her own experience to answer the question.

First she desired an attitudinal change, a definition of which missionaries often were unable to articulate succinctly.

> ....to my mind the ideal in India will be the self-reliant, self-support woman—a woman whose industry will be her panoply for her protection, be she single, a widow, or a deserted wife, and for this the woman must be trained to be industrious, prudent, virtuous, before she can attain to honourable self-support. But women should from the first, understand that they come to the mission to be trained to fight the battle of life as warriors of purity and courage and that they are not to be coddled all their lives without any thought as to what they shall eat or where with all they shall be clothed.

To extend Abbott's image, with what weapons did she propose to arm these women as they went into battle? She offered little but sewing, mending, silk embrodery, lace making and rug weaving. Sewing, or tailoring, was a field dominated by male *shimpis* or *durgas* in India, and not a field into which a low caste Indian woman could easily gain access. Lace making, or rug weaving, had limited usefulness to such a woman also, for the only market was among Europeans and Americans who would buy her products more from a sense of charity than of genuine need. Also, as

Marion Bemian was to point out later, most low-caste Indian homes were too dirty to allow for fine lace making for profitable sale to any European. In short, Abbott felt that Indian women were oppressed, "The utter dependence in which they live upon their fathers and brothers-in-law, degrades them in more ways than one. And she understood that this was at least partially due to their inability to support themselves economically. But recognizing that "all of us who are interested in the uplifting of the women of India must set our aims high for them," she could see no farther than "a scientific knowledge of the needle and the scissors is invaluable to their usefulless and their happiness."

What were the organized efforts made by the AMM to enable Indian women to support themselves when necessary? In 1902 a Lace Department was introduced into the Girls' Boarding School, over the opposition of some who felt it would detract from the school's academic reputation. The number of students taught in this department varied over the years, but for a decade or so after its initiation there were between seventy-five and a hundred women working the workroom. Their market was limited, and during World War I it collapsed entirely. Marion Bemian voiced sentiments similar to those of Churchill.

> It seems it serves the purpose (that is: keep our difficult girls busy) and makes the at least partially self-supporting, but if [other workers] can think of anything better—which I'm sure I'm not able to suggest—it would be a good thing to switch to it when they go in for industrial work here.

There were plans for a while to introduce the growing of silk worm cultures, but this project was an even more speedy failure than that of lace making. A few of the stronger girls from Alice House were sent to weave rugs at the Boys' Industrial Training center, but here, also there were problems of quality and market that could not be overcome. Despite the Mission's continuing flirtation with the notion of industrial training, for women especially they had little success.

But despite an ongoing and vaguely articulated feeling that women should be able to support themselves if circumstances made that necessary, the Mission continued to assume marriage was the best alternative for most women. working outside the house was only for those in trying circumstances:

> Girls who have not been married in infancy, or have been unfortunately wedded are beginning to think of an education as a means of securing a livelihood, and this is a hopful sign.

5

Problems of Woman's Freedom

The Population Problem—Woman's Emancipation and Fertility

Motherhood is sometimes inaptly, almost cynically, referred to as 'nature's handica.' While men are free to indulge in sex gratification without having to bear the consequent responsibilities and worries, woman is visited by the natural consequence of her act and, so long as gratification of the sex impulse and motherhood went hand in hand, complete freedom and equality of woman would have presented no problems in regard to the biological function of woman; for it is improbable that such emancipation would deaden the passion for sex to any noticeable extent. However, now that science, through contraceptives, has rendered possible the separation of the sexual act and its consequence, child-bearing, it is plausible to argue that full emancipation of women may lead to dwindling population figures. No psychologist of renown has yet conclusively established that the desire for motherhood is a natural instinct in woman. May it not then be argued that, once she is freed from her present social conventions and traditional mould of thought and is allowed to moor into the wide outside world, the urge to maternity may taper off? Contraception has reached a stage of success wherein it has severed parental instincts from their sexual precursors. It is therefore argued by some "that philoprogenitive instincts are alone too weak to effect social survival." The Roman matrons were socially the equals of men—where?—about the time of the *Punic* wars. At that time the Patrician Roman Class was dwindling and Roman civilization was decadent. The earlier Roman tradition expected the matron to be grave, self-contained, chiefly concerned with house-hold duties and she was to devote herself to the nurture of a sturdy and intrepid race. With the social equality and growing freedom of women, licentiousness inereased and, as a power, Rome no longer was held in esteem and awe. When the news of the earliest disasters at the hands of the invading Sueves and Goths reached his ears, Jerome exclaimed 'the barbarians are strong through our vice.' However, as Samuel Dill in his memorable treatise *Roman Society in the last century of the Western Empire* says, referring to the denunciation of contsemporary later Roman society women by S. Jerome and other Christian teachers, ".....It is hard to believe that the reserve and delicacy of so many generations of social culture should have grown so helpless in the face of evil... the warm imagination of S.Jerome has probable exaggerated the peril....There was much to amend in the morals of the Roman world. But we must not take the leader of a great moral reformation as a cool and dispassionate observer." Sir Henry Maine characterized Roman marriage 'the laxest the western world has seen.' True, divorce was free: but no one can justly be dogmatic, on the basis of what evidence we have, that the freedom of divorce in the early days of the Roman Republic led to private and social immorality. Actually, laxity seems to have set in later due to Greek and Oriental influences. In France, in the interwar period, womenfolk were 'possessed' by the New Morality and in 1940, after the capitulation of fallen France, Marshall Petain bewailed of 'dwindling numbers' as having been one of the contributory causes for France's humiliation in war. May not the apologists of restraints on woman's conduct point to these historical parallels and hint at the possibility that woman's freedom may lead to a stationary and even declining population and thereby to political and military weakness in a world of competing sovereign States? Does not Socialist Russia provide another instance? The revolutionary upsurge at first permeated every aspect in the social relations milien. Overnight a break with the nightmarish past was effected and woman's emancipation was consummated with a bang. The New Morality was intoxicating. In 1920 abortion was made legal. But by 1936 this zeal 'sagged' and, inspite of protests from women the code of family laws was substantially amended. In the planned drive for larger families, the Soviet State expects of her women "to fulfil their civic duty of child-bearing with greater assiduity than in the past." The Order of Heroine Mother was announced to be conferred on the prolific women. In the United Kingdom the continued stationariness of fertility and signs of its decline in the two decades before the war, the dislocation of family life during the war years, the problems confronting women disbanded from war and civilian work, have all led to the recent appointment of a Royal Commission on Population. In U.S.A."the two-child family is now a prevailing social standard: but it is not enough, on the average, to perpetuate the rece. Although the American population is not yet declining, the present increase is due only to increasing longivity. Given the present low birth-rate, a decline in numbers will inevitably set in between 1950 and 1980" (J.K.Folsom, *The Family and Democratic Society*). In Great Britain the Report published in 1942 by the Royal Commission on the Geographical Distribution of the Industrial Population revealed alarming trends in Britains' birth-rate position. If birth-rate continues to fall as at present, a peak population of 48 million—hardly two million more than in 1946—will be reached in about two decades (Manchester Guardian, 22 May, 1942). Since 1911, while the number of children under fifteen years has been decreasing, people over 65 years of age have been increasing. A declining population is, without exception, an aging population. This is a disquieting trend. The family pattern itself has been changing. All these changes have been seen in all parts of the country and among all classes of people, with slight deviations in extent and pace, in the past three decades.

Thirty years period increase in the population of Great Britain (percentage):

1821-1851—48

1901-1931—21

1909-1939—16

Over the past fourty years in the United Kingdom, a social psychology has imperceptible, nonetheless truly, set in, for a variety of reasons, which regards more than two or three children in a family unit as incompatible with economic resources and general happiness of a married couple. The natural result of this psychology has been that between 1931 and 1945 there has been no more than a five per cent growth in population. Between 1880 and 1945, the gross reproduction rate (fertility is best expressed so) has registered a 60 per cent decline from 2.28 to 0.90. While in 1939 children under 14 were 22 per cent of the total population in Great Britain, on the present showing, they will only be 10 per cent in 1970 and barely 4 per cent about 2000 A. D. (*Times,* leading article, 20 April, 1942). "If fertility and mortality remain what they have been during the last 10 years, the proportion of young people will have been reduced by one-third."

The problem of a threatened decline in population confronts such western countries like U.K., France and Sweden, whose population figures have actually become stationary and not countries like India whose problem is not one of man-power shortage but of 'teeming millions.' How to reduce the increasing rate of population growth is our problem. France already has a declining population. England is on the verge. The birth-rate problem is now common to western civilization itself. It has assumed such proportions that it can no longer be shelved. Our country, on the other hand, seems to be 'terribly full.' Our way of life is different and, let us admit, is one of abject ignorance. Here, all the causes, economic and social, that led to the widespread use of contraception and conscions limitation of family size in the west have failed to diminish the rate of procreation. For, brought up in our traditional, religious and ignorant ways, the very idea of consciously 'planning' the family size sounds blasphemous to our ears, for, can we dare negative the will of the Gods? If women's social freedom were to diminish the rate of growth of our population, it is a welcome effect.

Any attempt to extract a universal law from two or three such cases of parallelism or concurrence is clearly unwarranted. To seek to establish any casual connection between emancipation of women and decadence of society (from such isolated instances as of ancient Rome and Vichy France) is ridiculous. May be, the freedom of women has taken an unsocial turn in some instances, either in the direction of libertinism or towards aggressive feminism: maybe, some women, having grasped the fruits of individual liberty and social equality, have ignored their basic biological and other functions : maybe, they have become impatient of all social restraint: maybe, in certain instances, equality of women has led to a deterioration of the moral tone of the social structure as in France: but is fantastic to argue from these that woman's emancipation and equality is one of the basic causes that have landed modern civilization in sore staits. Because woman's uncharted freedom has been abused in certain countries in the past or may conceivably be misused in future, to suggest that we should flash back to the old order of sex relationships is irrational and exhibits a lack of faith in human progress. If democracy has improperly functioned in some countries if the recognition of the rights to free speech and expression has been abused by some unscrupulous people, does it follow that democracy and freedom of thought should be chosen for discard and are to be unceremoniously consigned to the much-heap ? Let us recall to our mind the parable in the Gospel. When the boat was about to capsize, while cowards stayed on, St. Peter jumped out into the whirling waters of the sea: when he too was sinking, was he told that he was a fool to have left the sinking boat? Was he not reminded that he was sinking because he had not sufficient faith in the wisdom of the step he had taken and was not striving his utmost to save himself? If in the past, particularly in the West, freedom of women has led to certain undesirable consequences, it should not induce one towards a nostalgic backward glance to revert to the dead past : it should, on the other hand, serve as a spur to stronger faith and more determined reformatory efforts.

Look Ahead and Not Back

The solution lies not in flashing back to the old order of things but in minimizing woman's cares, responsibilities and worries attendant on motherhood. Provision of maternal benefits, child welfare and health services, recreational and cultural facilities and other amenities, as of right, will be very helpful. Society should recognize woman's dual role—the biological function of motherhood and her active participation in social life as a free citizen. Neither should be secured at the expense of the other: for each is as important and complementary to the other. A fundamental change in social attitude towards woman's functions is necesary. The onus is clearly on the society to foster, and not to impede, the development of such a dual role. Motherhood may not be a natural instinct in woman. Neither reluctance towards maternity is natural or inevitable. It all depends on whether for the woman motherhood is a happy prospect to contemplate: society can contribute much in making the emancipated woman cherish motherhood with a feeling of pride. On the other hand, an unsympathetic and irrational society can generate *genophobia* in women—a dislike or shunning of children, an attitude of the mind which fears or shuns the advent of children. Emancipation of woman and her free participation in the affairs of the wider human world may in fact promote in woman a *genophilic* attitude if the community provides reliable prospects for the future welfare of children. If woman is assured of a happy and healthy home, motherhood holds no fears for the emancipated woman: on the other hand, love for children and an attitude of the mind that desires fuller family life is fostered (Dr. Spencer Paterson has coined these terms—*genophobia* and *genophilia*—*genophobic* and *genophilic*).

Are children important in married life? A recent investigation conducted in 1945 by Mass Observation in Great Britain revealed that, irrespective of the age group of the mothers and the period of their married life, eight or nine wives out of every ten believe that children are definitely important to the happiness of a couple (*Britain and her Birthrate*—The sixth of the 'Change' Wartime Surveys). It is only the tiniest minority of males and females that have as their ideal the childless marriage. The same is true of every modern country and this is the silver lining to the population problem that can be converted to good use in attempts to arrest and reverse the declining trend. But it should be realized that children are not wanted beyond a 'reasonable' number ; that they are wanted by the parents for personal happiness and not because of religious or governmental injunctions so that, unless the basic motivation of child-bearing is tackled, no social or governmental palliatives can substantially increase the average family size.

The Swedish Way is an Eye-opener

Swedish experience may have a lesson for others. In 1935 the Swedish Population Commission was appointed with a mandate by the *Riksdg* to suggest 'strong measures' to combat the problem of declining population. The Swedesh have been for centuries the foremost exponents of woman's equality. The Commission, inspite of the threatened population decline, did not suggest restrictive measures, that women should be precluded from public work and employment. Taboos on free contraceptive knowledge were not favoured. The Swedish population poilicy is positive and is a family welfare policy: for they believe that woman's freedom has little causal connection with population stagnation. They go a step further—even if it were a contributory factor, woman's full and equal participation in public life being indispensable for the development of her personality in society, other measures and policies should be devised by the State to increase birth-rate. It would be foolish to throw out the baby with the bath. "Inspite of clear data showing a correlation between the working of wives and low fertility, which could be easily used as proof that the former caused the latter if the nation's ideology favoured such an interpretation, the new policy makes no effort to restrict mothers, or women generally, from employment" (Folsom, *The Family and Democratic Siciety,*). In fact, according to a law passed in 1939, no employer can discharge or reduce the pay of employees who have been in service for two years, on account of pregnancy or child-bearing or marriage. Thus even the employment of married women and of mothers is not discouraged. To induce women to rear larger families the Swedish method is not curtailment of their physical, intellectual or cultural freedom : Sweden's two-planked positive policy *vis-a-vis* woman comprises of sex equalitarianism and promotion of security and happiness in family life through the provision of educational, medical and health services; recreational and cultural facilities, maternity and child-welfare benefits in cash as well as in kind.

Even in Great Britain, the decline in population growth is attributable to the desire of many women, particularly among the working classes, not to have large families.

This desire issued mainly out of the 'appalling' housing conditions, unemployment and economic insecurity (Margaret Goldsmith, *Women at War*). "Since the Great War" wrote no less an authority than Beatrice Webb, in her foreword to Richard Kathleen Titmuss's *Parents' Revolt* (1942), 'birth control has been practised by wage earners, suffering from long periods of unemployment and under-employment so drastic that it seemed abject folly to produce children who could neither be adequately nourished nor sufficiently educated to secure a satisfactory livelihood." Not the confinement of woman in an ignorant environment but the removal of social and economic deterrents to parenthood is the obvious remedy to the problem of population. Even accepting the volitional (as distinct from biological) hypothesis regarding the declining birthrate, that the population decline is attributable to the increasing effectiveness and use of contraceptives, should not a study be made into the economic, sociological and psychological factors, that have induced women to avoid pregnancy? If the basic maladjustments underlying the deliberate control of reproduction are analysed, steps can be taken by the community to mitigate these social disequilibria.

Every thinking mother has this viewpoint uppermost in her mind— "I want my child to have something to hope for when he grows up." A faith in future is therefore to be instilled. This is more important than the mere immediate provision of maternity and child allowances. While the negative approach lies in weakening the feeling against the large family, which itself is necessary, more permanent results can be attained by the positive approach of strengthening the motive for having children. "For the eugenic future, something deeper is needed — something which will make the thoughtful breed as much as the thoughtless, the well-nourished have as many babies as the under-nourished, the over-privileged as the under-privileged, the well-educated as those who left school at fourteen. A few extra shillings a week, an extra bedroom....these things may change decisions where the desire is there already and environment is at its worst....But for a quality nations the will to bring more children into the world must be stimulated where it is now weakest" (*Britain and her Birthrate,* op. cit.,). It is not negative or repressive measures to suppress the present means of family limitation that should be adopted. They will be little effective, because it is the fundamental attitudes of the people that are to be tackled. Of course all measures should be taken to check and reverse the declining trend in fertility. The State connot sit back and do nothing - *Laissez aller* is clearly not suggested. Some positive steps are needed to encourage fertility. It is to the economic resources and leisure available to the parents that we must turn our attention. 'Communalising' child care as in some countries of Continental Europe seems to be a short-cut: but like all short-cuts it has deep failings, if overdone. It is the wartime experience that children cannot be segregated from their parents for long without upsetting their moral and emotional stability. Of course, adequate provision of creches in work-shops, kindergartens, boarding schools, sohool mid-day meals, cheaper domestic service, are all wise steps. The granting of child allowances is a more ambitious scheme for making the arrival of more children in the household less unwelcome. For instance, in the Beveridge 'overall' Plan of social security, children's allowances are assigned a vital role. Education itself should be a means of popularising the large family, for ultimately it is the individual fathers and mothers that must develop more congenial attitudes towards large families. "In the long run,....any population policy, no matter how repressive legaily or how generous economically, is bound to fail unless the claims and sacrifices involved in parenthood are voluntarily accepted as part of a pattern of private values and social relations consistent with the material environment of the twentieth century" (*The Population of Great Britain,* Mark Abrams).

Woman and Society

While woman's individual personality has such definite claims on society, which society must realize or shall perish, woman herself should not pervert her freedom, should not 'go hang,' but should realize her responsibility towards society. Social progress has reciprocal claims on every individual member of the community. The modern woman should realize the importance of child-bearing, not only for ensuring the perpetuation of human society—(and in this world carved up into indepenent States, no State can be indifferent to dwindling numbers)—but for the success of her married life itself. "Marriage not only came into existence for the sake of the offspring but often becomes a lasting union though presence of children" (Westermarck, *A Short History of Marriage*). Dr. Willcox estimates that in U.S.A. chirldless marriages are between three and four times as likely to end in divorce as marriages with children. Since 1900 the same tendency has been observed in France. Instances can be easily multiplied. Woman should not retreat from her social responsibilities. If women were to be swamped in mere pleasure-seeking megalomania, liberty will end up in libertinism.

Again, freedom itself will turn out to be a fool's-gold concept if improperly applied. "The achievement of freedom, though a matter of justice, is not the end of the journey" (Mrs. Deighton Pollock, *Women of Today*). It is not so much the possession of a right as the use made of it that is of chief significance. It depends on how judiciously the power of choice is used. What for? is the basic question. Liberty and restraint: rights and duties: motivating energy and effective control: privileges and obligations go hand in hand. Woman should realize the need for accepting creative social restraints. Of what use is a great river to society if there are no dykes, no bridges, no dams, no quays? Such restraints are the essence of community living. While the individual personality of every single man and woman should be fostered by the group, every such single man or woman living within the community has reciprocal functions to discharge. These demands of society on the individual should not be whimsical or arbitrary or discriminatory ones but should be those subscribed to by the common will in the interests of promoting commonwell and social progress. It is to be emphasized that restraints on woman in society cannot be prescribed by men acting as law-givers but should be passed by men and women together participating in civic life as equal citizens. Nitzsche's penetrating distinction between 'freedom from' and 'freedom to' has great import. No one can be completely 'let alone' and all liberty that is not put to creative ends should be checked. Herein comes the need for power or authority in society. "I believe in Freedom because at the same time, I believe in Discipline (Havelock Ellis). Real freedom is not possible without power judiciously exercised. The harmonious blending of liberty and restraint is a very delicate task but there is no alternative. There is short-cut to the attainment of the highest 'disciplinary self-expression of the person.' "Behind democracy is freedom but behind freedom is the self-control of persons. The basic platform of democracy is self-restraint." This self-restraint is symbolized in the law of the land. Woman's freedom, no less than man's, should be subject to this law which should seek to be expression of a universal conviction, recognition of universal capacity, bulwark of universal rights and the medium of common good. "The outcome of such a legal theory, then, will be seen as the recognition of the individual, with this important proviso — the individual can be the possessor of no rights which run contrary to the common good" (Ralph Tyler Flewelling, *The Survival of Western Culture*). Such a conception of law effects a happy blending of *universalism* and *particularism* and this is the surest path to human harmony and progress. Law is properly social and, specifically, may be defined as "the minimum of morality that is indispensable for life in society and is imposed by material sanctions" (Henri Berr, Foreword to *'Rome the Law-giver,'* J. Declareuil). There must be a sociological synthesis between authority and liberty. Authority should be legitimate: liberty must be rational, so that, law may become the 'organic — social expression of morality.'

Woman's zeal for her emancipation, equality and assertion of her individual personality must not stampede her into running amock. Liberty under law was the shield-motto of one of the earliest of the thirteen American colonies. What you want must synchronize with common good. It is only through 'purposive freedom' that personality is developed fully. While society should recognize the *purpose* or *teleology* of the individual person, the individual should realize the *entelechy* or *organism* of human society. Human society is not a mathematical quantity of distinct particulars as Malthus surmised. The tell-tale of human evolution is not exclusively expressed in Herbert Spencer's immortal phrase 'survival of the fittest' but equally in Henry Drummond's striking variation of it 'the struggle for the survival of others'. Co-operation, not exclusiveness, is the basis of human civilization, Realization of personality is possible only in and through social progress. The flower yields its sweet honey to the bee: the bee furthers the propagation of the plant. Co-operation is the law of nature: selfish exclusion is the folly of man. Woman lives not in vacuum but in society. Let woman herself, as well as society, realize the implications of this simple truth. In the 'little lives' which we lead as individuals, men and women must have mutual respect: 'in the common life which is real life,' men and women must be equal and active citizens.

6

Woman and Sikh Religion

You must know who is the object and who is the subject of a sentence in order to know if you are the object or subject of history.

We have spoken of the subject but now we must turn to the object. We have been dealing with the world of ideas and words, so our epilogue must then quite literally be that which comes after the word, after the *logos*. But the Sikh Word is not a masculine *logos*, it is the beautiful and formless *bani*. The word proclaimed by the scriptures and secular writers of Sikhism is Women. We cannot underestimate the importance of this achievement in itself, but does anyone listen to the Word? Does anyone truly read it?

By the Word of the Sikh Gurus and poets we are invited to praxis, the third component of feminist ethics. But their word which empowers woman endangers man. The response has been either to shout it down or simply fail to hear it. In the writings of Guru Gobind Singh and Bhai Vir Singh, the feminine presences of Durga and Rani Raj Kaur are too central, too striking to be ignored, so instead they have been denounced. The patriarchal exegetes have declared that it would have been unworthy of Guru Gobind Singh to write of Durga, and so they have attempted to excise her from his works. They still argue that the compositions praising Durga under his name were written not by the Guru himself but by his contemporaries. Likewise, in the case of Bhai Vir Singh, the patriarchal literary critics have declared that the feminine nature and sentiment of his works is unworthy of the great writer. So they have described it as unfortunate weakness in his work, a lapse from their masculine standards.

That is where the twentieth century Sikh writer is misunderstood, or rather too well-understood and condemned for that very reason. The following words by a renowned Sikh scholar represent a point of view that is, unfortunately, all too common:

> It is in his diction bearing the perfume of Punjab's sacred literature and the expression of sensibility that Bhai Vir Singh achieves the poetic quality. Very often his sensibility declines to sentimentality and the feminine small-change of feeling — but rises with recurring spurts to the true emotional level.

In a metaphor that falls to the true sexual level, we hear that women experience the mere small-change of passive feeling and sentimentality, whereas men have sensitivity and true emotions that rise and gush out in recurrent spurts. The assessment that Bhai Vir Singh's "sensibility declines to sentimentality and the feminine small-change" only indicates the critic's glossing over the delicacy, the refinement, the multivalency attributed to the female person and psyche in the work of Bhai Vir Singh.

In the poetry of the Guru Granth itself, the importance of the feminine in a relation so vital as the one with the Transcendent has been neglected by the patriarchal exegetes. This neglect can be ascribed to a basic prejudice on the part of commentators, translators, and teachers of Sikh literature. Over the years, these scholars have been excising female symbolism and imagery and replacing it with a male one. Because the sacred text has not been meaningfully read, Sikh women do not enjoy the status that Guru Nanak wanted them to have. Its extraordinary potential for empowering women has been ignored.

The Sikh Gurus and the great modern writer who was so close to their spirit have been remarkably radical in supporting and under-girding social equality. Unfortunately, the subject of their sentences has been the object of history. She has not even been properly recognized by Sikh culture. Why she has such significance in Sikh literature but so low a position in Punjabi culture is extremely perplexing. Once again, the image of my grandmother comes back to me. I can see and hear her asking a male member to read her the opening of the *Barah Mah* on the first day of the new month, even though the bride is the central figure in this tex!

Guru Nanak did not want the feminine principle to be just a figure of speech or a literary device; the feminine principle was to pervade the life of the Sikhs. From the very beginning of the tradition, he took special care to give women a position of equality with men in matters religious and secular. In Guru Nanak's new community that grew on the banks of the river Ravi, men and women enjoyed complete equality. There was no priesthood, and men were not designated to play any more important role as liaisons between Humanity and Divinity than were women. When Guru Amar Das, the third Sikh Guru, organized districts of religious administration, women too were selected to head them. In the first Sikh society taking shape at Kartarpur, worship consisted of men and women sitting together and reciting and savoring the Divine Word in unison. Both men and women took equal part in day-to-day tasks as well: both drew water from the well, both reaped and ground corn, both cooked food in the kitchen, and both cleaned the utensils. The food was eaten in common by all, sitting in rows together as equals, irrespective of sex, caste, or rank. In the words of a Sikh woman scholar, "The transformation the Sikh Gurus brought in woman's status was truly revolutionary. The concept of equality of woman with man not only gave woman an identity of her own, but freed her from all kinds of fetters to which she was bound in the Hindu Society."

It is sad to see today that many Sikh women have their space confined to the kitchen and are bound within the home to carry out essential tasks. Women stay in the places ascribed to them in society and family by the male members — be they fathers, grandfathers, older brothers, brothers-in-law, or patriarchal bosses. The role of women is narrowly circumscribed. It is tragic to observe how the literature of this culture includes them so fully and the society excludes them so despairingly. The practice of *sati* was forbidden by the Gurus, and it is of course outlawed, but widows are still ostracized; they may not be forced to die like the Sati, but they lead a life that is almost dead. The Gurus rejected the notion of pollution. The Guru Granth celebrates womanhood and constantly reminds its readers of their origin from menstrual blood; in practice, however, menstruating women are discouraged from touching the Book that esteems them. The Gurus opposed the custom of *purdah,* but although women are not literally veiled, they are still marginal and almost invisible today, their voices are not heard, their desires are not discerned. It is indeed tragic to see that the birth of a daughter, who would have been honoured by Guru Nanak as a would-be bride, a would-be mother, a would-be queen, is to contemporary society a source of sorrow. Parents in the Punjab even weep at the birth of a daughter! The very female who would be opening up the way for liberation is imprisoned by her culture in the confines of her in-laws' home! Modern technology is abused to promote the abortion of fetuses that are determined to be female!

The societal and geographical context of Sikhism is another reason why the Sikh message has not been fully heeded and put into practice. The developing Sikh religion was surrounded and confined by an androcentric society. Guru Nanak tried to break the existing mold. But the overwhelming Hindu and Islamic presence has over the centuries reinforced and even today continues to reinforce patriarchal values which are difficult to break. The relatively young Sikh religion is unable to sustain the radical changes intimated in its sacred literature. The Sikhs after all constitute less than 2 per cent of the Indian population. The unique thealogical message of the Guru Granth remains buried under the weight of past tradition and the continued pressures from its environment. In the past many Sikh commentators have displayed a predominantly Hindu intellectual disposition. Udasi and Nirmala were two early schools of Sikh scriptural interpretation, and scholars within both these traditions were essentially reared on classical Indian exegesis. Saturated with Upanisadic and Furanic learning, the style and content of their analyses and speculations brought about a reincubation of Hindu ideology within Sikh exegesis itself. The Sikh vision of the Transcendent has been eclipsed by the Hindu *Zeitgeist*. My contention is that until the symbolic value of Sikh literature is truly understood and its difference from the neighbouring traditions is acknowledged, Guru Nanak's and his successor Gurus' aim of uplifting the role and status of women cannot be fulfilled. The new and separate message of Guru Nanak has to be re-cognized as new and separate. By continuing to categorize it under the rubric of Hinduism (or Islam or a syncretism of Hinduism and Islam), readers, hearers, and scholars unconsciously transfer the role and image of women in those societies over into the Sikh world. The issues and concerns raised by western feminists equip one with a sensitivity to avoid such a pitfall, to discover the centrality of the feminine in Sikh literature, and to re-cover the significance that is *hers*.

In addition to the context, the texts themselves present difficulties even for Sikhs. The poly-structured vocabulary of the Guru Granth, which includes Sanskritic, Arabic, and Persian terms, poses problems for an average Punjabi. Decoding the poetry of Guru Gobind Singh laced as it is with highly subtle and ornate metaphors and imagery, and replete with mythological allusions and linguistic innovations, is an even harder task. Furthermore, the British legacy spurs young Punjabi Sikhs to study English and western philosophies and literatures, drawing them away from their own mother-tongue and their own literary heritage. Indoctrinated in English-speaking schools which were founded by Victorian colonialists, many Sikhs thus do not even possess the basic linguistic tools to recognize the subtleties of their sacred text. Many youngsters are more familiar with Cinderella and Snow White than with Sundari or Rani Raj Kaur. The Guru Granth may continually be seen, read, and heard at all important occasions, during all rites of passage; some of Guru Gobind Singh's poetry may remain part of the daily regimen of Sikh prayers; Bhai Vir Singh's poetry may be read and memorized by young Punjabi students in schools and colleges without the import of these texts being really questioned. Thus the thealogy and feminist spirituality and power of Sikh literature remains closed.

Its disclosure can come about only through a feminist praxis. The moral sensitivity is there, and the ontological grounding is there; the words are there; the ideals are there; they have only to be read. Sikh literature is prescriptive, not merely descriptive; it is an empowering language, not "the feminine small-change of feeling." To unleash its power, every reader needs to be equipped with a poetic sensitivity and a real awareness of the primal context. Each word has to be chewed so that full nourishment and sustenance can be derived from it. Such knowledge is empowering, but it is also enjoyment; in it we find the climactic *jouissance* of Guru Arjun, Gaston Bachelard, Roland Barthes. To understand the choice of female models as representatives of the romantic and existential consciousness, to realize the overall importance of the varied feminine symbols and images, we need to make the translation from literary symbols to social and poilitical realities. The words should enable us to find the spark within ourselves, legitimate ourselves, fully validate ourselves. Guru Nanak's deep crimson *manjithara* — which corresponds with Alice Walder's Color Purple— radiates an energy that heightens and intensifies every experience in our social and political being. Women can articulate and construct their experience through the Sikh literary heritage and transform their lives in society. We can aspire to that ideal, aspire to that message, aspire to understanding that text. Surely, as Bachelard says, the "poetic image can be the seed of a world." It can deliver us a new world where women can enter the zone that we have been excluded from and that rightly belongs to us. "May she get out of the booby-trapped silence! And not have the margin or the harem foisted on her as her domain!" Sikh literature breaks this silence and provides a voice for women, though we speak in a booby-trapped world. It gives visibility and relevance to women, and it provides us with an opening towards real change, a bridge between the ideal and the real, mythos and ethos, being and becoming, moral sensitivity and social praxis.

The literature of the Sikhs raises feminist consciousness, and it gives a new meaning, a new direction, and a new authenticity to feminists in the West. Theirs is not simply a discourse developed in one particular place at one particular period in history; it is rather a voicing of an eternally and universally valid ontological perspective which has often been noticed but rarely acknowledged. The voice of western feminists is in perfect harmony with the literature of Sikhism, and it only remains to turn our mutually validating experiences into an envigorating dialogue. This dialogue calls for a vigorous interaction amongst Sikh women and other Asian women and feminists in the West. Together, we need to come close and understand one another and bring about change. I ardently await the day when the Punjabi culture which sustains the paramountcy of Woman in its literature will prove a model for her full equality in the social, political, and economic spheres, not just in India but throughout our common Matrix, the Earth.

7

European Writers and Indian Women

J.C. Archer has observed that there are two Nanaks: 'the factual' and 'the formless'; they are two in one, 'both in practice and in theory'. He goes on to add that the faith in him made him 'a compelling figure'. Archer rightly suggests that we are to judge 'this first Sikh in a fuller measure than himself, by other Sikhs and by what came after him'. As an appropriate epilogue to this study of Guru Nanak in history we may turn to the attitude of his successors and followers towards the founder of their faith. Our primary aim here is not to discover the Nanak of history behind the Nanak of faith, not even to distinguish the one from the other or to discuss all that came after him. Our limited aim is to consider, rather briefly, what Guru Nanak meant to the first few generations of the believers in his mission.

Guru Angad, the immediate successor of Guru Nanak, directly refers to the founder of Sikhism in these words:

> They need no other instruction whom Guru Nanak has given the understanding through his guidance and who, through (God's) adoration, are blended with the Truth.

Two aspects of this statement deserve attention. Nanak is being called 'Guru Nanak' and his 'guidance' is being regarded as superior to any other. Direct references to Guru Nanak in the works of Guru Arjan, the fourth successor of Guru Nanak, provide further insight into the image of the founder of Sikhism crystallizing among his successors. The path shown by Guru Nanak is 'the treasure' of God's *bhakti*. The idea that Guru Nanak has clearly shown the way to salvation occurs more than once. In the 'modern' age *(kaliyuga)*, Nanak is the true *Guru* and he is 'the greatest of all'. Indeed, the greatness of Guru Nanak has been made manifest for the entire *yuga*. Guru Nanak is also the *'hagat-guru'*. It is evident that in the eyes of his successors Guru Nanak occupies a unique position and his message possesses universal validity.

The last successor of Guru Nanak, Guru Gobind Singh too gives the same primacy to the founder of Sikhism. Guru Nanak 'established the true religion in the *(kal yuga)* and showed the way to all *sadhs;* whosoever follows his path becomes free from sins once for all; God removes all sin and suffering from those who join his *panth*; they never suffer misery and hunger, for they are released from the net of death'. In the *Bachittar Natak*, from which this extract is taken, the idea that Guru Nanak's religion was meant to transcend all previous dispensations is unfolded in clear terms in the context of what for Guru Gobind Singh was the universal history of religion.

The homage paid to the founder of Sikhism by his successors is not confined to upholding the uniueness or the universality of his message. Behind the religion of Guru Nanak they see not only the direct sanction of God but also a personality standing in a special relationship with God, without being His incarnation or His prophet. The concept of the Divine Preceptor in the works of Guru Nanak prepared the ground for this homage, for the same epithets could be easily applied to Nanak as the *Guru*. 'For Nanak the Guru was the voice of God withing the human heart, but with his own coming the function passed to the man himself. The function was vested in a particular man, Nanak, who, by means of his own exalted perception was qualified to instruct others. It was in this light that his followers understood his life and teachings and appended the title Guru to his name'. This title was appended to the names of his successors too.

The uniqueness ascribed to Guru Nanak's position thus reconciled to the continuity of his work through his successors adds a new dimension to the concept of the *Guru*. The immediate successor of Guru Nanak calls himself *'Nanak'*, a practice which is followed by his own successor also. The import is significant. There is no difference between Angad and Nanak as *Gurus*, for the office is derived from the founder. Guru Amardas, who was chosen by Guru Angad as his successor, is explicit on this point. The mingling of 'the light' of Guru Nanak with 'the light' of Guru Angad is in accordance with God's *raza*. Guru Nanak is the primeval source of *guruship* but he is not different from the successor. Guru Gobind Singh too invokes the idea of 'the light' of Guru Nanak to underline the unity of *guruship* from its inception to the time of his last successor. Guru Gobind Singh is quite emphatic about this unity; in his presentation Guru Nanak 'becomes' Guru Angad and Guru Angad 'becomes' Guru Amardas and Guru Amardas' 'becomes' Guru Ramdas. Indeed, only 'the foolish' failed to understand that the Gurus were all 'one form' and not distinct from one another.

It may be argued that the idea of the unity of *guruship* in Sikhism came into prominence in justification of the transition from nomination to 'hereditary succession'. But it is more valid to argue that this transition was made possible by the idea. Much before the time of Guru Gobind Singh the sanctity which was attached to the distinctive role of Guru Nanak had come to be associated also with his successors 'in all of whom thus appeared to shine the light of Nanak'. It must be emphasized that this conception of *guruship* safeguarded the distinctive position of Guru Nanak and, at the same time, bestowed upon the office of the *Guru* a legitimate authority for initiative. The successors of Guru Nanak were entitled to take vital decisions by virtue of their office and their decisions become 'the extension' of Guru Nanak's mission, both logically and historically.

Guru Arjan's decision, for instance, to compile a canonical scripture must be seen in the light of Guru Nanak's use of his own compositions for liturgical purposes. Guru Anagad had followed the example of his master not only by compiling the works of Guru Nanak but also by adding some of his own in a script significantly called the *gurmukhi*. Guru Angad's own example was followed by his three successors until in A. D. 1603-04 Guru Arjan compiled the *Granth* to enshrine 'in permanent form the teachings of the first five Gurus soon after the original delivery of those teachings'.

Furthermore, Guru Nanak's concept of the *Sabad* was imperceptible transferred to his *bani* and to the *bani* of his successors whose compositions 'read more or less like variations on the themes chosen by him for the edification of his disciples'. Consequently, the *bani* of the *Gurus* came to be regarded as the medium of communication with God. It may also be pointed out that the *Sabad* and the *Guru* were often equated so that the scripture compiled by Guru Arjan became an alternative to the personal *guruship* of Guru Nanak's successors. When Guru Gobind Singh decided not to nominate any successor to himself, he referred his followers to the 'eternal *bani*' for guidance and inspiration.

From the successors of Guru Nanak we may now turn to some of their followers for confirmation of what has been observed already and for further insight into their attitude towards the founder of Sikhism. Satta and Balwand refer to Nanak as the *Curu*. In the same sense, they refer to Guru Angad as '*satgur*' Baba Sundar in his *sadd* in *Rag Ramkali* refers to Guru Amardas as '*satgur purakh*.' Satta and Balwand are explicit on the point that the glory and greatness of Guru Nanak was transferred to Guru "Anagad who thus came to possess 'the same light'. Indeed, they are most emphatic about the unity of *guruship*: Guru Ramdas is 'the same' as Amardas, Angad and Nanak. Like Guru Nanak, Guru Angad is the medium of union with God. There are other ideas too in the *var* of Satta and Balwand which are associated with the *Guru*. The *Gurus* are 'true kings', and this *raj* was instituted by Guru Nanak on the firm foundation of the Truth. Also, the *Gurus* present resemblance with the *avatars* or the prophets of God or even God Himself. Furthermore, the office of the *Guru* is by 1.0 means an easy office.

For a more elaborate conception of Guru Nanak's place in the history of religion we may turn to Bhai Gurdas, 'the St. Paul of

Sikhism' whose *vars* are regarded as 'the key' to the Sikh scripture and appear to present 'an orthodox analysis of Sikh beliefs'. There is no doubt that Bhai Guradas's *varas* reveal his thorough familiarity with the works of Guru Nanak.

Our present concern, however, is only with the image of Guru Nanak as it was conceived and presented by Bhai Gurdas. This image is of obvious importance, for he was closely connected with Guru Amardas and associated himself with Guru Ramdas, Guru Arjan and Guru Hargobind. In a certain sense, therefore, he is 'an orthodox' spokesman.

Bhai Gurdas emphasizes the overwhelming greatness of Guru Nanak in the spiritual realm. He compares Guru Nanak to the sun, before which the stars fade away; to the lion, from whom the deer run away in panic; to the *garup,* from whom the cobras seek shelter in holes; and to the *shahbaz,* from whom the birds flee for refuge. Guru Nank is the herald of light which dispels the universal darkness of the *kaliyuga*. This darkness is vividly depicted by Bhai Gurdas in terms which often remind the reader of Guru Nanak's verses. The mission of Guru Nanak is placed in this context, and it is in this context that the well-known verse of Bhai Gurdas has to be placed:

Satgur Nanak pragtia miti dhundh jag Chanan hoa.

With the appearance of Nanak, the true *Guru*, the haze (of ignorance and falsehood) has vanished and the world is illumined with the effulgence (of knowledge and truth).

The uniqueness and the universality of Guru Nanak's message are taken for granted by Bhai Gurdas. In fact, he is explicit on the point that the message of Guru Nanak transcends all previous dispensations, particularly Hinduism and Islam. In the eyes of Bhai Gurdas affiliation to any of the four Hindu *virnas*, or to any of the 'religions' of Islam, is fruitless. Not the pilgrimage to Mecca, or to Benaras, but the adoration of God amidst the *sadh-sangat* leads to salvation; in the *sadh-sangat* are transcended all distinctions of caste and creed. As for the ordinary *gurus* and *pirs* and their following, 'the blind lead the blind to the ditch'. Both Hindus and Muslims are bound to suffer without good acts; their mutual wrangling has misled the world to the devil's path. The true *Guru*, on the other hand, has shown the highway to salvation. The 'light' of Guru Nanak shines in the entire universe; it cannot be concealed.

Jahar pir jagat-gur Baba!

Nanak, the *Guru*, has been made manifest for the whole of mankind.

In the *vars* of Bhai Gurdas, Guru Nanak's concern is with the salvation of the whole of mankind. Bhai Gurdas relates the *udasis* (travels) of Guru Nanak to his concern for the suffering humanity. Also, this concern becomes a spectacle of his unqualified triumph over the representatives of all other forms of religious belief and practice. On the assumption of the uniqueness of Guru Nanak's message, the entire world is alien to salvation 'without the *Guru*'.

Without the *Guru*, there is nothing but darkness! This verse is virtually a quotation from Guru Nanak's verses, but the import is very much different: Bhai Gurdas's reference appears to be to Guru Nanak himself and not to the voice of God within man.

It is highly probable, indeed, that the function of the true *Guru* of Guru Nanak's conception is often transferred by Bhai Gurdas to Guru Nanak himself. There is no understanding without (Nanak) the true *Guru*. Without the true *Guru*, the fear (of Death) is not eradicated. The true *Guru* has provided the remedy for the disease of *haumai*. The true *Guru* alone is perfect and there is no salvation without the perfect *Guru*. For Bhai Gurdas, Nanak the *Guru* is in fact beyond time (*akal rup*); he is like God. Quite frequently, Bhai Gurdas poses an equation between the *Guru* and God. The idea of Nanak as the last and the eternal spokesman of God assumes great importance in the *vars* of Bhai Gurdas.

Bhai Gurdas often conceives of the position of the *Guru* in terms of sovereignty. The true *Guru* is the 'true king'. The *Guru's panth* is his coin. And the *panth* is compared by Bhai Gurdas to 'the eight-metal coin'. Temporal authority fades into insignificance before the sovereignty of the *Guru.* It is in this context that Babur is vanquished by Guru Nanak in Bhai Gurdas's reference to a meeting between them. Also, the *Guru* as the true sovereign commands exclusive allegiance: those who do not submit to the *Guru* are 'rebels'. Bhai Gurdas does not make any distinction between Guru Nanak and his successors, for they too are the *patsah* of both *din* and *dunia.*

The idea of the unity of *guruship* is clear and consistent in the *vars* of Bhai Gurdas and the conception of the Guru appears to crystallize in a form that would endure.

> Nanak struck his coin in the world and instituted the pure *panth.* In his lifetime he installed Lehna, with the umbrella of *guruship* over his head. Blending light with light, the true *Guru* Nanak changed form, and performed a wonder of wonders which is beyond the comprehension of everyone. In Lehna's body was infused the form of Nanak.

The characteristic phrase expressing the unity of *guru*ship in the *vars* of Bhai Gurdas is 'blending of the light' (of Guru Nanak) with the light (of Angad) and, by inference, the transference of the light from the predecessor to the successor. Another variation is that of a limp being lightened by another. Also the mingling of water with water or even 'apparentation' suggests the relations between the predecessor and the successor. All these mataphors are used to underline the unity of *guru*ship.

Bhai Gurdas appears to attach a good deal of importance to the fact that the appointment of Lehna was made by Guru Nanak himself. Guru Angad in turn could appoint a successor to himself. Angad 'received' the *guru*ship from Nanak and 'transferred' it to Amardas as a divine gift. Bhai Gurdas explicitly traces the *guru*ship of Hargobind from Guru Nanak, successively through Angad, Amardas, Ramdas and Guru Arjan. The right to nominate a successor goes with the office of the *Guru* and, to Bhai Gurdas, it is immaterial whether the nominated successor is from amongst the disciples of the *Guru* or from amongst the members of his own family. The nomination by Guru Ramdas of his youngest son, Arjan, is as meaningful and legitimate in the eyes of Bhai Gurdas as the nimination of Lehna by Guru Nanak. Bhai Gurdas's ardent support to the 'new measures' of Guru Hargobind springs ligically from the assumption that Guru Hargobind as the legitimate successor of Guru Nanak was vested with the authority of action by virtue of the office he had come to hold.

For Bhai Gurdas, the office of the *Guru* is more important than the person. Guru Nanak performed 'a wonder of wonders' not simply by nominating a successor in the ordinary sense but by transforming a disciple into the *Guru*. Bhai Gurdas appropriately uses the simile of the water running upstream. In his *vars* there are frequent references to the *Guru* being the *chela* and the *chela* being the *Guru*. The positions of the master and the disciple are interchangeable precisely because in Bhai Gurdas's conception of the *Guru* the office is distsinct from the person. Much before the author the *Ramkali Var Patshahi Dasven ki* praised Guru Gobind Singh for becoming the *chela* as well as the *Guru* (of the *Khalsa*), the idea had been popularized by Bhai Gurdas.

It has been remarked recently that with the death of 'the tenth and last *Guru* we come to a third stage in the development of the doctrine of the *Guru*' in Sikhism. The function which was exercised for about two hundred years by a succession of men had now come to be vested, according to Sikh belief, jointly in the scripture and in the corporate community, the *Khalsa*. That this development was made possible by ideas coming into currency during the second stage itself may be evident from Bhai Gurdas's conception of the *Guru-sabad* and the *Gurumukh-panth*. Bhai Gurdas uses the term *narmal panth* also for the followers of the *Gurus*. More frequently he uses the term *sadh-sangat*. There is no doubt that Bhai Gurdas is keenly conscious of the distinct identity of the Sikhs. Also, the *sadh-sangat* has a certain amount of sanctity for Bhai Gurdas. In fact, the *Guru* is in the *sadh-sangat*. Similarly, the *Guru's sabad* is the *Guru*. And, for Bhai Gurdas, the *sabad* primarily connotes the *bani* of Guru Nanak and his successors.

According to a Sikh scholar, the possibility of miracles is admitted in Sikhism but the True Name is enormously more valuable than the power to perform miracles. This is certainly true not only of the successors of Guru Nanak but also of the best minds among the followers of the Sikh *Gurus*. Bhai Gurdas was easily among those best minds. He appears to have grasped nearly all the fundamental teachings of Guru Nanak. In his *vars*, the insistence on the True Name is quite remarkable. Nevertheless, he attributes to Guru Nanak the actual performance of miracles in certain situations. It may be safely inferred that the lesser minds would look upon the supranatural powers of Guru Nanak as an impressive, or even an essential, trait of his personality.

Within fifty years of Guru Nanak's death traditions regarding his life and teachings began to grow in the Punjab, and in the first half of the seventeenth century attempts were made to compile them as '*janam-sakhis*' of Guru Nanak. This tradition of preserving or compiling the *janam-sakhis* of Guru Nanak has survived into the present century and even today some of these compilations are popular among the followers of Guru Nanak. The earliest of these are the *Puratan Janam-sakhi* which are fairly well-represented in the *Puratan Janam-sakhi* compiled and first published by Bhai Vir Singh in 1926. The other compilation of the first half of the seventeenth century is known as the *Miharban Janam-sakhi*, though only its first volume, the *Pothi Sach-Khand*, is the work of Sodhi Miharban, the nephew of Guru Arjan. These two works may therefore be regarded as the most relevant to our present purpose.

It has been observed recently that in the *janam-sakhis* of Guru Nanak we find 'the image of the *Guru* seen through the eyes of popular piety seventy-five or a hundred years after his death'. *Sakhis* appear to have been used by the followers of the *Gurus* for propagating the faith of Guru Nanak among Sikhs and non-Sikhs alike even before attempts were made to compile them. At any rate, they appear to have been a most popular medium of propagation and, hence they have an importance of their own. The *janam-sakhis* are, first, a testimony to the impact made by Guru Nanak's personality; also, they reflect the ideals and values of those among whom they were popular. In a certain sense, therefore, the *janam-sakhi* image of Guru Nanak is the more important, for it is the more popular, image.

In this popular image the power to perform maracles is an important aspect of the personality of Guru Nanak. The supranatural powers of Guru Nanak are not unobtrusive in the *Puratan Janam-sakhis* or the *Pothi Sach-Khand.* These powers are revealed by effecting change in the chemical state of an object and in the physical state of matter or even changing it into life, reviving life in a dead animal or a human being, surmounting the insuperable barriers of the physical world or exercising control over the objects of nature, for instance. In certain situations, the performance of a miracle is the clinching argument in a contest; it is a token of Guru Nanak's overwhelming greatness. In some other situations, the miracle is performed to help an individual, to provide food or to heal, for instance. Occasionally, the supranatural element is brought in apparently for no meaningful purpose: understanding the language of birds, for instance, or meeting the personified *Kaliyuga.* In the latter case, it is true, there is a meaningful import. In his encounter with *Kaliyuga*, Guru Nanak not only reveals his greater control over the physical world but he also rejects the offers of wealth, women and temporal power made by *Kaliyuga.* Nevertheless, this moral superiority of Guru Nanak could easily be conveyed in some other way, as indeed it is done elsewhere in the *janam-sakhis.* It appears, therefore, that a strong belief in the supranatural world was as much a part of the psychological makeup of the followers of Guru Nanak as of their contemporaries in general.

It must be added, however, that the supranatural powers as such are subordinate to the power of the True Name; they are even seen as meaningless; and, in the possession of Guru Nanak, supranatural powers are a token of his special relationship with God. For instance, a boat can sail against heavy odds when '*Satguru Nanak*' is written on it. Or, a pitcher miraculously stuck to the head can come off when '*Wahguru*' is uttered. Occasionally, the performance of a miracle is presented as the infringement of God's *hukam*. Indeed, Guru Nanak is presented at times as discouraging the performance of miracles, or even implying that miracles could not be performed. There is no doubt that in the eyes of the believers the True Name was to be preferred to the possession of supranatural powers; but when it came to revealing those powers, there was none to match Guru Nanak, the *zahir pir*. His miracles were surely a sign of God's grace. That is why the shade of the tree under which Nanak sleeps does not move with the sun advancing on its natural course. It is in this light that Rai Bhoa is made to look upon the incident in the *Pothi Sach-Khand*.

The believer's faith in the *Guru* as an extraordinary man of God, combined with the belief in the existence of a supranatural world, enables him to visualize a meeting between Guru Nanak and God Himself. God *(Par-Brahm)* calls Guru Nanak to the Realm of Truth, praises him and asks him to sing His praises. Guru Nanak first expresses his inability to praise God's ineffable greatness and then recites the *So-dar* passage. At another occasion God *(Parameshar)* calls Guru Nanak and asks him to have whatever he likes; Guru Nanak asks for the Name, in preference to riches and honour. Similarly, Guru Nanak rejecsts rulership in favour of the Name. Eventually, God chooses Nanak from amongst all His *bhagats* as the best: 'Nanak'! now you go to the world and save mankind. With this divine sanction, Guru Nanak does not remain different from God. His mere glance even at the funeral pyre of a sinner saves him from hell *(narak)*. At any rate, there is no salvation without the *Guru*.

Nanak the *Guru* is the preceptor of all, irrespective of one's caste, creed, country or sex. It may be pointed out, first, that the *janam-sakhis* are not, strtictly speaking, the biographies of Guru Nanak. In them there is no attempt to see the spiritual growth of the man leading to a discovery of the truth for himself. At his birth, the thirty-three crores of Gods and Goddesses, the eighty-four *joginis*, the fifty-two *birs*, the six *jatis*, the eighty-four *siddhs* and the nine *naths* how to him in reverence: the child is 'a God' for the Hindus and 'a *sadiq* of *Khuda*' for the Muslims. At the age of seven he teaches the *pandit* true gnosticism. He teaches the *mulla* too; and everyone says 'he is no ordinary child; he has on him the seal of God'. At Sultanpur, on Guru Nanak's enunciation that there is no Hindu and there is no Musalman, people say: 'God is speaking through Nanak'. Guru Nanak refuses to identify himself with any creed or sect; he wears a dress which in neither Hindu nor Muslim, but both. The dispute between Hindus and Muslims over the disposal of the dead body of Guru Nanak appears to symbolize the acceptance of his position as the *jagat-guru* by both Hindus and Muslims.

The *udasis* (travels) of Guru Nanak become a spiritual conquest of the four quarters of the world. He meets the Jaina monks and triumphs over them; he meets the *shaikhs* and the *'ulama* of Islam; he meets the orthodox *pandits*, the Jogis, the Vaishnava *bairagis* and the *sanniyasis* and he meets the *sant-bhagats*. They all acknowledge his superiority. For instance, the Vaishnavas in Bikaner are completely convinced of Guru Nanak's greatness and they fall at his feet, uttering '*dhan* Guru Baba Nanak! *Satguru* Baba Nanak! *Wahaguru* Baba Nanak. Similarly, the great Kabir himself acknowledges that Nanak is the *Guru* of the World. Those who become the followers of Guru Nanak do not belong to one particular creed or class or country: they include Hindus and Muslims, holy men and *thags, rajas* and *nawabs*; and they belong to near and distant lands.

The *janam-sakhis* do not always present the ideals of Guru Nanak in the light of their original significance. It has been observed recently that in the *janam-sakhis* there is a marked deference to the ascetic ideal and this in some measure is a departure from the teachings of Guru Nanak. Occasionally, the 'law' of *karma* appears to overshadow the merit of *satsang*. Guru Nanak is presented at one place as cursing the pious and blessing the wicked. In spite of the clever explanation that the pious once uprooted would infuse piety among others wheresoever they go and the wicked would remain stuck to their village, the anecdote does no justice to the Nanak of history. Similarly, Guru Nanak is presented sometimes as causing the death of an opponent with a curse. Though there is a repeated insistence upon the absolute efficacy of the Name in the *Puratan Janam-sakhi*, the Name means the mechanical repetition of the single word 'Ram'. In the *Pothi Sach-Khand*, the mere utterance of 'Har' enables Guru Nanak to be transporterd instantly from an unknown land of darkness to the banks of the Ganges.

This is not to suggest, however, that in the *janam-sakhis* deviations from the teachings of Guru Nanak are more marked than the positive acceptance of his ideals. In fact, departures are rather insignificant compared with the insistence upon the essential teachings of Guru Nanak. In the *janam-sakhis* there is, first, a strong opposition to notions of caste and ritual purity. There is also a strong opposition to ritualistic practices and customs, and to attachment to *maya*. But for the element of miracle, the import of the *Babar-vani* verses, and of those having a bearing on the moral and political condition of the time of Guru Nanak, is quite close to the original. In the *Pothi Sach-Khand*, the primary duty of the ruler is explicitly mentioned: to be just. There is a similar emphasis upon the unity of God, His ineffable greatness and His *hukam* and His omnipotence, His omnipresence and His immanence in the macrocosm and the microcosm. To adore God, to love Him and to offer exclusive devotion to Him, to make one's worship really meaningful, to discard heedlessness and to search for salvation,— all this is commendable. So too is the 'true trade', the 'true farming' or to be a *gurmukh* and not a *manmukh*. The only thing that God does not possess is 'falsehood' *(na-haqq);* He is all Truth; and Guru Nanak is His disciple.

In the *janam-sakhis*, Guru Nanak bequeathes his office to Lehna and, through him, to the other successors of Guru Nanak. Lehna becomes Angad, a part of Guru Nanak, and also his *Guru*. Guru Nanak grants to Angad the boon of the *Sabad*, which is the *bani* as well of Angad and his successors as of Guru Nanak. Furthermore, the *panth* of Guru Nanak has behind it the Divine sanction: 'Go Nanak ! Your *panth* will flourish', says God. The followers of Guru Nanak are to be called the *Nanak-panths*, with their distinct form of salutation and with their distinct places of worship; their watchwords are to be *nam, dan* and *asnan*; their aim is to spread true religion; and they are to live pure amidst the impurities of attachment. Thus is reflected in the *janan-sakhis* 'a developing self-consciousness, a growing awareness of the community's nature and function as a distinctive *panth*'.

In retrospect, it is possible to see that Sikh institutions during the first two centuries of their history developed in close relationship to some ideological developments. Nearly all of these were seen as interpretations or extension of Guru Nanak's mission. If we were to choose one key-idea which lends unity to all these developments, it is surely the concept of the *Guru*, which at once reconciled the uniqueness of Guru Nanak's position to the authority vested in his successors through that office and which, at a different level, brought the *bani* and the *panth* into parallel prominence with the personal *Guru*. The unity as well as the end of personal *guru*ship, which today is the fundamental belief of the majority of the followers of Guru Nanak, is a legacy from the times of his successors. This may be regarded as perhaps their most creative response to the greatness of the founder of Sikhism.

8

The Socio-cultural Trend

Introductory

Any Assessment of the status of women has to start from the social framework. Social structures, cultural norms, and value systems influence social expectations regarding the behaviour of both men and women, and determine a woman's roles and her position in society to a great extent. The most important of these institutions are the systems of descent, family and kinship, marriage, and religious traditions. They provide the ideology and moral basis, for men's and women's notions about their rights and duties. The normative standards do not change at the same pace as changes in other forms of social organization brought about by such factors as technological and educational advance, urbanization, increasing population, and changing costs and standards of living. This gap explains the frequent failure of law and educational policy to produce the desired impact on social attitudes.

The social status of women in India is a typical example of this gap between the position and roles accorded to them by the Constitution and the laws, and those imposed on them by social traditions. What is possible for women in theory, is seldom within their reach in fact.

Religious Traditions

The religious traditions have a deep bearing on the role and status of women.

(1) *Hinduism* : In Hinduism, a multitude of derogatory attributes have been ascribed to women. Like the Shudras, she must not

study the Vedas or perform any sacrifices. According to Manu, "In childhood a woman must be subject to her father, in youth to her husband, and when her lord is dead, to her sons. A woman must never be independent", She is viewed solely as the mother and the wife, and these roles are idealized. The ideal wife is faithful and uncomplaining, and her virtue lies in the services she renders to her husband. Practices like giving away of girls in marriage and the importance attached to sons for maintaining continuity of the line have strengthened the patrilineal social structure of Hinduism. The impurity associated with menstruation and childbirth, which restricts women from joining religious ceremonies strengthens the view that they are naturally inferior to men. Since marriage and motherhood are considered essential, a Hindu woman is expected to perform special *vratas* (rituals) to obtain long life and special protection for her husband and sons. A widow, on the other hand, is associated with misfortune and is regarded as inauspicious. She cannot participate in socio-religious activities as she may bring misfortune to others. Remarriage was not permitted for high caste widows by the Great Tradition, which continues its influence to this day, in spite of the legal sanction for remarriage provided since 1856. Castes in which remarriage has been traditionally allowed, imposed other disabilities on widows, and secondary marriages are most performed with the same pomp and ceremonial. Many of them even adopt a ban on widow remarriage to establish their claim to a higher status in the caste hierarchy. The Hindu male is not subject such restrictions or conditions. He does not wear any diacritical marks to indicate his married state, does not observe fast for his wife and suffers from no restriction on remarriage. A widower is not considered inauspicious.

Protest movements within the Hindu fold, like Buddhism, Jainism, Vaishnavism, Veerashaivism, and Sikhism contributed to some improvement in the status of women, particularly in religious and spiritual activities. But they also continued to regard women primarily as mothers and wives, and inferior to men in society. In Buddhism, the male monk is given a higher status than the nun. In the religious teachings of Jainism, women are severely condemned even though they are given a legitimate position in congregational life. Veerashaivism permitted divorce and remarriage. The Bhakti movement, by permitting women to seek spiritual solace independently of intermediaries, and throwing open religious pursuits to the languages of the people, enabled many women to become saints and religious leaders. These movements however failed to rectify in any significant manner the subordinate position attributed to women by both the Great and Little Traditions in Indian society. Later religious like Islam, Christianity and Zoroastrianism which brought with them their distinct images of women, adapted themselves to the Indian context, often drawing on the prevalent customs and practices.

(2) *Islam* : The Koran regards men and women as being equal and does not regard women as an impediment in the path of religion. Though it provided women with a much higher status than was prevalent at the time, various interpretations of Koranic injunctions over the centuries accorded women an inferior position in many respects, reflecting the cultural norms of those periods. Though equal as a believer, a woman cannot be a priest, nor can she lead the prayers. She has no place in the formal religious organization and legal affairs of the community, and cannot be a Kazi. Emphasis on modesty, decorum, and chastity led, through conflicting viewpoints, to the practice of seclusion and veiling. In India, the *burqa* and seclusion were more characteristic of the upper and the middle strata of society, particularly in urban areas. Though declining among these sections, it has now become more of a lower middle-class phenomenon, and a status symbol among the working classes, to indicate a rise in their social status. Seclusion imposed many restrictions on women's behaviour and deprived them of the right to participate in communal prayers.

The marriage contract gives very unequal rights to men and women, permitting polygamy and unilateral right of divorce to the husband. The bride's consent to the marriage is a mere formality, and the institution of marriage-guardian places her in a subordinate position. Religion makes the husband the family head, and demands obedience and service from the wife. Widow remarriage and divorce, though permitted for womens are generally frowned upon, specially among the middle classes. Though some security for women against the possibility of divorce is provided by *Mehr* (dower), very few women are able to assert this chain; and while Islam recognizes women's right to inherit property, in practice these rights are not upheld. Women lose their rights because of ignorance and inability to assert them.

(3) *Christianity* : Like Islam, the basic tenets of Christianity have intermingled with local traditions of the various communities which follow this religion. The Biblical image of woman as the tempter and seducer has strengthened the husband's right to control the wife and her property. However, the emphasis on the mutually dutiful and respectful relationship between the husband and the wife has helped to weaken the authority of the extended family or the patriarch, and thus accorded a relatively higher status to the woman through the nuclear organization of the family. Even among communities which retain the joint family, the daughter-in-law is not relegated to the background as in Hindu families. She is free to move with her husband, and it is recognized that her primary relationship is with her husband.

Emphasis on monogamy is the one enduring factor which has raised women's status in Christianity. However, the concept of permanency of marriage with no place for divorce has affected adversely the status of women among Catholics and some other groups. Though these women enjoy greater security of home and the company of their children, they are more subject to the husband's authority, being deprived of legal rights and an independent existence.

The Bible emphasizes certain qualities of a woman such as her capacity to work, caring for her family, kindness and charity for the needy outside the home, and wisdom. She can participate in all religious ceremonies, though she has not been granted full ecclesiastic responsibility in the church organization (except among Methodists). Christianity does not not emphasize marriage as a woman's sole destiny. She has an independent moral entity and responsibility. Because of this tradition, Christian women were the first to enter the field of education and employment as nurses, doctors, or teachers. Though the taboos on women are less in Christianity, the basic concept of their inferiority to man is beyond dispute.

(4) *Zoroastrianism* : This religion, practised by the Parsees in India, gives women a position of honour in the family and society. They are entitled to property, religious as well as secular education, and permitted to divorce and remarry. Traditionally, Zoroastrianism imposed menstrual taboos demanding segregation and non-participation in religious activities. Polygamy and child marriage, which had crept in under Hindu and Muslim influence, were fought against and removed by the Parsee Panchayat in the nineteenth century. But while a man's marriage to a non-Parsee involves no disgrace, and his children are accepted as Parsees, the same right is not given to the Parsee woman who marries outside the faith. Even her right to enter the Fire Temple is not accepted.

(5) *Tribal Religions* : Women have a role to play in the religious activities of the family and the group, but have no place in the special worship of tribal deities. In matrilineal tribes, women worship ancestral deities. Menstruation is associated with impurity throughout tribal India and leads to the exclusion of women from positions of ritual importance. Their contribution to economic activity results in considerable freedom in social behaviour, but they play no role in the enforcement of community discipline and public morality, which is the function of the Panchayats or Tribal Councils.

The forgoing discussion will show that there is no radical difference in the position attributed to women by any of the religions. The reform movements of the nineteenth and twentieth centuries, like the Brahmo Samaj, Arya Samaj, or Prarthana Samaj among the Hindus and similar movements in other communities, attacked practices like child marriage or ill-treatment of widows and pleaded for women's education and their rights to property. The leaders of these movements realized the difficulty of separating social from religious reform, but their aim to reform all religions together could not be realized as both the ruling power and religious orthodoxy in all communities resisted such attempts. Consequently, the scope of these movements was generally estricted in two ways: (1) they developed within the folds of each religion rather than as a unified movement for a transformation of the whole society; and (2) their objective was to change the position of women within the domestic framework only and to ensure for them a position of dignity and respect within the family. Their impact has, however, been most pronounced on the urban middle-class and the goals of the reform movements have become part of the general cultural heritage of this section of Indian society. Being more concerned with the disabilities of women in the higher classes, the reformers did not challenge the universal suppression of all women perpetuated by their subordinate position in society and did not consider the need and problems of their participation in the wider social process. It was left to Mahatma Gandhi and the Freedom Movement to place the movement for women's emancipation in its proper perspective, as part of the larger movement for the removal of inequalities that oppressed all the weaker sections.

Descent Systems

There are two main descent systems in India, matrilineal and patrilineal.

(1) *Matrilineal:* Matrilineal communities are concentrated in the South-Western and North-Eastern regions of the country, among the Nairs, Thiyars and Moplahs of Kerala, in Lakshadweep, and among the Khasis and Garos of Meghalaya and Assam. Islam and Christianity, accepted by a large percentage of the population in these regions, did not affect the patterns of kinship and marriage substantially. Since the close of the nineteenth century, however, changes have been brought about by the development of a market economy, education and occupational mobility, which have influenced patterns of marital residence, rules of inheritance, and other related matters.

In a matrilineal system, the lineage is counted through the woman but power rests with the men in the woman's family.

Matriliny is associated with an economic system in which women are not dependent on men (except among the landed Nairs, whose women do not engage in productive work, though they enjoy full property rights). Constraints on women are found in those areas where there is greater concern with the maintenance of group boundaries and retention of family and caste status. The Nairs impose many restrictions on women, but the Garo, Khasi, and Lakshadweep women enjoy greater freedom of movement because of the contribution that they make to the economy.

Matrilineal systems display some inherent conflicts. Authority rests with men, while group placement is determined through women. A husband is not incorporated in the wife's kin group, and has minimum rights over hs wife and children. The property is controlled by the wife's brothers, father, or uncles. Occupational mobility, resulting from modernization, increases a man's control over his wife and children if they move with him, but disrupts the matrilineal system. The Nair Taravads have been disintegrating partly because of political and economic change, and partly because of the new laws of marriage which confer rights, on individual members to demand their shares. The Nair women have benefited from educational opportunities and continue to enjoy respect as property-holders and as perpetuators of the line. But the restrictions that bound them to their homes, unlike other matrilineal groups, have coincided with the adoption of Sanskritic rituals of marriage and institutions like dowry which have contributed towards lowering of their status.

(2) *Patrillineal* : The majority of the Indian population follows the patrilineal mode of descent. The male is the perpetuator of the line and of the family name. The girl's contribution is made in another patriline, so the system emphasizes the transferability of the daughter at marriage to the husband's kin group. This affects the position of a woman in society, is reinforced by socialization, and has a bearing on her jural rights. Only the son can perform certain religious duties for the family. The socio-cultural compulsion to get a daughter married had led to a girl being regarded as a burden, especially as she has to be brought up and trained without the parents receiving any economic support from her. Discrimination

between the sexes in nutrition, medical care and education is directly related to this attitude.

In tribal and rural areas the girl's rights to property are extremely limited. Men are the possessors and inheritors of land and its resources. A widow's right of usufruct over her husband's land is subject to her not remarrying. In the event of divorce or separation, children may accompany the mother, though they have to return to the father when they grow up. The cultural notion that a woman's role is only supportive has to be traced to patrilineal descent and patrilocal residence.

Family Organization

The most common family organization, the joint family, is composed of a group of patrilineally related males who have equal rights to property, sharing a common budget, residence and hearth, though this pattern of living has been considerably affected by modernization, urbanization, and socio-economic change. The type of joint family depends on such factors as the caste, community, or age of marriage. Joint family living is more characteristic of the land-owning, trading classes and other upper castes. Among tribal groups, the nuclear household is the culturally approved form of the domestic group.

A woman is expected to adjust to her father-in-law's household to which she goes after her marriage. She is placed under severe restrictions and has little or no say in decision-making and is directly subordinate to her mother-in-law. Her status in the family depends greatly on her husband's contribution to the family economy, and in the middle and upper classes, on the amount of dowry brought by herself.

Mothers of long standing in the middle classes enjoy considerable respect and authority in the family and have a say in decision-making. Our survey, however, reveals that women as a whole play a marginal role in decision-making. Their role is slightly higher for decisions affecting the daughters. The mother's authority, which often reduces the position of a daughter-in-law to that of a miserable drudge, may decline with old age, widowhood, and the daughter-in-law's coming into importance as a mother and wife of the principal provider.

Our survey also revealed varying degrees of observance of *purdah* before the husband's kin. The highest percentage of *purdah* before the father-in-law was found in Haryana (72.61%), Rajasthan (62.18%), and Delhi (60.78%). This is low in Southern States, where *purdah* was never so prevalent. Women settled away from the patrillocal villages and in urban areas have greater freedom of association and movement, particularly if they also contribute to the family economy. The woman's role is less restricted in a simple family where she is not subordinate to any other woman and is the mistress of the house.

Marriage

In patrilineal societies marriage signifies a transfer of a woman from her natal group to that of her husband. Arranged marriages at a young age are considered most desirable for girls, as these notions are related to the importance of virginity and the restrictions placed on marriage within the same *gotra* or clan lineage. This restriction is absent among Muslims, who prefer marriages between close relatives, as they help to keep the property within the family. In the South, cross-cousin marriages among Hindus is the accepted mode.

Education and liberalization of ideas in urban areas have led to certain changes in patterns of selection of the marriage partner. Some recent surveys conducted have, however, revealed a greater preference for arranged marriages among the young generation. In the pre-independence period young people preferred self-choice of partners.

Arranged marriages have many features which highlight the unequal status of a woman. She has to present herself before marriageable boys and their relations for acceptance. The ceremony of *Kanyadan,* where the virgin daughter is given to the bridegroom by her father, is another indicator of the inequality of status between bride-givers and bride-takers. This is particularly prevalent in Northern, Central, and Western India. In the North, the son-in-law and his parents are entitled to receive gifts from the girl's parents but the latter are not supposed to accept any food at the son-in-law's house.

The practice of hypergamy, where a marriage is arranged between a man of a higher caste and a woman of a lower caste, is extremely detrimental to the status of women. It is prevalent among Rajputs and Jats of North India, Maithil Brahmins of Bihar and some other groups. Female infanticide among these communities was partly a consequence of hypergamy as it was difficult to find a suitable match for girls of high castes. Conseqently, dowry is very high in hypergamous communities.

Polygamy: Both variants of polygamy, viz., polygyny (plurality of wives) and polyandry (plurality of husbands) are found in India. Polyandry is confined to certain Scheduled Tribes like the Todas in the Nilgiris, the Khasas in the Jaunsar Bawar District of Uttar Pradesh, and the people of Lahaul, Kinnaur, and Spiti in Himachal Pradesh.

Polygyny was much more prevalent in most parts of India. Social reaction against this practice as an indignity offensive to the status of women was one of the most marked features of the nineteenth century Reform Movement. While the acceptance of monogamy became widely prevalent among the educated classes, reformers differed on the action necessary for the eradication of polygyny. Some wanted legislative prohibition, others believed that it would die out with the spread of education. Partly because of this social reaction and partly due to "declining material prosperity" among the classes which had practised polygyny earlier, its prevalence has declined considerably over the past 100 years. This demand for legislative ban gained momentum under the influence of Mahatma Gandhi and women's organizations, and laws were passed in some provinces and princely states even in the pre-independence period. Finally, the Hindu Marriage Act, 1954, prohibited it for all Hindus.

Under the existing laws, polygyny is permitted only among Muslims. A census study in 1961, however found the practice to be still prevalent among most communities to a certain extent, though its incidence had declined over the decades. The overall incidence of polygyny found by the study was 5.8% among Hindus, 5.7 among Muslims, 6.7% among Jains, 7.8% among Buddhists, and 15.2% among tribal communities. The tribal communities were the only ones where the incidence of polygyny had increased over the years. While most tribal groups permit this practice, we were informed that it is mainly practised by chiefs and headmen. Barrenness of the wife, economic advantages, and gain in prestige are the usual justification for plurality of wives among the tribes. We were informed that such marriages take place even among the Christian tribals and receive customary sanction though they are not performed by the church.

The cultural motivation for plural marriages operates among non-tribal groups also, barrenness or sickness of the wife, the absence of a son, and the custom of marrying a brother's widow (still prevalent in some communities) providing the usual reasons. Another social reason which has become more important in recent years is the cultural and communication gap between an illiterate or uneducated wife and an educated husband whose social aspirations are influenced by modern norms. These are generally cases of child marriage. The women are often not able to seek a divorce because of their economic and social dependence on their married status. Resistance of their family to a divorce is an added reason.

Economic gain is an important motivation for polygyny among communities where women contribute substantially to the family economy. Some artisan groups, both Muslim and Hindu, find it cheaper to have a number of wives as extra hands than hiring labour. The wide prevalence of polygyny among the middle classes in Manipur has a clear link with the economic independence of Manipuri women who not only support themselves and their childred by their earnings but also contribute to the husband's income.

Though the incidence of polygyny among Muslims is not as high as commonly believed, we found widespread resentment among Muslim women against legal sanction of this practice. They observed that any protest against this institution always resulted in acute oppression against which Muslim women received no protection from society. Though law alone cannot eradicate this practice, its existence acts as a norm setter and arouses public coscience. We cannot, therefore, appreciate the denial of this support to Muslim women in their struggle against this social custom.

The continuation of this practice among the Hindus now is mainly due to custom, women's lack of knowledge of their legal rights, and social acceptance of the situation. We were informed that sometimes wives are compelled to sign a document permitting their husbands to remarry, believing that such a document deprived them of their legal right of redress. It is necessary for women's voluntary agencies to launch a campaign against such marriages by ostracizing the men who commit bigamy and mobilizing public opinion against this practice.

Bride Price and Dowry: The two major types of transfer of material wealth accompanying marriage are bride price and dowry. The latter is transferred along with the bride whereas the former moves in the opposite direction.

Bride price is customarily prevalent among patrilineal tribes and the middle and lower castes of the non-tribal population. Theoretically this payment in cash and kind is made to the bride's father in exchange for authority over the woman, which passes from her kin group to the bridegroom's kin group, but the idea of compensation for the loss of a productive worker is implicit in it. In communities which follow this custom, a daughter is not regarded as a burden and parents do not dread the thought of her marriage. She brings wealth to the family both before and as a result of her marriage. However, the flavour of a market transaction (*i.e.*, buying of a bride) is not altogether absent.

There is also a custom that permits a wife to leave a husband who ill-treats her, by paying some compensation. This is welcome as it gives her a chance of a freedom from an unwanted partnership. However, this practice is sometimes abused and a woman may be transferred from one man to another even against her wishes in return for some monetary compensation. We found considerable resentment against this custom known as *Reet* (Himachal Pradesh) and *Natra* (in Madhya Pradesh) among women.

Among some of the poorer communities, the custom of bride price has been responsible for indebtedness resulting in a state of servitude to the money-lenders who are generally landowners. We received reports that, among some Scheduled Castes and Tribes of Uttar Pradesh, wives have been sent for prostitution to clear the debts incurred by the husband at the time of marriage. The custom of bride price needs to be eradicated in order to change the concept of women as someone's possession as well as to improve the conditions of life of these communities.

Changing from bride price to dowry is an attempt to improve the social status of a family or a group, because dowry is associated with the higher social groups. This change has been reported from different regions and indicates a loss of status for the girl in her father's family where she becomes a liability rather than an asset. This is undoubtedly a consequence of the withdrawal of women from productive activities and of the loss of their productive skills.

There are baffling regional variations in people's understanding of dowry. It may be seen as (a) the gift given to the bride and often settled beforehand, which may not be regarded as her property; (b) a gift given to the bridegroom before and at the time of marriage; or (c) a present to the in-laws of the girl. There are a number of social and cultural sanctions for the practice of dowry among both Hindu and Muslim communities. Some see it as a *pre-mortem* inheritance from the bride's natal family; some as an insurance for the bride against any economic crisis; some as the means to set up a new home. In reality, however, dowry has come to be regarded as essential to obtain a suitable match for a girl with a view to ensuring a high or a higher standard of life for her. The increase of social and economic inequality has been one of the most important inducements for dowry and operates at all levels of the society. The amount of wealth involved may range from a few hundreds to lakhs, from utensils and jewellery to refrigerators, cars, and air-conditioners, but behind each such transaction is the desire for social status for the daughter and indirectly for her parents' family. The desire to obtain security and good status for the daughter places the bride's parents in a vulnerable position where they may face demands which bear no relation to their actual economic capacity and may reduce them to a state of indebtedness. The present reality, therefore, bears no relationship to the traditional sanctions for this practice.

Throughout our tours the increasing incidence of this custom was brought to our notice. Originally an urban practice, it has now penetrated rural areas and to communities which had never practised it before. The increasing demands for gifts and ostentatious expenditure on weddings impose a tremendous strain on the family finances and expose young girls to an extremely unfair competition, in which their own worth is hardly recognized. The aura of a market transaction colours marriage negotiations and inculcates the values of a high consumption society with its false ideas of prestige and ostentation. It encourages the belief that women's work in the home is non-productive and puts a premium on a parasitic existence for women. Black money and unaccounted earnings provide an impetus for the increase of dowry and ostentatious expenditure in weddings and expose families of honest means and moderate income to indebtedness. We received bitter complaints about the high interest rates at which money has to be borrowed for a daughter's wedding. While the groom's family demands dowry as compensation for expenditure on his education, parents of many girls have to sacrifice educating their daughters to avoid the double expenditure expenditure. It has also been found that the rates of dowry increase with the education of girls because the higher educated boy expects a larger dowry.

In our view, the spirit of dowry, apart from exposing many young women to extreme unhappiness and mental breakdowns, goes against the goal of a socialist society and needs to be combated in a multi-pronged manner—by arousing consciousness among men and women; reforming and simplifying marriage customs; increasing opportunities for women's employment and condemning the ideal of a parasitic existence for them; reassessing the value of house work and home-making as socially and economically productive; enforcing the Anti-Dowry Act; and banning display of gifts and ostentatious expenditure on marriages. Women's organizations and the mass media should play a definite role in organizing active propaganda against these practices and to make women conscious of their demeaning implications.

Widowhood: According to our estimates, based on the census of 1931 (the last census which enumerated population by castes), 13.9% of the Hindu population at that date did not customarily practise widow remarriage. In spite of their small proportion in the population, and the role played by leaders from this section in bringing about legal reforms, the remarriage and condition of widows still constitutes a problem which cannot be described as insignificant. The census of 1971 reported 23 million widows as against 22 millions reported by the census of 1951. While the percentage of widows decreased from 15.5% in 1961 to 12.5% in 1971, their ratio of 2,772 per thousand widowers and the fact that they outnumber the latter in all ages indicate that the deterrents to remarriage of widows are still fairly high. The fear of losing the children particularly prevents women from seeking remarriage.

Social attitudes towards widows differ at different socio-economic levels, but a change in the life-style of women after widowhood is characteristic of most sections of Indian society. According to our survey, 59.52% Hindus, 61,49% Muslims, 62.16% Jains, 52.94% Parsees, and 44.2% Christians approved changes in the mode of dress of widows. There seems to have been some improvement in the attitude to widows' participation in auspicious ceremonies. Interestingly enough, the approval of such participation is the highest among upper caste Hindus and the lowest among the Scheduled and other lower castes.

In spite of such marginal changes in attitudes, the condition of widows continues to be a blot on our society. We met a large group of widows in a state of destitution in Banaras: they had been unashamedly abandoned by their families and were eking out an existence through begging or various petty trades. Most of them were more concerned about the future protection or security for their children rather than their own.

For widows with property, however, the legal reform of securing their right to a share of the husband's property has improved conditions considerably. The decision of the government to provide family pensions to widows of government servants for their life time with additional allowances for children during their minority has also guaranteed a degree of security.

Age of Marriage: Though there is a distinct rise in the age of marriage for women in India, in rural areas the marriage of very young girls is still quite prevalent. Rules of endogamy, other norms of restrictions and preferences for marriages between certain groups, and the strong emphasis on the purity and chastity of women encourage early marriages. Significantly, most tribal communities do not have child marriages. We came across some child wives in different parts of the country, but in discussions, practically everyone observed that 14 to 15 was the desirable age for marriage of girls. According to some reports, early marriages are essential for Scheduled Caste women to protect them from the lust of men of upper groups who wield economic power over them. Early marriage and lack of education constitute a vicious circle, affecting population growth and the health of the mother and the child, and the status and education of girls. In urban areas, education and need for employment of boys has raised the marriage age of girls also. Attitude studies among urban middle and upper classes suggest 16 to 24 as the age for marriage of girls.

Customary Marriages: While marriages among the dominant higher castes are performed by ritual ceremonies, there have been various forms of customary marriage practised by other castes. They are normally conteminous with easy forms of divorce and secondary marriages. The secondary marriage of a widow or a separated or divorced woman is accompanied by a nominal ceremony varying from region to region. Most tribes prefer marriage by negotiation, but they also provide for unions established by elopement and an emphatic choice by the girl is generally respected.

Women's Role in a Changing Society

Role Differentiation: While the Indian polity recognizes equality of rights between men and women, society implicitly accepts a sharp distinction in their roles and spheres of activity. True parity will be possible only when the implications of the Constitutional equality are accepted in people's minds. Even with regional variations, basic notions about male and female roles display some common features. A woman is primarily associated with the home, is expected to look after domestic chores and her typical roles are those of a housewife and mother. In the cultural understanding of the people, home-making, like child bearing and child rearing, is identified with femininity. Whether women work in the fields, factories or mines, at construction sites, or in white-collar jobs, all of them are expected to be home-makers in the same manner as women who confine themselves exclusively to home-making activities. Their role in the outside world has not yet been accepted in the same manner as men's.

Decision-making for the community and the exercise of political power is still regarded as an exclusive male preserve: this is clear from the entirely male composition of the traditional panchayats, either of villages or of caste groups (including some Muslim castes). Men may engage in manual work outside the home but such work inside the house is considered derogatory and is expected to be done by women. Cooking, tailoring can be taken up by men as a profession but inside the house, these are left to women.

Regional differences in the type and quantum of work expected of women expose the hollowness of the myths attached to these sex-linked roles. In the North-Eastern region, weaving is the monopoly of women but there are parts of India where a woman may not touch the loom. Embroidery work is a male activity in Kashmir and a female one in the Punjab and elsewhere. In agriculture the variations in women's tasks in different regions prove the invalidity of the assumption that men are supposed to do the heavier work. In the Northern hill regions, women carry heavy logs weighing 200 to 300 lbs, slice the timber, and help in wood chopping. What is important is that the tasks assigned to men are considered more prestigious in most communities and regions. Women are generally the unpaid family workers.

In the middle-class, however, the spheres of men and women are more sharply demarcated. There is a clear distinct between work done for one's household and that done for others. Women are supposed to do only the former. Where they assist the family business like grocery, tailoring or knitwear, food processing, etc., by preparing things in the home, their contribution is not to be acknowledged, with the result that they are not recorded in the census as workers. It is considered unfortunate for women of these classes who have no other qualifications and skills to engage in these jobs as a means of earning a livelihood because the prestige of the family suffers when their women have to work for others.

This traditional concept is changing with girls taking up white-collar jobs. Parental inhibitions are breaking down where girls have to earn sometimes to provide their dowry and marriage expenses and sometimes to support their parents and younger members of the family. Cases where parents do not want their daughters to marry out of a fear that this would deprive them of her earnings are no longer rare in lower middle-class families.

Among the well-to-do, women are spared of much of the drudgery of house work because of domestic help, but they are expected to run the home and bring up the children. Home-making is raised to a fine art, and trifling details assume exaggerated importance. The precise activities may depend upon the locality, educational level, and extent of modernization, but the real differentiation remains.

These distinctions in roles within and outside the family, in decision-making, in management of expenditure and incomes were clearly indicated by our survey in which the number of respondents who claimed that these activities are equally shared by men and women was very small.

These norms of behaviour influence the bringing up of boys and girls. While enlightened families take pride in not discriminating between boys and girls in educational opportunities, the emphasis on feminine tasks and feminine abilities remains and there is distinct difference in the degree of protection considered necessary for boys and girls. Boys are not asked to share in domestic work though they may lend a hand in marketing, running errands and doing escort duty to their mothers and sisters. Boys with an aptitude for cooking or tailoring are ridiculed and discouraged. Studies and career motivation are emphasized for boys but few parents visualize a career for their daughters. Marriage remains as the goal and education as only a security against unforeseen eventualities. Excellence in studies or any other field does not provide a justification for a girl's lack of interest in household work. This distinction in expectations inevitably affects the allocation of family resources for the education of boys and girls, irrespective of their aptitudes and abilities.

This emphasis on feminine roles has an inevitable effect on girls' personalities and identities. They learn early in life the need for flexibility, adjustment, and submissiveness, and hesitate to develop strong opinions and commitments which they may not be allowed to pursue after marriage. These constrictions and inhibitions affected most women in their later lives, particularly when they have to compete with men in their careers. Among the poorer sections, where girls contribute to the running of the house as well as to the family economy, their education is often sacrificed, while the boys are encouraged to study. We saw many cases of this type during our tours, in both urban and rural areas. Apart from the economic reasons, there is also a lurking fear that education may alienate girls from their conventional roles and make them less submissive to the family.

Home and Work: The relationship between earning capacity and status and autonomy within the family for the woman depends, to a great extent, on the status of her earning activity. Since manual labour has a low status in our society, women employed as wage labourers or unskilled and menial workers do not enjoy a better status, while women in high prestige jobs may do so.

Women of the poorer sections whose days are spent on hard labour (in earning and house work) are extremely overworked and can give little attention to the bringing up of children. Among the middle classes, the lot of women who have to cope with both house work and employment outside the home is not much easier. While urban life brings certain aids and makes house work easier (for instance, she may not have to fetch water and fuel from a distance), she is expected to give greater care and attention to the children and their studies, to keep the home in a better and more attactive manner, provide more varied menus and play hostess to guests and friends of the family more frequently than her counterparts in rural areas. This overwork explains the persistence of the desire for a leisured life for their daughters even among these working women. For this class of women, there has been considerable role expansion since they are called upon to assume many new roles, in addition to their traditional ones. The efficiency that is required of them in full time employment with its consequent professional responsibilities, as well as in running a modern home with its extra familial dimensions, create considerable psychological stress which make their life very difficult. Only few such women have the income as well as understanding and sympathy from the family which can ensure some rest and leisure for their self-improvement, or enable them to adjust the patterns of social interactions demanded by their jobs with the demands of the home.

The change in attitudes to women working outside the home or participating in public life has been slow and uneven, because they are related to deep-rooted prejudices about a woman's inherent aptitudes and capacities, her proper sphere of work and man-woman relationships. Thus, the teaching profession or medicine is considered more respectable for women because it does not conflict with traditional norms of femininity. Nursing, on the other hand, though not in conflict with feminie roles, involves contact with impure objects, male patients and doctors, and odd hours of work and has still not attained the same degree of acceptability among the middle classes, except in a few regions and communities. Prejudices against the performing arts are, however, breaking down rapidly because of the chances of high income associated with them.

The pace of change in these attitudes is even slower in small towns where it is more difficult for women to take up unconventional work because of the social attitudes. Because of the post-independence entry of women in the administrative services, prejudice against this career is breaking down fast. But in smaller towns men still do not relish working under a woman boss. These traditional concepts of a woman's limitations and her proper place were responsible for the well-known episode in Uttar Pradesh when the Chief Minister decided .that women officers should not be entrusted with administrative responsibilities. These views are shared by many, both men and women, and form a current theme in literature, the mass media, and social research.

Society's ambivalence regarding the gainful employment and independence of women is demonstrated in many ways. Her income is appreciated because it raises the standard of living and lessens financial burdens, but the freedom of association and movement needed for outdoor work is not approved by many who continue to put a stigma on working women. Men may come late from work, and may take time off from family responsibilities in the interests of their carrer, but not so women. We received many complaints that even men who helped with domestic chores when abroad, do not do so after their return to the country. A few who do are criticised and disparaged by neighbours and relatives. A belief that working women are bad mothers and inefficient housewives, is widspread. An improvement in the financial condition of the family often precipitates women having to leave their jobs. Most working women develop a sense of guilt and tend to pamper their children to make up for what they consider to be lack of proper attention on their part.

The problem of role conflict manifests itself in various ways, particularly where there is a difference between the job status of husbands and wives. Husbands who have a lower status job than their wives find adjustment difficult because they consider the situation a reversal from the normal, where the husband is the principal breadwinner and enjoys superior authority in the family. On the other hand, it is also considered demeaning for wives of men in high status occupations to take up low-paid and relatively lower status jobs. An idle wife attuned to the life patterns of the husband is appreciated more. Many women who continue in employment after marriage in order to support their needy parents and siblings have to face tremendous misunderstanding and lack of sympathy from their husbands and inlaws.

These problems of adjustment will remain unless the distinction between men's work and women's work within and outside the families is removed through the socialization process in the home and the school. It is also necessary to provide supportive institutions in the way of creches, easy transport, labour saving devices, and changes in life style to make home-making an easier and less time-consuming process. If household work and the rearing of children are recognized as socially and economically productive, then sharing such responsibilities need not disgrace a man and they need not become obstacles to a woman's right to play the multiple roles required by a modern society. Recognition of a house-wife's work for purposes of national accounting as a contribution to national savings and stability of economy would enhance women's status and acknowledge society's debt to them rather than its present attitude where she has to shoulder the drudgery and the sacrifice without any recognition.

Special Problems

The gap in the perception of women's needs and available opportunities leaves them open to exploitation which cannot be offset by laws or development programmes only: an understanding of the magnitude and intricacies of these problems and institutional support is necessary. In a rapidly changing and culturally differentiated society, the slow process of adjustment in social institutions and values to changing needs gives rise to certain problems and deviant behaviour which can only be removed with structural changes in the socio-economic system. These special problems include prostitution, the problems of women prisoners, suicides, unmarried mothers, and aged and destitute prisoners, suicides, unmarried mothers, and aged and destitute women.

(1) *Prostitution:* The commercialization of this old profession is a recent phenomenon. The emphasis on chastity, child marriage, denial of widow remarriages, dowry, and inadequate employment opportunities for women, have always been the major factors contributing to the spread of this evil. Industrialization and urbanization have helped to transform trafficking in women into a highly profitable industry, and changed its character from the traditional institutions sanctioned by social and religious customs for certain castes, into a widspread industry in vice. Recent studies of prostitutes prove that while a large numbers are descendants of these traditional groups, there are many new entrants to this profession who are victims of social oppression and poverty. In the absence of adequate employment opportunities, families in poorer and even the middle classes are compelled to allow prostitution of their women. Wives of bonded and other agricultural labourers take up (and are sometimes forced to) this occupation to free their families from indebtedness. In certain areas girls are encouraged to practice this profession to earn their dowries. Recent additions to this group are from middle-class families driven by economic necessity and in a few cases by their desire to keep up an appearance of affluence. Even educated women are found in their ranks because of difficulties in obtaining other types of employment.

While there is no doubt of the historical or traditional origin of this profession in India, it represents in our view the exploitation of the poor by the rich and of women by men. If women are to become equals of men in society, society must ensure economic, social, and psychological security for them and protect them from this worst form of exploitation and inequality. The growing incidence of prostitution in metropolitan cities and urban areas indicates growing demand on the on hand and poverty on the other. The increasing commercialization has resulted in the emergence of a host of intermediaries and allied traders who profit from this traffice. Lure of the high profits from this trade has encouraged the exploitation and seduction of women from tribal communities, and even other sections of the population who never practised this profession.

The Suppression of Immoral Traffic in Women and Girls Act, 1956, aimed to suppress this commercialization and did not attempt to penalise individual prostitutes or prostitution itself. The only case where an individual prostitute can be punished is when she carries on her trade in the near vicinity of public places or places of religious worship. According to senior police officials, this lacuna and the necessity of having women witnesses during a raid have severely restricted their powers to suppress this traffic. Social workers and police officers agree that the punishments imposed under the Act are most inadequate. We understand that amendments of the law are under consideration. We also suggest better preventive and rehabilitation measures in the way of homes for abandoned and illegitimate children, special counselling service for women in moral and social danger and economic rehabilitation of women rescued from this trade.

(2) *Women in Prisons:* The condition of women prisoners has not received adequate attention since they constitute a small segment of the total convict population (4.3% of convicts and 3.2% of undertrials). About 72% of the female convicts are between 21 and 40 years of age and around 10% are between 16 and 20. About 12% are illiterate, 15% are unmarried, and 12% are widows. A large majority are mothers. It has been found that their crimes are mainly caused by poverty or helplessness in certain social matters. Most of them are beginners in crime, for whom prison life is extremely unhealthy. The Law Commission has recommended that convicts on short-term sentences should not be sent to prison.

We were informed that in some prisons, lunatics—both criminal and non-criminal—are housed with women prisoners. This dangerous practice will prevent both reform or rehabilitation of the convicts and 'the treatment of the insane.

Another problem brought to our notice was that most women prisoners are sent away from their place of residence because of accommodation difficulties in prisons. Their isolation from the family increases difficulties of rehabilitation and readjustment to family life after release. We feel that problems of women prisoners deserve special attention, particularly with regard to their rehabilitation and education, and care of their children. It has been suggested that women's voluntary organizations should be involved in arranging useful educational and recreational work programmes for women in prison.

(3) *Suicides:* Suicide is a 'reaction to problems that apparently cannot be solved in any other way—a final response which a human being makes to inner emotional distress'. Cultural patterns, socio-economic conditions and group activities act as inhibiting or encouraging factors for suicides. In India the earliest instituionalized form of suicide for women was *sati,* which arose out of a social system that degraded widows. It was legally banned in the 19th century.

The overall incidence of suicide by women was reported to be higher than that for men in 1966 and 1969. In 1970, 41.4% of those who committed suicide were women. The highest incidence of suicide among women has been found in the age group 15 to 34, followed by the 35 to 54 age group. The causes of suicide have generally been found to be despair over dreadful diseases, quarrels with parents-in-law, and quarrels with married partners. While there has been no national survey of the causes of suicide, the increasing incidence of female suicides on Gujarat resulted in the appointment of an Enquiry Committee, which found that the number of women committing suicide was larger than men when the causes were physical, mental, social, and domestc, while the proportion of men was higher when the cause was economic. About 62% of women who committed suicide were illiterate and the large majority were married. The Enquiry Committee emphasized child marriage, lack of freedom in the choice of partners, and joint family relationships as the major causes of female suicide. Two earlier surveys of suicides (Bombay State 54-57, and Saurashtra 52-55) had also found the rate of female suicide to be higher in certain districts of Gujarat.

In our view, the increasing burden of economic insecurity and the breakdown of the family economy in the absence of social security and adequate employment opportunities explain the recent cases of women committing suicide along with their children. Suicides thus represent a serious malaise in social organization which may increase if life becomes harsher with increasing poverty and destitution.

(4) *Unmarried Mothers:* One of the causes of a high suicide rate found by the Suicide Enquiry Committee was illegitimate pregnancies. Before the passing of the Medical Termination of Pregnancy Act, 1971, unmarried mothers had either to risk their lives through criminal abortions or become destitutes or prostitutes. While some illegitimate pregnancies are caused by rape, most are due to unhappy or maladjusted family life, broken homes, or sexual ignorance. We met some of these women whose lives had been wrecked completely by the refusal of the family to accept or assist them in any manner. In one case the father had ordered the girl's death and her escape to a women's home was arranged by a village school teacher. The number of such homes are most inadequate, nor are they known to most people.

Since this problem is already on the increase with growing urbanization and the disintegration of traditional social norms, we feel that it requires much greater attention that it has received so far from official agencies and voluntary welfare organizations. It is important to collect information, provide counselling and assistance to these women to rehabilitate them in their families and society.

(5) *Aged Women:* Traditional Indian society had ensured the

care of aged persons through the joint family. But disintegration of this pattern of family organization and values have left a large number of aged women economically helpless. We found many such women to destitute homes because no other homes were available for them. They are seldom visited by the family.

Though a few State Governments are operating schemes for old age pensions, reports indicate that the amounts are very meagre and reach very few persons. Illiteracy and helplessness of the recipients are exploited by intermediaries who charge commissions for help in obtaining the pension. Greater care and attention to this problem by state and voluntary agencies is necessary, because aged women are being increasingly regarded an encumbrances by their families in the changing milieu.

(6) *Destitute Women:* The number of destitute women has been increasing in recent years because of poverty, loss of employment and breakdown of the family. We met many of them in both rural and urban areas. Many of them are widows or deserted wives who swell the ranks of beggars or are exploited for immoral traffic to support themselves and their children. We believe that the government's estimate that about 100,000 women in the age-group 20-44 become destitute every year falls short of the reality. Institutionalized services for them are highly inadequate, in both numbers and types of services provided for rehabilitation.

Conclusion

Our review indicates that society has failed to frame new norms and institutions to enable women to fulfil the multiple roles expected of them in India today. The majority do not enjoy the rights and the opportunities guaranteed by the Constitution. Increasing dowry and other phenomena, which lower woman's status further, indicate a regression from the norms developed during the Freedom Movement. The content analysis of periodicals in regional languages revealed that concern for women and their problems has suffered a decline in the past two decades. The new social laws have remained unknown to the large mass of women.

While social attitudes and institutions cannot be changed rapidly, this process can be accelerated by deliberate and planned efforts. Responsibility for this acceleration must be shared by the state, the community, and all who believe in the equality of women. We urge all of them to mobilize public opinion and strengthen social efforts against oppressive institutions like polygamy, dowry, child marriage, ostentatious expenditure on weddings and to mount a compaign the increase women's awareness of their legal rights. The mass media, which we find have contributed little to changing attitudes in the needed direction, or in conveying basic knowledge to women about their rights and responsibilities, should be activised for this purpose. Films and advertising should seriously consider the complaint made to us repeatedly, that they are degrading the image of women by using them as sex symbols, and contributing to the increase in sex crimes and deviant behaviour that threaten women's status in society.

9

Educational Development

Education has been regarded both as an end in itself and as a means of realizing other desirable ends. It develops the personality and rationality of individuals, qualifies them to fulfil certain economic, political, and cultural functions and thereby improves their socio-economic status. It has been recognized as a major instrument which societies can use to direct the process of change and development towards desired goals. It provides for vertical mobility and can thereby help to equalize status between individuals coming from different social strata. The Universal Declaration of Human Rights regards it as one of the basic rights of every human being.

The movement for improving women's status all over the world has always emphasized education as the most significant instrument for changing women's subjugated position in society. The Indian social reformers of the nineteenth century also accepted this view. Their aim, however, was to use education to make women more capable of fulfilling their traditional roles as wives and mothers and not to make them more efficient and active units in the process of socio-economic or political development. The colonial authorities generally supported this limited view of women's education. The expansion of education and health services in the twentieth century, however, precipitated a need for women 'teachers' and doctors and resulted in the incorporation of these two non-familial vocations in the programmes for women's education.

The attainment of independence and the constitutional guarantee of equality introduced new dimensions with the call on women to play multiple roles in the polity, the economy, and the society. In the years after the second world war, international agencies also emphasized the role of education as an instrument that can equip women to build the new social order. In spite of this new emphasis, however, attitudes to women's education in India have displayed an ambivalence between the traditional, limited view on the one hand and this broad new concept on the other and it is this ambivalence which has influenced academic planning, allocation of resources and development of values in society, both for men and women.

Progress of Women's Education : Quantitative Aspects

We have examined women's educational development (1) by quantitative indicators like enrolment, outturn, educational facilities, literacy rates, and total stock of educated women, and (2) in the light of the stated national objective of integration of women as equals of men in all aspects of national development.

(1) *Enrolments* : The constitutional directive to provide free and compulsory education for all children up to the age of 14 years has remained unfulfilled till now. Educational experts admit that this failure is mainly due to the slow progress of education among girls. Scheduled Castes, and Scheduled Tribes. In the age group 6-11 only 66% of the girls were in schools at the end of the Fourth Plan period. In the age group 11-14, this figure was only 22%. The comparative figures for boys were 100% and 48% respectively.

When compared to the progress of women's education in the pre-independence period, however, the development of women's education in the post-independence period has been phenomenal. The expansion of women's education, which began at the primary stage, was also mostly confined to that stage only in the earlier period. In 1947, the number of girls enrolled in primary schools (3,475,165) represented 83% of all the girls in the educational system. The middle schools had an enrolment of only 321,000 and represented 9% of the total enrolment. The secondary schools with their enrolment, of 281,000 represented only 7% of the total enrolment; and even though the Indian universities had proved to be more liberal than their western counterparts in admitting women, their enrolment in higher education (23,000) was only less than one-half of 1% of the total enrolment. The number of girls per 100 boys at different levels in 1947 was 36 at the primary level, 22 at the middle level, 14 at the secondary level, and 19 at the university level. By 1973-74, the number of girls enrolled at different stages as well as their proportion to boys had increased tremendously. At the primary level, girls enrolled numbered over 24.4 million (ratio 62 per 100 boys), at the middle level, over 4.5 million (ratio 43), at the secondary level, over 2.3 million (ratio 36) and in colleges and universities, about 0.9 million (ratio 31). The distribution of all girls enrolled between different stages of the educational system also changed during this period. By 1970-71, 73% were in primary schools, 14% in middle schools, 7.3% in secondary schools, 2.4% in universities and colleges, and 3.3% in professional schools.

In spite of this unprecedented advance, the overall situation left a good deal to be desired. Some of the major weaknesses of the position were the following :

(1) In classes I to V, one girl out of three is out of school. The drop-out rate is also high—of every 100 girls enrolled in class I, only about 30 reach class V.

(2) In classes V to VIII, only one girl out of five is at school. The steep fall from an enrolment of 66% of the population in the age group 6-11 to 22% in the age group 11-14 indicates the tremendous drop-out rate between the primary and the middle stages.

(3) At the secondary stage, the proportion of girls enrolled drops to only 12% of the population in the age group 14-17 which implies that only one girl out of eight is in school. Secondary education, even now, is largely confined to the upper and the middle classes in urban areas. In the rural areas, it is mainly utilized by well-to-do families, particularly from the middle classes. According to the Educational Survey of 1965, less than 17% of rural children in secondary schools were girls.

(4) At the university stage, the proportion of girls is higher at the post-graduate than at the under-graduate level. In professional education, women have substantial enrolments in teaching, medicine, and fine arts but meagre ones in commerce, law, agriculture, or engineering. Higher education of women is even more confined to urban upper and middle classes.

(5) The National Committee on Women's Education (1958-59) had been perturbed by the widening gap in the education of boys and girls and recommended special programmes and efforts to close this gap in as short a time as possible. As a result of special efforts, girls, enrolment was stepped up from 1960. We regret to observe, however, that these efforts were slackened after 1966. The quinquennial growth rate in enrolment of girls declined at the primary stage from 56.1% in 1961-66 to 30.7% in 1966-71. At the secondary stage, the decline was from 70.6% to 30.5%. At the university stage, however, the decline was relatively less, from 109.4% to 78.4%. In professional and special schools the decline was from 74.6% to 34.6%. This is a matter of deep concern.

(6) While enrolment is generally regarded as the main indicator for measuring educational progress, the problems of wastage and stagnation impose certain limitations. The all-India average of drop-outs at different stages of the school system has always been higher for girls than for boys. The Education Commission had found this to be 62% at the lower primary stage as against 56% for boys. At the higher primary stage, it was 34% as against 24% for boys. A later study found the rate of wastage and stagnation to be 62.3% for boys and 71.3% for girls in primary and middle schools, the maximum difference being in grades I and II.

(2) *Outturn* : In the outturn of students from students from and the university system the most significant features are the slower rate of increase in number of girls per thousand boys who pass the matriculation and higher secondary examinations and the much faster rate of increase at the university stage, particularly at the first degree level. The gap between qualified men and women

is declining more rapidly in higher education than at the school level. Since higher education in India is still confined to a small minority, the impact of this trend on the educational development of women as a whole is marginal. During 1947-48 to 1965-66, the number of girls per thousand boys passing the matriculation examination increased from 12 to 31. At the first degree level, the increase has been from 18 to 43, at the second degree from 14 to 37 and for doctorates from 4 to 19. For professional degrees the increase was from 9 in 1950-51 to 16 in 1965-66.

In professional education, the only courses open to women before independence were medicine, education, nursing and law. Admission to engineering and technology became possible only after 1948. Considering this late start, women's success in these courses has been significant, though their representation in other professional fields still remains very low. Similarly, women's entry into research was mainly a post-independence development and their progress at this level is satisfactory. The earlier widespread beliefs that girls have less aptitude and intelligence than boys for higher studies, particularly in subjects like mathematics or science, has been disproved by their success, which often outstrips that of boys, in various examinations.

(3) *Growth of Institutions :* The National Committee on Women's Education had advocated provision of separate institutions for girls to break down the prejudice against their education. In the period after 1960-61, exclusive institutions for girls multiplied rapidly. In 1947-48, these represented only 10.3% of the total number of educational institutions. By 1967-68, they formed 29% of the total, the number increasing from 16,951 to 230,032.

While welcoming the growth of institutional facilities for spread of education among women, we have to point out some adverse features of this rapid growth. The large number of single-teacher primary schools suffer from frequent closures because of absence of teachers, which has discouraged many parents from sending girls to school. Many girls' schools at the middle and secondary level suffer from inadequate teaching facilities and low standards, particularly for subjects such as science and mathematics, limiting the students' choice of subjects. The extremely rapid expansion of women's colleges (from 81 in 1953-54 to 435 in 1971-72) has introduced a number of institutions with very low enrolments (250 have less than 500, 55 less than 100), which are financially non-viable and provide very low standards of teaching. This has been possible because of the policy to encourage women's colleges by reducing eligibility conditions for recognition and provision of special financial assistance by universities and government. In our view, the spread of sub-standard or limited education will not help the achievement of equality of opportunities and may even damage the cause of women's education. Vigilance regarding standards is imperative and must form a part of the policy of encouragement and assistance.

(4) *Women Teachers* : It has always been recognized that increasing the number of women teachers is an essential condition for development of women education. In 1947, only 14.4% of school teachers were women. In 1973-74, their proportion had increased to 26% in primary schools, 37% in middle schools, and 30% in secondary schools. In the universities and colleges their proportion increased from 8.5% in 1950-51 to 15% in 1970-71, the highest representation being in education (23.9%), arts (19.7%), and medicine (19.2%). They constituted 13.6% of the university teaching staff in sciences and 10.8% in law, their position in other faculties being negligible. The low proportion of women among primary school teachers is mainly due to difficulties that women have to face in serving in rural areas, caused by resistance from their families, the fear of insecurity in villages, and the lack of physical amenities such as accommodation schooling, transport, and medical facilities. In our view these need to be solved on a priority basis to reduce the present imbalance in the development of women's education between urban and rural areas and to prevent increasing unemployment among trained and qualified women teachers. We were also informed that the inadequacy of women inspectors creates certain difficulties for women teachers, particularly

in single teacher schools. In some States which do not have a women's cadre of inspectors, women teachers complained of misbehaviour, blackmail, or exploitation by male inspectors.

Literacy

In spite of all the expansion that has taken place in the formal educational system, the vast majority of Indian women have remained outside the reach of all education and are illiterate. While the female literacy rate has increased from 0.69% in 1901 to 18.4% in 1971, and the number of literate females per thousand males from 68 to 435, the number of literate women has also increased from 161.9 million in 1950-51 to 215.3 million in 1970-71. The comparable figures for illiterate males are 139.9 million and 172 million. In the 15-24 age group, 29.8 million or 67.5% of the women are illiterate. In the 25 and above age group, this number increases to 94.5 million or 88.6%. Of the small proportion of literate women in these two age groups. The large majority have only primary and middle level education.

The challenge of this widening illiteracy gap will have to be borne in mind in determining priorities in educational development in the years to come. The claims of the formal educational system which can cater to the needs of only a minority, and mainly the younger generation, will have to be balanced against the educational needs of this group of adult women who constitute the workers and the mothers of the society.

Attitudes to Women's Education

Social attitudes to girls' education vary from acceptance to absolute indifference. According to our survey, only 16.8% of the respondents felt that girls should not be given any education, but 64.5% observed that girls should not go in for higher education even if they are very intelligent. About 77.5% both male and female, supported compulsory education for girls up to the 8th class. Educationists and administrators were generally in favour of compulsion for this purpose. We found the acceptance of girls' education to be far wider in urban areas, being the highest among the middle classes. A small group of affluent families still oppose it for traditional reasons, but others regard it as an accomplishment and a symbol of modernization. Among the lower middle-class, an increasingly large section is now ready too make substantial sacrifices for girls' education because of economic need, but a very large section still finds itself unable to do so for economic and social difficulties. For the majority of the people below subsistence level, poverty is the predominant factor that governs their attitude to girls' education.

A large majority of girls have to undertake domestic chores, including looking after the siblings, by the time they reach the age of 8 years. A very large number are also engaged in earning for the family. We found girls from the age of five working with their parents in bidi factories and other industries in the unorganized sector for 12 hours a day and also as helpers of their mothers in domestic service. Some teenagers were supporting entire families of sick and unemployed parents and young siblings on their sole earnings. It should be noted that girls constitute a higher proportion of a unpaid family workers throughout the country and that is a major reason for their exclusion from schools. Other social reasons for this adverse attitude to girls' education are early marriages or betrothal, though these are on the decline, except in the admittedly educationally backward States of Bihar, Orissa, Madhya Pradesh, Rajasthan and Uttar Pradesh. The social restriction on girls pursuing their studies after marriage, is however, considerably less now. The other reasons mentioned to us, which stand in the way of girls education, are inadequacy of facilities, particularly distance of schools; irrelevance of the content of education; and fear of the alienation of girls from their environment as a result of education.

The strongest social support for girls' education comes from its increasing demand in the marriage market. About 64.5% of our respondents stated that education helped to improve the girls' marriage prospects. This relationship between marriage prospects and education, however, operates in different ways. Since it is considered necessary to find bridegrooms with still higher education,

education of girls contributes to an increase of dowry, and the double expenditure acts as a deterrent to girls' education. We were told by many parents that this was the reason for their withdrawing their girls from schools after the primary stage.

Other Imbalances in Educational Development

Education is a double-edged instrument which can eliminate the effects of socio-economic inequalities, but can also introduce a new kind of inequality between those who have it and those who do not. Apart from the sharp increase in the number of illiterate women and the disparity in educational development between rural and urban areas, there are severe imbalances in educational development between advanced and backward classes and between regions. Imbalances in women's education and literacy are the consequences of these regional disparities, which reflects, to a great extent, variations in regional attitudes to women. A detailed analysis of State-wise progress in women's education at different levels revealed that while all of them have made rapid progress, the rate of progress has been uneven between different States. While Bihar and Rajasthan show uniformly lowest performance at all levels, States such as Andhra Pradesh, Assam, Maharashtra, Karnataka, Uttar Pradesh, Himachal Pradesh, Manipur and Tripura have achieved a higher rate of progress at the primary level. The only States where progress of enrolment at both primary and middle levels have been equally high are Jammu and Kashmir, Kerala, Nagaland, Delhi and Tamil Nadu. The case of West Bengal is rather unique, as it has merely maintained its position at the primary level and lost ground at the middle level during this period. At the secondary level only Kerala, Tamil Nadu, and Delhi registered definite progress. At the university level, the majority of the States registered a distinct improvement, but progress in vocational and technical courses at the school level, has been slow and even static in many States, with the exception of Assam, Maharashtra and Delhi. Progress in professional and technical education at the university level is marginal in all States. This is not conductive to the diversification of women's education or to the employment of educated women.

While we found a significant correlation between the growth of girls' education and the female literacy rate, no such significant relationship could be established between girls' education and (1) per capita income of the State; (2) density of population; and (3) sex ratio. Female literacy rate, in turn, in influenced greatly by population composition. Cities and regions with a high proportion of Muslim or Scheduled Castes and Tribes are marked by low literacy rates, while those with a relatively high percentages of Christians have a high literacy rate. While there is a big gap in urban and rural literacy rates, broadly speaking, the southern States have always maintained a higher rate of female literacy.

Apart from the lower literacy rate among Muslim women, our survey of minority communities definitely revealed that the number of Muslim women with no formal education continues to be very high even in those States which have otherwise progressed considerably in the development of women's education (e.g. Kerala). Similarly, women of Scheduled Castes and Scheduled tribes continue to lag behind other women and the men in their own communities very greatly in both literacy and education. According to the census of 1961, the proportion of illiterate Scheduled Caste women was 975 per thousand of their female population in rural areas and 900 in urban areas (the comparable figures for males being 866 and 696). The large majority of the small literate group are literate without educational level.

The influence of these sociological factors on women's education reduces the value of national or State averages in assessing educational progress. Female literacy rates in different districts of the same State very sometimes from 6.4 to 29.5% (Andhra Pradesh); 4.8 to 33.8% (Uttar Pradesh); 4% to 31.4% (Madhya Pradesh). In our opinion, plans for educational development which do not take these social and regional imbalances into account, will intensify inequalities between different sections of the population. It is necessary to identify factors responsible for them and seek their removal with the aid of special programmes.

Co-Education

Co-education represents a controversy of longstanding in Indian education. While arguments in its defence from the point of view of fuller utilization of resources and economy are gradually gaining ground, it has been generally objected to by the defenders of women's education out of an apprehension that social prejudices against women's education can be removed more easily if girls are taught in separate institutions. We found continued evidence of this divergence of view during our investigation. Communities which observe *purdah* naturally demand separate schools. There was, however, no such demand in Kashmir.) In some areas this resistance to co-education is higher among Hindus than Muslims. We also found this resistance to be more of an urban middle-class phenomenon, explained by the increasing indiscipline and rowdyism in institutions for secondary and higher education. The under-privileged classes, whether in urban or rural areas, do not have such objections to co-education. A few argument in favour of co-education coming even from an educationally and socially backward State like Bihar is that co-educational institutions provide better teaching standards and show better performance of students. An opinion poll among officials, from Directors of Public Instruction to field staff working in rural areas, elicited a strong support for co-education at the primary and middle levels.

In our opinion, the considerations of efficiency, economy and equal opportunities require the acceptance of co-education as a long-term policy. However, in view of the divergent social attitudes, we recommend:

(1) its adoption as the general policy at the primary level;
(2) provision of separate schools at middle and secondary levels in areas where there is a great demand, along with an effort to persuade public opinion in favour of co-education;
(3) its adoption as a general policy at the university level, discouraging opening of new colleges exclusively for girls;

(4) removal of ban on admission of girls to all-boys' institutions;
(5) vigilance regarding required standards in all exclusive institutions for girls;
(6) acceptance of the principle of mixed staff as the condition of recognition for all mixed school—to be reviewed a few years after implementation; and
(7) provision of separate toilets and retiring rooms for girls in all mixed institutions.

Curricula

The traditional view regarding women's education had resulted in an emphasis on different curricula for girls, with accent on subjects' which were considered specially suitable for them such as domestic science, needle-work, or fine arts. This also resulted in failure to provide subjects such as sciences and mathematics in most girls' institutions. This practice was challenged by the Committee on Differentiation of Curricula for boys and girls (1964) which recommended a common course at all levels to counteract the influence of traditional attitudes which regard certain tasks as 'manly' and others as 'womanly'. The Education Commission (1966) endorsed these recommendations. We found wide acceptance of this new trend of thought, but some States continue to prescribe different curricula for boys and girls.

We recommend a common course of general education till the end of class X with all optional courses open to boys and girls. Simple needle craft, music and dancing should be taught to all children at the primary stage. From the middle stage, variations may be permitted under work experience with no compulsion or exclusion for students of either sex. Vocational and technical courses in classes-XI and XII should be open to girls.

Pre-primary School

Good pre-school education helps children to overcome their environmental disadvantages and to develop egalitarian values as they are unaware of differences of caste, class, creed, or sex at this age. We were greatly impressed by the achievement of the rural Balwadis in this respect. These pre-primary schools also help to relieve mothers of small children and increase the chances of schooling for older girls. We recommend the provision of three-year's pre-school education for all children and special efforts to increase the number of Balwadis in rural areas and in urban slums. They should be located as near as possible to the primary and middle schools of the locality.

Primary and Middle Level Education

We recommend (1) provision of primary schools within walking distance from the home of every child within the next five years: (2) establishment of Ashram or residential schools to serve clusters of villages scattered in difficult terrains; (3) mobile schools for children of nomadic tribes, migrant labour, and construction workers; (4) sustained propaganda by officials and non-officials to bring every girl into school; and (5) provision of incentives (including mid-day meals, free uniforms, scholarships and stipends, free supply of books and special awards or recognition to the community, teachers, students) in order to prevent dropouts: (6) provision of at least two teachers in every school and raising the proportion of women primary teachers to 50 or more; (7) adoption of the multiple-entry system and a system of part-time education for girls who cannot attend school continuously on a full-time basis: (8) provision of some space in every school for the care of younger siblings who are the charges of school-going girls: and (9) provision of sex education from the middle stage in schools. An expert group should be appointed to prepare graded teaching material for this purpose.)

We recommend (1) free education for all girls up to the end of the secondary stage (2) improving teaching facilities in science, mathematics and commerce; (3) introduction of job-oriented work-experience relating it to the needs, resources, and employment potential of the region; (4) adequate arrangements for co-curricular activities; and (5) greater provision of need-cum-merit scholarships and hostel facilities for girls.

Higher Education

While progress of women in this sector has not been an unsatisfactory as at the school stage, we disagree with the view which considers higher education of girls as a waste because many of them do not use their knowledge for any social purpose. It is for the society to provide greater opportunities for such educated women to be of social use by utilizing their talents for social and national development. We therefore recommend (1) development of more employment opportunities, particularly of a part-time nature; and (2) improvement in employment information and guidance services for women entering higher education.

Non-formal Education

The greatest problem in women's education in India today is the provision of some basic education to the overwhelming majority who have remained outside the reach of the formal system because of their age, social disabilities on the literacy gap. In order to integrate women in the process of national development, it is imperative to provide some education to the vast mass of illiterate and semi-literate women in the 15-25 age group. The government's efforts in the field of adult literacy and education have been rather ineffective so far; and even the non-formal training programmes such as functional literacy for women and non-student youth, show surprising biases by drawing distinction in educational content for men and women and emphasizing family life, health, nutrition, and child care for the latter. In our view, these distinctions have now become meaningless, since a proper management of family life requires joint efforts of men and women. At the same time, women's needs for vocational and occupational skills have become even greater than those of men. The greatest handicap of these programmes, however, is their *ad hoc* approach and the lack off co-ordination between different agencies that take up such programmes. There is considerable wastage of resources on duplication of administrative machinery. What is necessary, now, is to design a non-formal system of education using all available educational resources in the community (e.g. teachers, health service personnel, agricultural extension, workers, successful farmers, mechanics, welfare workers, and other educated persons). The system should be continuous and emphasize learning useful things in spare time, the object being to provide women with easy access to information and use of information for better participation in social life. Functional literacy would certainly have to form the core of the package.

In our view, the organization and management of this programme for women could be entrusted to the women's panchayats that we have recommended. Government's role should be limited to providing technical guidance and advice, permitting government functionaries at the local level to participate in the programme and supportive assistance in the form of literature and reading material, and development of basic libraries in villages and slum areas. We recommend concentration of government efforts on providing this infrastructure.

Equality of Sexes as a Major Value to be Inculcated Through the Educational Process

The educational system is the only institution which can counteract the deep foundations of the inequality of the sexes that are built in the minds of men and women through the socialization process. It must make a deliberate, planed, and sustained effort to replace the traditional value system, based on inequality, by the new value system which accepts equality of the sexes. Unfortunately, the educational system, instead of accepting this responsibility, has helped to perpetuate traditional prejudices through its curricula, classification of subjects on the basis of sex and the unwritten code of conduct enforced on the pupils.

10

Political Status

The Political Status of women can be defined as the degree of equliity and freedom enjoyed by women in the shaping and sharing of power and in the value given by society to this role of women. The recognition of women's political equality in the Indian Constitution was a radical departure, not only from the inherited norms of traditional Indian society, but also from the political norms of most advanced countries at that time. The two major forces which acted as catalysts in the achievements of political equality of women were the national movement and the leadership of Mahatma Gandhi.

The nineteenth century reform movements had limited their efforts to improving the position of women within the traditional family structure. The turn of the century, however, saw a minority of women participating voluntarily in social welfare activities outside their homes, particularly in the cause of women's education, welfare of the weaker sections in society and relief to distressed persons. A still smaller group participated in the revolutionary movement. The early twentieth century saw the birth of women's organizations and the beginnings of the demand for political rights. In 1917, a deputation of Indian women led by Shrimati Sarojini Naidu presented to the British Parliament a demand for the enfranchisement of women on the basis of equality with men. The Reforms Act of 1921 extended the franchise only to wives who had property and education. The foreign rulers could not believe that Indian society would ever regard women as equal partners of men. Nor did they regard women as a separate political force.

In sharp contrast to such attitudes was that of Mahatma Gandhi. He had declared himself to be uncompromising in the matter of women's rights'. He believed that women had a positive role to play in the reconstruction of society, and that the recognition of their equality was an essential step to bring about social justice. He had also extended his continued and unqualified support to the ennfranchisement of women. This, added to the massive participation by the women in the Freedom Movement, had a direct impact on the political and social elite, including women of these classes. In 1930, a meeting of representative women's organizations demanded immediate acceptance of adult franchise without sex discrimination. Though rejected by government, the Karachi Session of the Indian National Congress in 1931 accepted the demand and committed itself to women's political equality, regardless of their status and qualifications. This promise was redeemed after independence, when the Constitution pledged the nation to the principles of equality and dignity of the individual, and proclaimed the fundamental right of women to political and legal equality and guaranteed non-discrimination in employment and office under the state.

In examining the impact of these rights in the years since independence, our basic position is the same as that of Mahatma Gandhi who looked upon them as instruments for achieving general equality of status and opportunities and social, economic and political justice. We also propose to use three main indicators to assess the political status of women, *viz.*, (1) participation in the political process as voters and candidates in elections; (2) political attitudes such as awareness, commitment and involvement in politics and autonomy inn political action and behaviour; and (3) their impact on the political process.

Participation as Voters and Candidates in Elections

Election statistics indicate a general trend of increase in the turnout of women voters. Their percentage increased from 46.6% in 1962 to 55.4% in 1967 and 49.1% in 1971, when there was a general decline in participation of all voters. The difference between percentage turnout of men and women voters declines from 15.4% to 11.8% during this nine year period. The States of Orissa, Bihar, Madhya Pradesh, Rajasthan, Uttar Pradesh and Himachal Pradesh which are generally known for the educational and social backwardness of their women have had persistently low mobilization of women voters during elections. While States with a high literacy rate show a higher mobilization of women, it is not possible to establish a similar correlation between education or economic development and exercise of franchise by women. Patterns of political behaviour from different regions indicate influences of various inter-related factors such as the social status of women, their economic position, the cultural norms, and the overall regional outlook towards women's participation in the wider society.

In the case of candidates, the difference between men and women is much sharper. For the Lok Sabha, only 17% of the total seats were contested by women in 1971, the highest so far. As compared to the total number of candidates, women have never exceeded 4%. Interestingly enough, the maximum number of candidates are found in Uttar Pradesh, Bihar, and Madhya Pradesh, where the general mobilization of women voters has been consistently low. This indicates that there is no correlation between the level of women's participation and the selection of women candidates. Punjab, where women voters have outstripped the men in the urban areas, had an extremely poor number of candidates. Kerala and Maharashtra, with high level participation, show a slow increase in the number of candidates over the years, and West Bengal a sudden one in 1971. But the most visible trend is of stagnation or even decline in their number in most States. Karnataka, which is not a backward State, did not put up a single woman candidate in three of the general elections, and only one in the other two. Women in Manipur, Andhra Pradesh, Tamil Nadu, Karnataka and Orissa were extremely vocal in criticizing the political parties for not sponsorinng women candidates. In their view, the small number of candidates represented not the aspirations of women, but the indifference of political parties.

Apart from election data, our discussion with different groups of women lead to certain general conclusions:

(1) The steady increase of women voters at each election shows that the response of women to the political rights conferred on them by the Constitution is improving. Keeping other things equal, development of literacy, and mass communication may help to draw an even larger number of women into the political mainstream.

(2) While there has been a substantial number of new entrants among women candidates, a large number of the older ones have also dropped out from active participation in politics. Where these come from families with long political traditions, such drop out indicates a degree of disillusionment with the political process.

(3) Muslims and tribal women show a lower level of participation, both as voters and as candidates, although there are exceptions to this rule. Our survey of Muslim women indicates that a large number of the respondents had also voted in the previous election. We also met tribal women in Tripura, Meghalaya and Bastar (M.P.) who, though not formally educated, took a keen interest in politics and participated regularly.

(4) Women of the intermediate and scheduled castes have a higher participation rate. We met many women from these communities in villages in different States and found them determined to participate in elections.

(5) Rural-urban difference in voting participation of women is narrowing down, though the belief in the lower participation of rural women still remains widespread. Our investigations indicate that urbanization does not have much influence on women's participation in politics. On the other hand, urban women, particularly those from the middle classes, plead that domestic duties prevent their participation.

(6) Awareness of the power that the right of franchise gives to them is far more widespread among women than is generally believed. We found evidence of this even among Muslim, tribal and Scheduled Caste women in villages of Madhya Pradesh, U.P., and Tripura. Most of these women were also aware of the reasons for the secrecy of the ballot and observed that this permitted them to exercise their independent judgment in voting.

(7) There is a general feeling that political parties have neglected their task of politically educating and mobilizing women adequately.

(8) The majority of women candidates come from relatively well-to-do families, with a sprinkling of members of old princely houses. Most of them are educated though the levels of their education vary. A smaller group comes from families with fairly long traditions of political activity. Consequently they are more articulate and have continued in the struggle for power for a longer period. The larger group are new entrants, with no previous political experience; and their entry into the political arena has been through elections only.

(9) Factors which deter women from active participation in politics are: the increasing expense of elections (this constitutes the biggest handicap, as the majority of women do not command any independent means); threats of violence; and character assassination. The two latter factors have increased recently and have also prevented many women from contesting elections.

Political Attitudes

Levels of political awareness of women vary from region to region, class to class, and community to community. They are conditioned greatly by the political culture of the area, the approach of political parties to women, and the quality of the local leadership. We found that the influence of education, urbanization, and exposure to mass media is not always uniform. While literacy seems to have a direct influence on both awareness and participation, the relationship between education and awareness does not always extend to participation. Political awareness of women also does not differ significantly between urban and rural areas.

On the whole, working women, including professionals, have greater awareness but this is not always reflected in participation. Nor is there any positive relationship between higher socio-economic status and political awareness. Some of the studies initiated by us revealed that political awareness is less among women in the higher income groups, who have a negligible interest in politics, though many of the women legislators come from well-to-do families.

The influence of husbands on women exercising their right of franchise seems to be on the decline. In rural areas, the influence of village elders is still strong, but there are significant exceptions to this rule. In spite of such changes, the differences in the level of political information and understanding between men and women still continue, mainly due to the indifference of political parties to women. Women's organizations and pressure groups have also failed to provide political education to women.

There is some evidence of disillusionment among women with the political process, partly because of the prevalence of corruption and inefficiency in political circles, and also because women feel that politics has not solved the problems which affect their daily lives. About 42% of women interviewed in a study supported revolution for social progress as opposed to the 'ritual' of election. The majority felt that the greatest problems before the country were unemployment and poverty, rising prices, corruption, and breakdown of law and order.

Our investigation in different States indicates one common trend, that women are more concerned with problems that affect their day-to-day lives. They have shown themselves ready to protest against rising prices, adulteration of food, unemployment and poverty. The unity between political, economic, and social issues that characterized the freedom movement was one of the causes for the high degree of women's participation. The absence of a similar movement in the period after independence and the divorce between social problems that affect women directly and the political process has been one of the major Causes for lower participation of women in politics in recent years.

Impact of Women on the Political Process

Women's participation in politics has not been reflected in their record of success at elections. The number and percentage of successful women candidates for the Lok Sabha has been declining steadily from 33 (50.6%) in 1962 to 21 (25.9%) in 1971. The sharp decline in 1971 is due to the increase in the number of independent women candidates most of whom were defeated. The increase in independent candidates was mainly due to the failure of the parties to sponsor an adequate number of women. It has generally been found that the success of women candidates depends upon party backing, the campaign strategy adopted and the personality including the family background of candidates. Since 1952, 212 women have served in the Indian Parliament—129 in the Lok Sabha, and 83 in the Rajya Sabha. In the State legislatures, the most significant trend is either a decline or stagnation in the percentage of successful candidates.

Women leaders in the period immediately after independence were mostly veterans from the freedom struggle. They had also worked in the movement for women's welfare and development, were spokesmen of the women's cause in the representative bodies, and played an important role in mobilizing public opinion in support of the social legislation that changed the legal status of women within the first few years after independence. Some of them also helped to shape the policies and the programmes for women's development that were taken up by Government at that time. Most of these leaders, who had attained a national stature during the freedom struggle, became members of the Central Government or Parliament. In States, a new generation entered politics. Our investigations suggest that while experience of social work among women is still considered a qualification for candidates to local bodies, it has ceased to be so far entry to the legislature. We were informed by political workers that politics at the State level seldom reflects social differences at present. The women involved in State politics mostly come from the economic and political elite of States and enter the representative process, more because of support within a party, rather than through work among the people.

Women form the minority among the party workers. When elected to the legislature, they see their role as representatives of the people with no special responsibility to women. In earlier years, their championship of women's causes was concerted, cutting across party lines. In recent years, however, women legislators have not shown such concern or interest in problems that affect women specifically. This criticism was voiced by many women outside the circle of active politicians. Debates and discussions in the legislative bodies have given very meagre attention to women's problems.

We are of the view that the political elite of the country, of both sexes, has perhaps come to believe that the problems of women had practically been solved with the legal and administrative measures adopted in the first few years after independence. The very articulate debates of earlier years on women's problems, in which women members played a major role, have not been repeated since. The absence of an active women's movement and the failure of political organizations to mobilize women for the solution of their problems have prevented women from exerting adequate pressure on political institutions. The small number of women in the legislatures and their lack of position in the decision-making bodies within the parties have limited their capacity to voice women's problems in these institutions.

Political Parties and Women

The election manifestoes of the political parties agree that women constitute a backward section of the society to whom special privileges have to be granted to bring them at par with men.

(1) The *Indian National Congress* whose recent manifestoes have emphasized development of education and employment opportunities for women has been sponsoring the largest number of women candidates at all elections, but has still failed to reach its repeatedly stipulated target of 15%. In spite of a woman being the undisputed leader of this party, women's position in the party hierarchy is not particularly impressive. Though the Working Committee contains three women out of a total of twenty-one and two out of four General Secretaries are women, it is evident that, without pressure from the Working Committee, party committees in many States would exclude women. Women workers in the party complain of denial of opportunities to develop or demonstrate their organizing ability and of neglect of women's demands by the leadership.

(2) The *Communist Party of India* believes that women can be fully liberated only in a socialist system. They must play a role in bringing about the social revolution. It has, therefore, been demanding equal pay for equal work and removal of all restrictions and discriminations against women in employment inheritance of property, education and social laws. The party claims that 5% of its members are women. The National Council of the Party with a membership of 110 has four women members. Their representation on State bodies of the party is, however, uneven. The party's representatives emphasized the removal of economic dependence and poverty to enable women to enjoy their legal rights, and argued that, without fuller participation in the process of social production, reservation of jobs in selected industries, free legal aid, and greater educational opportunities, it will be difficult for women to achieve the equality to which they are entitled by law.

(3) The *Communist Party of India (M)* holds similar views regarding women and is critical of the poor progress in the field of

women's welfare since independence. The nation cannot progress if its women remain in their present condition as victims of obscurantist customs and prejudices and with limited opportunities for development. Women constitute about 1% of the party's membership with one woman out of a total of thirty-one members in the Central Committee. Their representation on State Committees varies according to regions. The representatives of the party emphasized the need for economic independence without which women were as good as private property of men. The growing problem of rural unemployment with increasing landlessness and decay of village industries threatened the security and status of women in these areas, and made them unable to enjoy their constitutional and legal rights, even more than urban women. The party suggests mass employment and mass education (including the education of women about their emancipation), inclusion of the principle of equal pay for equal work in the Fundamental Rights, and equal shares of land and job facilities for peasant women, as necessary steps to achieve genuine equality for women.

(4) The *Bharatiya Jana Sangh* supports advancement of women and special steps to remove their social and educational disabilities, without any change in the traditionally established principles of social organization. The Central Executive of the party has five women and the All-India Council eighty-three. The constitution of the various committees of the party provides for inclusion of one or more women though it has been found difficult to meet this target at the level of local committees. The party's representatives emphasized the need to increase political participation and consciousness of women since the conservation of women presents an obstacle to their development. They criticized the use of female figures in advertising and the image of women projected by other mass media as derogatory to women's status.

(5) The *Indian National Congress (O)* promises to implement the constitutional guarantees and Directive Principles of State Policy regarding women. Out of a total membership of twenty-

eight in the Working Committee, two are women (one of them is the General Secretary). The 20% quota reserved by the party for women candidates has not been filled due to decline in political interest among women and in members seeking nomination. In the opinion of the party's representative, economic backwardness and competition in obtaining nominations at different levels deter women candidates.

(6) The *Socialist Party* believes that women still suffer from social inequalities. The party's representative emphasized the ignorance and indifference of women regarding their legal and constitutional rights. A determined effort has to be made by social workers to remove this difficulty. Government and other institutions should educate men and women against outmoded traditions and superstitions. The women's front of the party has adopted a charter of Women's Rights, demanding free education, vocational and technical training, part-time employment, uniform Civil Code, social mobilization against dowry and greater scope for women in elections and party organization.

Positions in Government

Though only a few women reached the highest level of power and authority, those who did so have been recognized for their administrative skills and capacity to manage their own affairs. Since 1952, thirteen women have served the Union Government as Ministers and several have served as Chairmen of both Houses of Parliament. Many have been members of Standing and *ad hoc* Committees. In States, two women have been Governors, two Chief Ministers, one Speaker, and one Deputy Speaker. Though few have held Cabinet rank, women have held office in most of the States. Compared to their overall number in the legislature, the number of women holding offices was not low.

Effectiveness of Campaigns to Mobilize Women

Though women constitute nearly 50% of the electorate, the experience of all the general elections proves that they are not aware of their strength nor has this source been adequately tapped by any political party. There has not been any bargaining on the part of organized women with political parties for their support, except in Jammu. The parties generally tend to seek the support of the male active heads of families expecting that their wishes would prevail with the women, particularly in rural areas. In larger cities, some attempt has been made to activize women voters, making specific promises to them and using a house-to-house approach.

Among the non-political organizations, the most important are the All-India Women's Conference, the National Council of Women in India, the Bharatiya Grameen Mahila Sangh, and the National Federation of Indian women. The first two are mainly deliberative bodies and have concentrated more on welfare and relief activities. The Bharatiya Grameen Mahila Sangh works among rural women and has been active in rural development. The National Federation aims to raise the political and social awareness of women and has been mobilizing women's protest against such issues as rising prices, hoarding, and adulteration. All these organizations admit that they have not been fully successful in carrying the message of their new rights to all women in the country.

While women leaders in the trade union movement have played a major role in bringing about changes in labour laws to provide protection to women, most trade unions admit that they have not made many efforts to mobilize women to assert their legal and constitutional rights. Whenever these organizations have worked together to defend the rights of women, however, their influence as pressure groups has been fairly effective. They played an important role in the enactment of social laws after independence.

We find that, in spite of increase in participation, women's ability to produce an impact on the political process has been negligible. Parties have tended to see women as appendages of the males. Among women, the leadership has become diffused and diverse, with sharp contradictions in their regard and concern for the inequalities that affect the status of women in every sphere—social, economic and political. The revolution in status of women for which constitutional equality was to be only the instrument, still remains a very distant objective. While the position of some groups has changed for the better, the large masses of women continue to lack spokesmen in the representative bodies of the State. Though women do not constitute a minority numerically, they are acquiring the features of one by the inequality of class, status, and political power. The chasm between the values of the new social order proclaimed by the Constitution and the realities of contemporary Indian society as far as women's rights are concerned remains as great as at the time of Independence.

The right to political equality has not enabled women to play their role as partners and constituents in the political process, because Gandhiji's message to treat political rights, not as an end, but only as a means, has been forgotten. Instead, these rights have helped to build an illusion of equality and power which is frequently used as an argument to resist special protective and ameliorative measures to enable women to achieve a just and equal position in society. In spite of special powers provided by Article 15(3) of the Constitution, almost no efforts have been made to redress the unequal status of women in different spheres. The fact that the country has been ruled by a women for the past nine years is not an indicator of the real status of women in this country. Though men recognize and advocate the desirability of giving equal opportunities to women in economic and political spheres, the norms and attitudes regarding a woman's role in society remain traditional. In this sense, the new rights provided to them seem to be only concessional.

Women in Local Bodies

In order to provide greatest opportunities to women to actively participate in the decision-making process, it is imperative to recognize the true nature of the social inequalities and disabilities that hamper them. This can best be achieved by providing them with special opportunities for participation in the representative structure of local government. The present form of associating women in these bodies, through co-option or nomination, has become a kind of tokenism. The time has come to move out of this token provision to a more meaningful association of women in local administration, and to counteract the general apathy and indifference of the local bodies to women's development and change of status. We therefore recommend the establishment of statutory women's Panchayats at the village level with autonomy and resources of their own for the management and administration of welfare and development programmes for women and children, as a transitional measure, to break through the attitudes that inhibit most women from articulating their problems and participating actively in the existing local bodies. They should be directly elected by the women of the village and have the right to send representatives to the Panchayat Samitis and/or Zila Parishads. A viable relationship with the Gram Panchayats should be maintained by making the Chairman and Secretary of both bodies *ex-officio* members of the other.

At the level of municipalities, the principle of reservation of seats for women is already prevalent in certain States. This should be adopted by all States as a transitional measure. In addition, permanent committees should be constituted in municipalities to initiate and supervise programmes for women's welfare and development.

Reservation of Seats in Legislatures

Political parties should adopt a definite policy regarding the percentage of women candidates to be sponsored by them for elections to Parliament and State Assemblies. While they may initially start with 15%, this should be gradually increased so that, over time, the representation of women in legislative bodies has some relationship to their position in the total population of the country or the State. We also received a demand for reservation of seats for women in State Assemblies and

Parliament, but rejected the suggestion after examination, with two members dissenting.

Association in Important Bodies

Women should be included in all important committees, commissions, or delegations that are appointed to examine socio-economic problems.

11

Woman in India

For centuries, women in India have been deliberately denied opportunited of growth in the name of religion and ancient socio-cultural practices. At the advent of independence, women were prey to many abhorrent customs, traditional rigidities and vices due to which their status in the society touched its nadir. To be sure, the situation of women was bleak all-round. At the *personal-social plane,* women were victim of widespread illiteracy, feeble-health, segregation in the dark and dingy rooms in the name of *purdah,* enforced marriage before marriageable age, indeterminable widowhood, rigidity of fibelity and opposition to remarriage of widows turning many of them into prostitutes, curse of polygamy degrading scared rites of matrimony to a system of shameful traffic, putting to death to female children, violence used to make women follow *sati,* commercialized marriage through-dowry, and, above all, the complete dental of individuality. At the *economic structural plane,* the women were prey to economic dependence, early tutelage of husbands and in-laws, heavy domestic workload and invisible 'unpaid' and unrecognised work, absence of career and mobility, non-recognition of their economic contribution, poor work conditions and wages, and monotonous jobs which men denied to do. At the *socio-political plane,* women suffered from the dential of freedom even in their own homes, repression in some direction and unnatural indoctrination in others, unequal and inferior status everywhere, rigid caste hierarchy and untouchability. Most women were reduced to 'dumb driven cattle' and led an inhumane, beastly life. In pre-independent India, two major forces, among others, which acted as catalyst in creating awareness and hopes among women were nationalist movement and the leadership of Mahatma Gandhi. Despite their miseries and misfortunes, thousands of women of different communities and all walks of life came out of their homes to join the nationalist movement as political campaigner; participate actively in the protest marches and demonstrations; face *lathis* and bullets; and suffer galantly the police repression, privations, tortures, incarceration in prison and other indignities at the hand of the British imperialist.

Scores of women were in the vanguard of the nationalist movement. In the world ascribed to Nehru:

> "Our women came to the forefront and took charge of the struggle. Women had always been there of course but there was an avalanche of them which took not only the British Government but their own men-folk by surprise. There were these women, women of the upper or middle classes leading sheltered lives in their homes, peasant women, working class women, rich women—pouring out in their tens of thousands in defiance of government orders and police lathis. It was not only the display of courage and daring but what was even more surprising was the organisational power they showed."

Not only that women sweeped in the high tide of the struggle for independence, but they also lauched a separate movement of their own to fight for their rights. While breaking the chains of India's slavery, they broke their own age-old shackles. They fought orthodoxy, superstition and communal separation. They proved themselves of extraordinary capacities and projected a free, strong and courageous image of Indian womanhood. Events evinced that without the co-operation of women, the freedom struggle will not succeed.

This kind of participation in the nationalist movement had a direct impact on the attitudes of women. They pinned high hopes in the solemn declarations made during the struggle for independence. Mahatma Gandhi—the Father of the Nation—at whose call thousands of women of all classes plunged in the political movement, declared that the *leitmotif* of the independence struggle was:

> "to gain independence not for the literate and the rich in India, but for the dumb millions,... I shall work in India in which the poorest shall feel that it is their country in whose making they have an effective voice, an India in which there shall be no high class and low class of people".

And, Gandhiji's half of India's 'dumb millions' were women, for whom he wanted independence along with other half consisting of men. One of the goals Gandhiji wished to achieve through the nationalist movement was equality for women. In fact, his life-mission was to bring women on equal footing with men which he declared in no uncertain terms:

> "Iam uncompromising in the matter of women's rights. In my opinion, she should labour under no legal disabilities and suffered by man. I should treat the daughters and sons on a footing of perfect equality."

> "Women is the companion of man gifted with equal mental capacities. She has the right to participate in minutest details of the activities of man, and she has the same right of freedom and liberty as he .... By sheer force of a vicious custom, even the most ignorant and worthless men have been enjoying a superiority over women which they do not deserve and ought not have?"

Women were Gandhi's 'last persons' whose tears he wanted to wipe and without whose liberation, he thought, the independence was superficial. Since the majority of Gandhiji's 'dumb millions' and the 'last persons' lived in rural areas, he wished that the *Antyodaya* must seek their welfare.

With the declaration of Independence and the transfer of political power, the pith and marrow of women's movement of yesterdays suddenly subdued. Only a minority of erstwhile radical women leaders carried their activities beyond into post-independence period. Since the ultimate mission of struggle for independence was fulfilled, many women activists saw no reason to continue their activities. Some of them retreated to the security of their homes. The ordinary women became busy in the task of recovering their lost homes. Only a small section of wealthy and well-to-do women could go in for politics or enter any one of a number of professions. Barely within a year since Independence, Mahatma Gandhi—the champion of women's cause—was gone for ever from the scene. The Independence, thus, by no means automatically improved the lives of women. Several barriers—many old and many new—stood in the way of improvement in the condition of women in different domains of their life.

Without doubt, independence brought the promise of actual liberation and equality. And, in the years following freedom, tremendous changes were felt in the status of women in Indian society. Perhaps influenced by Gandhiji's exhortations and Nehru's convictions about giving woman an equal status, the first major document—the *Constitution of India*—was adopted barely within three years of independence—on 26th January, 1950. In the *Constitution*, the ideals of Indian society were very clearly laid down. The *Preamble* of the *Constitution*, which is a great declaration of the ideals and objectives that Indian people desire to achieve through the political edifice they have set forth for themselves, lays down that

> "We, the people of India, having solemnly resolved to constitute India into *Sovereign Socialist Secular* Democratic Republic, and to secure to all its citizens: Justice: social, economic and political; Liberty of thought, expression, faith, belief and worship. Equality of status and of opportunity; and to promote among all; Fraternity assuring the dignity of the individual, and the unity and integrity of the nation.

To attain these national objectives, the Constitution guarantees certain fundamental rights and freedoms such as freedoms of speech, protection of life and personal liberty. Indian women are the beneficiaries of these rights in the same manner as Indian men. Article 14 ensures 'equality before law' and Article 15 'prohibits any discrimination'. Article 15(3) empowers the State to make 1any special provision for women and children', even in violation of the fundamental obligation of non-discrimination among citizens, *inter alia*, of sex. Article 16(1) guarantees "equality of opportunity for all citizens in matters relating to employment or appointment to any office under the State." And Article 16 (2) forbids discrimination "in respect of any employment of office under the State" on the grounds only of "religion, caste, sex, descent, place of birth, residence or any one of them."

The *Directive Principles of the State Policy* enunciated in Part IV of the *Constitution,* like the *Preamble,* reflect high ideals of liberal democratic polity. They embody the major policy goals of the Welfare State. The Directive Principles are declared non-justiceable; but nevertheless fundamental in the governance of the country," and the State is charged with "a duty...... to apply these principles in making laws" [Article 37]. Some of the Directive Principles concern 'women indirectly or by necessary implication, while a few are women specific'. The *Directive Principle that concern women indirectly or by necessary implication include:* Article 38 directs the State to secure a just, social, political and economic order, geared to the welfare of the people; Article 39 (b), (c) and (f) relates to the distribution of ownership and control of material resources of the community for the common good, prevention of concentration of wealth and means of production to the common detriment, and protection of childhood and youth against exploitation and moral and material abandonment; Article 40 concerns the organization of Village Panchayats to promote self-government; Article 41 appertains to right to work, education and public assistance in cases of unemployment, old-age, sickness, disablement and other types of underserved wants; Article 43 contains provision of work, a living wage, condition of work ensuring a decent standard of life and full enjoyment of leisure, of social and cultural opportunities and the promotion of cottage industries; Article 44 calls for Uniform Civil Code; Article 45 ensures free and compulsory education for all children upto the age of 14; and Article 47 relates to raising the level of nutrition and the standard of living of the people and improvement of the public health. The *Directive Principles which concern women directly and have a special bearing on their status include:* Article 39 (a) — right to an adequate means of livelihood for men and women equally; Article 39 (d)—equal pay for equal work for both men and women; Article 39 (e)—protection of the health and strength of workers—men, women and children from abuse, and entry into avocations unsuited to their age and strength; and Article 42—just humane conditions of work and maternity relief.

The Fundamental Rights and the Directive Principles are the instruments to attain our national objectives-equality, liberty and justice. The special attention given to the needs and problems of women to enable them to enjoy and exercise their Constitutional equality of status, along with other specific provisions relating to hetherto suppressed section of society, have led scholars to characterize the Indian Constitution embodying the objectives of a social revolution.

True to these objectives, the Constitution abolished all discriminations flowing from *sex,* caste, creed, colour and place of birth. Women were placed on par with men in all respects. Women's sacrifices of the pre-independence days were rewarded by the Constitutional fundamental right of equality between the sexes. The *Constitution of India* has not only provided equal rights and privileges between men and women, but has gone a step further to make provisions for special measures to be taken by the Government to improve the conditions of women by enacting laws and establishing separate institutions. Thus, the Constitution has once for all settled the position of women in society. And, this recognition of political equality of women was a radical departure from the socio-cultural norms prevailing in the traditional India and even from most advanced countries of the world.

Since the Constitution stresses the need for promoting with special care the educational and economic interests of weaker sections of the people, the welfare and development of women received particular attention from the beginning. Nehru wrote:

> "We talk about the Welfare State and direct our energies towards its realization. That welfare must be the common property of everyone in India and not the monopoly of the privileged groups as it is today. If I may be allowed to lay greater stress on some, it would be the welfare of children, the status of women and the welfare of the tribal and hilly people in our country. Women in India have a background of history and traditional behind them, which is inspiring. It is true, however, that they have suffered much from various kinds of suppression and all these have to go so that they can play their part in the life of the nation.

In order to translate the ideals and objectives into social reality and build on egalitarian, secular, democratic society, the era was begun of economic planning, of Five Year Plans, and all its other appurtenances. And, a great many instrumentalities were brought into play. Underneath the planning and implementation of the programmes, the noble intentions were implicit: the last persons' were to be looked after first, the welfare services were to reach to persons and groups who by reason of some handicap—social, economic and physical—are unable to avail of, or traditionally denied, the amenities and services provided by the community; the benefits were to flow in the more backward and underprivileged sections of the community, and all sorts of disparities were to be removed. Women were considered in such categories of people. And, in all these years, the basic values of a society based on egalitarian ideals and betterment of common man and the weaker and disadvantaged sections of society were never allowed to slip, or, so it is claimed.

By now six Five Year Plans have been completed and the Seventh Five Year Plan has started. A close look at the performance during the first fourty years of India's independence reveals a mixed record of achievements and failures on the women's liberation front. If there are some monumental accomplishments, there are colossal debacles too. And, to be fair, it is but natural that the change from a position of utter degration of women throughout history to a position of equality barely within four decades of India's independence is not a simple case of progress.

The wise and determined leadership was able to attain a measure of national integration, establish a stable regime, institutionalise political conflict, and contain a variety of communal, regional and parochial interests. India's democratic polity could weather several storms without succumbing to anti-democratic forces that swept several post-colonial countries.

However, while ensuring the political stability, India has to pay the heavy price in terms of slower economic development. It is not to say that there was no economic development. In fact, in all these years, there was a decisive economic spurt, much greater and much intensive than at any other time since India was appended by the British imperialists to its chariot. On the agricultural and industrial fronts, the country's performance is not as poor as some of its crities—foreign and native—make out. In fact, the real income per person has gone up. But, even a steady increase of the rate of economic growth has failed to solve the problem of poverty. Despite raising the real income per person, India still contains very many 'Ultrapoor'. Even when Indian average real income is, at least, 40 per cent higher than in 1951, the Indian poor are scarcely less poor. The gap between the rich and the poor is too wide. The share of the bottom 60 per cent in income ranges from 6.7 to 14.3 per cent, while that the richest 20 per cent is 48.9 percent. As revealed by the various estimates poverty—whether striking optimistic or pessimistic notes—a vast majority of india's population lie below the breadline and the majority of these poor live in rural areas where the condition of women is worse than that of their men counterparts.

While such is the situation of gains and losses at macro-politico-economic fronts, it would be in order to see the impact of efforts on women's cause. Before we proceed, we must go by a caveat, and it is that the condition of women in Indian society has been very complicated and contradictory. So many of the recent changes in the status of women in India may not be a sign of real progress; it may just be some amelioration. An official document, *Towards Equality,* which examined for the first time the status of women in independent India in depth and detail, drew pointed attention to a number of developments that demonstrate decline and, not the progress, in the status of women since beginning of the twentieth century.

The First five Five Year Plans passed without integrating women into development process. The planners and policy makers relied on "trickle down" or "oil stain" theories of development whereby it was assumed that the prosperity in one sector, in one class, or growth at macro-level, would spread gradually to all others. Consequent upon such development ideology, women were not made participant and beneficiary in India's planned development. So the planning benefited women only incidentally and residually, and often bypassed some of their special requirements and problems. Since they were not seen equal claimants with men, the gains did not filter down to the vast multitude of women who remained shackled and servile.

The growing widespread disenchantment with the "trickle down" approach of development led the planner to recognise women as a specific critical category requiring special attention in development strategies. It was in the Sixth Five Year Plan (1980-85)—i.e., after over three decades in India's planning history, that a separate chapter to "Women and Development" was provided in the plan document. However, this, too, lacked the instruments that could help the rhetoric rise to the level of a force capable of changing the harsh realities of women's life. The Seventh Five-Year Plan (1985-90), which has now begun, adopted the same set of policies as in the previous plan; it wants to give added impetus to the ideas and efforts initiated during the preceding Plan.

Although there is paucity of data on the indicators of the situation of women in India and the national data system suffers from sex biases, even we would like to assess the gains, disabilities and constraints of women with the help of the available statistics.

Let us begin with the *socio-demographic* status of women. Needless to say, the demographic situation affect, to a large extent, the life, living and role of women and indicate to a certain degree their status in Indian society. In 1980, the world population numbered to 4.4 million mark and three-quarters of this world population resided in developing countries of Latin America, Asia and Africa. Rural women constituted the majority (70 to 90 per cent) of women in developing countries. India alone shared 684 million of world's population on March 1981, out of which there were 354 million males and 331 million females. In 1985, the total population of India touched 761 million mark of which 367 million were females and 394 million males.

A simple index which gives a comparative picture of the growth of male and female population is sex ratio which is defined by Indian Census as the number of females per thousand males. The ratio of females to male population in India has been low for a long time and this ratio has been declining since 1911, registering the steepest fall between 1961 and 1971. For example, the sex ratio in 1901 and 972; if declined to 946 in 1951, 941 in 1961, and 930 in 1971. For the first time in history of post-independent India, the sex ratio has increased during the decade 1971-81: while it was 930 in 1971, it become 933 in 1981. This is a welcome feature of the situation. But the slight rise in the sex ratio in 1981 must be treated with caution. Though the figure has improved during the last decade, it is still much below the figure of 972 in 1901. This shows that the demographic imbalance has hardly improved. Further, a detailed study of the sex ratio shows that the increase has not been uniform in the country. An overall picture that emerges from the preceding data is that the proportion of women in the population has been decreasing since the beginning of the century.

The mortality rate is greater among women than among men at all ages, but more so in certain age-groups—between 1 and 5 years and between 15-34 years. Ashok Mitra has found that Indian female babies and girls (age 0-9 years) have a much higher mortality rate than boys, and that this rate has gone up consistently between 1941 and 1971. This period also witnessed the increased mortality rate of women as compared to men in the other age groups, particularly in the age-group of 20 and 45 years. A similar bleak picture emerges from an analysis of the maternal mortality rate. In rural India, it was 573 per 10,000 live births in 1968, whereas in the U.S.A. it was 32 (1965), in the U.K. 29 (1968), Hong Kong 44 (1966), Malaysia 200 (1965) and Sri Lanka 300 (1968).

In the absence of adequate and reliable data, it is not possible to give definite causes of the decline of the sex ratio, female mortality and differential improvement in the health condition of the sexes. Nevertheless, some causes mentioned most often, may be mentioned. They are: (1) the marked preference for sons and the consequent neglect of female infant in the patriarchical Indian society; (2) the lower status of women; (3) the higher mortality rate; (4) the adverse impact of frequent and excessive child bearing on the health of women; (5) the higher incidence of certain diseases in women; (6) reproductive years being the most arduous years in woman's life spelling out hard physical labour for most for survival; (7) malnourishment of pregnant women; (8) differential health treatment and nutritional standards of female and male; (9) the sexist ideology-women eat usually what is left over; and (10) penetration of capitalism creating disparity between the sexes with regard to their chance of physical survival and employment.

The life expectancy at birth is a measure of the state of health. During, 1941-51, the expectation of life at birth was 32.5 years for males and 31.7 years for females. In the next decade, i.e., 1951-61, the figures were 41.9 years for males and 40.6 years for females. During the decade 1961-71, the expectation of life at birth for males was 46.4 years, while it was 44.7 years for females. The last decade (1971-81) has shown some encouraging signs of a somewhat higher expectation of life for females: male life expectation was 50.9 years, while female life expectation was 50 years. In 1985, life expectancy for male was 56.7 years and for females

56.6 years. These trends strike some encouraging note on the health front of women, but we should not be complacent in view of other disturbing demographic trends within overall improvement.

Let us now look at *women and the law*. "The tasks of social reconstruction, development and nation-building all call for major changes in the social order, to achieve which social legislation is one of the main instruments. It can act directly, as a norm setter, or indirectly providing institutions which accelerate social change by making it more acceptable." In the post-independent India, we have a series of laws for the advancement of women. The legislations have been brought out in order to give equal rights and privileges with men, eliminate discriminations against women, abolish inequality between the sexes, and remove external barriers coming in the way of their self-realization and development.

Some of the important enactments affecting women can be recalled in passing. The Hindu Code Bill of 1955 prohibited Hindus from contracting a biogramous marriage and outlawed polygamy. It gave the wife right to obtain divorce in certain circumstances. The Specieal Marriage Act of 1954 (for civil marriages) and amendment to it in 1976, treats men and women as equal in matters appertaining to property and inheritance Hindu Succession Act of 1956 gave women equal rights to succeed with the son and his children, to all property of the parent. The Child Marriage Restraint Act, 1976 has barred child marriages and raised the age of marriage for girls and boys. The Dowry Prohibition (Amendment) Act of 1984 (initially pased in 1961) has put restraint over dowry. The Hindu Minority and Guardianship Act has now empowered mother to be the natural guardian of child's property. The Suppression of Immoral Traffic in Women and Girls (Amendment) Act, 1986, has come heavily against flesh trade among women. There is plenty of legal protection for working women in the Factories Act, 1947. Equal Remuneration Act, 1976, guarantees women equal pay for equal work. Maternity Benefit Act, 1961, allows maternity relief to women.

These, and several other laws, have brought a radical change in the Hindu social system and many new laws, both general and special, are on the anvil. The raising of the age of girls at marriage, the recognition of the claim of daughters to inherit share in the family property, and the right of the widow to an independent share in her husband's property, you will nitice, denied the very basis of the Hindu joint family and became reality which was impossible for more than 2,000 years. And, the claim of the daughter, the wife, and the widow in the property of the family involves a sort of social revolution unseen, but fundamental to, the Hindu life. The erstwhile ideal of looking upon the husband as a God — *Patidevata* — has either disappeared or is disappearing fast. Some of these laws are the most progressive in the world and, at least, in terms of laws, Indian women are better off than their sisters in most Western countries.

Yet, in real sense, liberation of women is not merely a sum of legal enactments and constitutional sanctions. While not denying the importance of an effective legislative policy, it was not possible to bring about a change in the status of women through legislative action alone. One must acknowledge that there is a large gap between the law and social attitudes and beliefs which act as barriers in the enforcement of laws for women's emancipation. The complex system of social institutions, norms of behaviour and religious prescriptions, some of which have congealed and hardened like statutory laws, come in the way of proper implementation of special protective legislations for women. Consequently divorce remains, at best, a theoretical possibility due to women's economic dependence on men and the social ostracism a divorced woman suffers from. The scope of marriage, though enlarged in law, stands to be narrow in practice: it is very difficult to marry across the barriers. The law exists, but women are scared to seek remedy through law enforcing agencies. The Suppression of Immoral Traffic Act has been messed up defeating the purpose for which it exists. The Succession Law is unsuccessful. Many legislations suffer from gender bias and discriminate against women. Dowry has been outlawed, yet it remains a fundamental part of most marriage negotiations even today. The widow remarriage has yet to be an universally acceptable social system. The protective legislation for working women is actually beginning to work against them; employers are reluctant to hire women due to legal safeguards. Despite legislative restriction on the age of marriage, child marriage is a common practice. Though the Constitution provides for equality between the sexes with special protection for women and children, Indians, in their family life, have been governed by personal and religious laws which fail to give women their due. In spite of the medley of laws, women in India still continue to live under the stress and strain of male domination that manifests itself in the form of various kinds of cruelties to them.

Education has been identified as the major instrument for raising the status of women. Hence, with the acceptance of gender equality of access to education for women on par with men was accepted. And, the rapid strides in education during the last fourty years have affected women in a number of ways. It has created awareness among women and enabled them to be self-reliant. It has brought women in contact with the philosophy of liberalism and the democratic traditions of the West. It has deferred the age of marriage, postponed the mothering responsibility, and enabled them to seek a career. It has given rise to new equations in the relationship between husband and wife and enabled women to exercise their choice in the selection of the life partner.

Education is not available to all equally. There is widespread illiteracy among women and great disparity between male and female literacy rate. According to the Census 1981, the number of literates in the total population was 237, 991, 932 or 36.17 per cent out of which men were 158, 837, 215 or 46.74 per cent and women were 79, 154, 717 or 24.88 per cent. To put it differently, while women constitute 48 per cent of India's population, only less than 25 per cent of them are literate. By contrast, while men constitute 52 per cent of the country's population, nearly 47 per cent of them are literate. Thus, the female-male literacy ratio of 25.47 per cent reveals glaring educational disparity between the sexes. In the literacy sector, there has been only a 6 per cent increase in literacy during the decade, the figures being 18.70 per cent in 1971 and 24.82 [er cemt om 1081. In fact, the literacy growth rate had been shrinking over the last two decades—from 102.3 per cent in 1961 to 75.6 per cent in 1971 to 63.75 per cent in 1981.

The total number of illiterate females has been increasing steadily from 161.9 million in 1951 to 185.2 million in 1961 to 215.3 million in 1971 to 24116 million in 1981. With the progress of education, the sex ratio among illiterates changed to 1055 women for every 1000 men in 1911 to 1138 in 1951 to 1250 in 1961 to 1248 in 1971 to 1322 in 1981.

The gap in rural-urban literacy is very high. In 1971, the percentage of literacy for the total population was 34.1 for the age group 15 years-and-above of which it was 60 per cent for urban and 27.2 per cent for rural areas. In 1971, there were 45.5 per cent urban literate females as compared to 13 per cent rural literate females. As per 1981 Census, 29.65 per cent of the rural population and 57.4 per cent of the urban population was literate. In 1981, the female literacy in rural area was 17.96 per cent, whereas it was 47.82 per cent in urban areas.

Taking the entire intercensal period (1971-81) into account it is found that more girls are in schools at all levels of education in 1981 than in 1971. However, the enrolment figures indicate that the gulf between boys and girls exists at a high proportion. Over 55 per cent girls at primary level, more than 75 per cent at the middle level and more than 85 per cent at the secondary level are out of schools. The corresponding figures for boys are 20 per cent at primary, 57 per cent at middle and 71 per cent at the secondary level. At the graduate level, the proportion of women's enrolment to total enrolment increased from 20.70 per cent in 1970-71 to 27.70 per cent in 1981-82.

Women confront a lot of difficulties in education. Also, there is slow growth of women's education. There are discriminations in the curricula for girls and for boys.

Coming to women's *economic status*. The status of women is intimately connected with their economic position which, in turn, depends upon rights, roles and opportunities for their participation in economic activities. The economic status of women is now accepted as an indicator of a society's stage of development. However, all developments do not result in improving women's economic activities. Patterns of women's activities are affected by prevailing social ideology and differ according to the stage of economic development.

Without doubt, the scope of women's career has expanded during the last fourty years; it is no longer limited only to the household chores. They are now employed in teaching, medicine, law, film industry, public service, fine arts, literature, sports, factories, mines and plantation, just to cite a few. The rural women have been working in the field and farms who constitute about 80 per cent of women in India. But, most spectacular increase has been in the employment for women of the middle classes, who are working in secretarial and administrative capacities or as stenographers, clerks, telephone girls, saleswomen and receptionists.

But this is only part of the reality. The 1981 Census puts female participation through employment at 20.95 per cent, while in 1961 it was 28 per cent. Between 1971 and 1981, the overall Work Participation Rate (WPR) for males declined by one point from 52.61 per cent in 1971 to 51.62 per cent in 1981. For females, WPR increased from 12.06 per cent in 1971 to 13.99 per cent in 1981. Of the total labour force of the country in 1985, only 31 per cent were females out of which 12 per cent were in agricultural labour force.

The poor women are ready to accept any form of employment however arduous and at whatever wage. The most important and the largest sector for employed women is the unorganized sector, employing 94 per cent of women workers. This sector includes landless agricultural labourer, workers in traditional village and cottage industries, migrant to the cities in domestic service, day labourers, street vendors, etc. In 1971, 80 per cent of women workers were in agriculture, 10.5 per cent in industry, and 9.4 per cent in service. They accounted for 17.35 per cent of the total workforce and 11.86 per cent of the total female population. Most of this female labour force in the rural areas (92.1 per cent as per 1971 Census) is illiterate. Women and children are more vulnerable for exploitation and also earn lower wages than men — a generalization that applies to all countres. The work at home women do is traditionally devalued and is, thus rendered invisible and the Indian State refuses to treat them works.

The employers in organized sector prefer not to employ women if they are forced to comply with laws governing working conditions for industrial workers. The conditions under which millions of women workers work in organized sector is very old and they find themselves faced with many a health hazard and risk to life. Their hours of labour are long and often arduous. Women are struggling hard against occupational segregation and unequal wages. They are forced to accept the low paid jobs. Nearly 80 per cent women in Central Government offices hold the lowest paid jobs. Studies by Employment and Manpower Division of the Planning Commission show that 75 per cent of women in organized sector continue to work as handcart pullers, the sanitary servants, construction workers, laundry servitors, scavengers and so on. New technology has not helped women in several ways.

There seems to be a close connection between the employment of women in production and their proportion in the total population. Women seem to be increasingly losing ground in both employment and population since 1911. The Indian Council of Social Science Research (ICSSR) brochure. "Critical Issues on the Status of Women", states:

> "In the 40 years between 1911 and 1951, the gap between men and women in the population increased by 27 per cent. During the same period, women's proportion to the total worldforce declined from 525 per 1000 males (1911) to 408 per 1000 males (1951). In the 20 years between 1951 and 1971, the gap between men and women in the population

> rose from 8.9 million to 19.9 million. In the same period, the number of women workers in agriculture ndeclined from 31 to 25 million, while (the number) of men increased by 34.3 million. In the non-agriculture sector, women workers declined from 9.3 to 6.2 million, while men increased from 32.8 to 48.4 million. The total number of men workers increased by 27 per cent while women suffered a decline of 12 per cent — reducing their ratio in the workforce to 210 per 1000 men.

A closer analysis of the female work participation shows how women in the rural sector are affected by these trends. Women have lost ground in all industrial categories where they had been employed since 1911 and the sharpest decline was between 1961 and 1971. Eighty per cent of female workers are employed in the rual sector. The most dramatic decline in female employment has been in the secondary sector, i.e., the industries, in trade and in commerce. But between 1961 and 1971 this trend could also be observed in the traditional agricultural occupations and household industries. Whereas the number of female cultivators dropped by 52 per cent, the number of male cultivators increased by 6 per cent cent. This is a clear indication of the fact that women are losing control over land as a means of production—that is, they are gradually becoming pauperized. Similarly, the female agricultural labourers increased by 43 per cent, whereas the male agricultural workers increased by more than double that rate (88 per cent). Women are also not becoming proletarianized at the same rate as men.

Whereas until 1961 the proportion of women among cultivators had been between 289-498 per 1000 men (with the exception of 1931), this ratio fell steeply between 1961 and 1971 to a mere 135 women to 1000 men. Similarly, the female ratio among agricultural labourers had been relatively stable since 1901, but between 1961 and 1971 it dropped from 819 women per 1000 men to 498 women per 1000 men, a decline of about 40 per cent. What happened between 1961 and 1971 can be seen as the accentuation of a long-term tendency towards both proletarianization and marginalization. Even as wage-earners women generally get one-third less than the male agricutural labourer. In 1975, women in agriculture got only 68.8 per cent of the earnings that males received.

The *political status* of women "can be defined as the degree of equality and freedom enjoyed by women in the shaping and sharing of power and value given by society to this role of women." Participation in politics has to be viewed at the levels of acquisition and exercise of power and exercise of the rights of citizens. Political participation of women can be measured both as candidates and voters in general elections.

In the post-Independent India, women contest elections and are elected to the legislative bodies at the centre and in the States. They have accepted and successfully carried out the responsibilities of the high offices of Prime Minister, Ministers, Governors, ambassadors and the like.

In the first General Elections held in 1952, several women stood for the membership of Parliament as well as of the States legislatures. As many as 23 women were elected to the Lok Sabha and 19 women were elected or nominated to Rajya Sabha or the Upper House raising their number upto 42. As many as 58 women were elected to the State Legislatures and 20 were elected or nominated to the State Upper House. Thus, as many as 120 women were sitting in the Central Legislatures in 1952. In the 1957 elections, there were 27 women candidates for the Rajya Sabha and 342 women for the State Assemblies of which as many as 195 women were elected. Thus, there were altogether 245 women members in the legislatures in 1957. In 1962 elections, there were 36 women in the Lok Sabha and 18 in the Rajya Sabha. In 1967 elections, 31 women were returned to the Lok Sabha and 21 women in the Rajya Sabha. There were more than 140 women in the State Assemblies. These data show that there was spectacular increase from 120 women in 1952 to 245 women in 1957. But since 1957, the figure has not increased. Whereas in 1962, 33 women were elected to the House, the number dropped to 28 in

1980. However, the number of women candidates contesting elections has increased. In 1962, only 65 women contested the elections, whereas there were 142 women candidates in 1980, the majority of which were independents. The increase in number of women in election fray reveals women's growing desire to play an active part in politics. While there were 514 male members of national legislative bodies, there were only 28 females in the year 1980-84.

Looking at the population of women, it is clear that they have certainly not flooded the portals of Lok Sabha and State Assemblies as its members. However, the percentage of women MPs in India is larger than that of the U.S.A. Great Britain, Japan, West Germany, France, Yugoslavia and Norway taken together.

The number of female ministers in India is higher than in other countries. In addition to Parliamentary and State Assembly elections, a large number of women also contested elections and got elected to the local bodies municipalities, district boards, and Taluka Boards.

The Franchise to women has been acceded on equal terms with men. The voting figures during elections show that there was a big increase in the proportion of women exercising their franchise. While in 1952 elections, only 30 per cent women exercised their votes, it went upto 39 per cent in 1957 and 47 per cent in 1962. In the 1984 Lok Sabha elections, the women voted in larger numbers than ever before. In between 1957 and 1980, the percentage of female turn out at elections has gone up by 12 per cent and that of men by just 6 per cent. In each election less women than men have voted. However, the larger gap between male and female voters has narrowed from 17 per cent in 1957 to 11 per cent in 1980 at all India level. But in most cases, men tell women where to vote. Long back Gandhiji declared: Women must have votes and equal legal status. But the problem does not end there. It only commences at the point where women begin to affect the political deliberations of the nation."

This evinces that there was an increasing awareness in women regarding their political rights, duties and responsibilities as citizens even though on a limited scale. The fact that less women were elected can be explained by the prejudices of male voters towards women.

And, finally, a word about the *socio-cultural* setting of women's status. Social structure, cultural norms, and value systems are important determinants of women's role and their position in society. The social framework influences social expectations of the sexes both as individuals and in relation to each other. The emerging values and norms must be seen in relation to the social traditions, for, the latter shape the attitude and behaviour of members of society to a large extent.

Social structure can stimulate certain trends of change, but, at the same time, it can also prove an impediment in their path. Changes in the normative structure and changes introduced in the organizational forms of society are many a time at variance and do not change in unison. In respect of the status accorded to women by law and by the Constitution, it is found that there is a hiatus between the theoretical possibilities and their actual realisation. Religion, family and kinship, roles and cultural norms delimit the scope of women's activities due to which full and equal participation of women in society is hindered and the realisation of their full potential blocked.

Religion shapes and sustains certain images of women. Various communities of Indian society profess diverse religious faiths. Consequently, various systems of personal law exist. But because of the secular character of the polity, the State does not make any uniform civil law and makes many compromises and adjustments. Religion provides moral bases for the accorded and institutionalized role of women in society. Each religion has a store of myths and legends to define woman's characteristics, her assumed virtues and vices.

The forms of social organization that exert the greatest pressure on women's roles and status are descent and kinship systems, marriage and family organisation. The modes of descent, types of family organization, and nature of institution of marriage provide the major contours of the socio-cultural setting in which women are born, brought up, and live their lives. These institutions have implications for the status of women in society. The overwhelming majority of the Indian population follow the patrilineal system of descent. A boy is the perpetuator of the patriline and a girl is of no use in this respect. This has direct relevance to place of women in society: a girl is said "a bird of passage", "another's property", "a guest of parents house", " a thing to be preserved for an outsider", and the like. Discrimination between sexes in the allocation of scarce resources in various fields, such as nutrition, medicare and education, is linked with the greater destrability of the son. Even after marriage, a woman remains an inferior partner.

Family in India largely exists in the framework of patrilineal descent. Such families put great emphasis on adjustability in the socialization of girls. Many problems of major importance for women are linked with marriage. Various issues like age at marriage, procedures for contacting and executing marriage, customs of dowry and bride-wealth, divorce, separation, widowhood and remarriage speak about the status of women.

The women confront constraints due to distinction between men's sphere and women's sphere and between masculine roles and feminine roles. Woman is primarily associated with the home and man with the outside world. The home-makers women look after domestic chores. Women's contributions go unrecognized, invisible and unpaid. Housewives and mothers are the feminine roles. In the cultural understanding, child-bearing and rearing cannot be distinguished from feminity. The quantum of labour put by women is devalued. This division of labour leads to the seclusion and segregation of women.

Women suffer from some special problems. In a fast changing society, a slow process of adjustment in its social value system results invarious forms of incongruous behaviour. Prostitution "is the worst form of exploitation of women and as an institution it speaks of man's tolerance of this exploitation on an organised level in society. Women is viewed solely as a sex object and as an outlet for man's baser instincts. The most recent statistics on the cases registered under Suppression of Immoral Traffic in Women and Girls Act reveals that a total of 15,658 cases were registered during 1980, showing an increase of 9.4 per cent in 1981 over 1980 despite statistical sleight.

Women's poor status in Independent India is reflected from other events as well. For instance, the suicide by female is on the increase. In 1983, 41.4 per cent of the total suicides in the country were committed by women. This state of affairs has, to quote Shah, 'a compelling message for self-introspe election and for a critical reassessment of our domestic and social life, the customs and traditions which prevail in this domain and the relationships between men and women.'

Women lack channels to express their opinions. Rarely are women, even when recipients of specific policy programmes, consulted. They suffer from a great many hurdles. Most women are scared of a police station which is the last place they would go to if they were in trouble. They lack insurance against future hazards. The fruits of progress are not reaching women. The religious practices, rituals, scriptures and precepts are still the forces which continue to create women's existing secondary status in society. The traditional attitude towards women persists till now. Many leaders, intellectuals, and enlightened persons believe till today the primary duty of women to be the proper management of home.

A Pause

In what preceded, the status of women in India was analysed on the basis of some selected indicators of the social situation of women. We may pause to give a close look at the conditions and constraints women confront in India today.

The demographic data denotes a disturbing direction. There is imbalance in the sex ratio: the number of males exceeds the number of females. What is more distressing is the fact that there has been a steady decline in the sex ratio since 1901. A wide gender differential in mortality rate continues, even though there has been general reduction in female mortality. Needless to say, the health status of women is always worse in rural than in urban areas. Thus, the situation causes grave concern with regard to health status of women.

On the face of it, the legal status of women with reference to marriage, divorce, abortion, guardianship of children, maintenance and inheritance, matrimonial property and criminal law for the protection of women seems to have improved, for, there are laws on the Statute book to tackle these problems. But, in reality, every legal measure designed to translate the constitutional norms of equality of special protection into actual practice has had to face tremendous resistance from the legislative and other elites. Even after the promulgation of these laws, the protection enjoyed by the large masses of women from exploitation and injustice is negligible. The desired transformation in women's status through legislative action confront persistent issues which had constrained that role. There are lacunae and differences in the various systems of personal law in the absence of a uniform civil code. Certain outdated provisions in criminal law exist which bear little relationship either to the constitutional directives or the emerging, social reality. There is absence of adequate enforcement mechanism which had made many laws ineffective. Inadequate efforts to educate women regarding their legal rights, particularly to those who are illiterate and poor, has made these laws redundant.

Education is a major instrument for raising women's status. With the acceptance of gender equality in the Constitution, the principle of equality of access to education for men and women was accepted. It is a matter of consolation that there is a relatively faster rate of progress recorded in the education of women during all these years. But the sharp increase in the number of illiterate women despite rapid expansion of education of women at various levels, points to severe imbalance in the distribution of enducational effort among different sections of the population. Education plays the double role; it can eliminate the effects of socio-economic inequalities, but it can also introduce a new kind of inequality between those who have it and those who do not. The disparity between rural and urban areas is marked and significant. There is a wide disparity of educational development between the advanced and the backward classes and regions. The progress made by women within the formal system of education indicates its severe limitations — the system now covers only 10 per cent of the total female population. Social attitude to the education of girls vary from acceptance of the need to one of absolute indifference. There is a marked difference in the enrolment of boys and girls. Still, there are several serious problems, such as illiteracy; widening gap in access to elementary education through problems of non-enrolment, wastage and drop-out; imbalances in educational development; and ideological imbalances among educational planners and administrators regarding the objectives of women's education.

The status of women is closely linked with their economic position. "The emancipation of women and their equality with men," said Marx, "are impossible and must remain so as long as women are excluded from the socially productive work and restricted to housework, which is private." Women's participation in labour force is necessary for society's development as well as women's survival. In terms of absolute numbers, women's participation in work-force has increased in both organized and unorganized sectors. However, the majority of women workers are engaged in the unorganised sector of the economy where they work in worst conditions and are exploited in terms of wages, overwork etc. Even in the organized sector, jobs women do are of lower status. The services and professions have provided relatively greater opportunities to women in the post-independence period, but they are confined to women coming from higher strata of society. However, technological changes in some of the urban occupations like industry, trade and commerce and in public offices not only reduced the rate of absorption but also involved displacement of some labour, thereby increasing the number of the unemployed. The equalisation of wages led to retrenchment of women workers who are usually employed because of their cheapness. Labour laws began to act against women, for, the employers are reluctant to recruit women due to legal protection. Women have suffered a decline of economic status.

Women's political participation is considered necessary for raising their status. Participation can be viewed from different levels—from within the family to decision-making in different positions of power and authority. Looking only at two levels—representation in legislatures and exercise of franchise, it can be said that women's participation in the political process has shown a steady increase. However, either as representatives or voters, women could not have impact on the political process. No doubt, the position of some groups of women have changed for the better by opening to the positions of power and dignity, but the large masses of women continue to face powerlessness and indignities. Political equality for women still remains a distant reality. The right to political equality has not enabled women to play their roles as partners and constituents of the political process. In fact, the political rights granted to women have helped to build an illusion of equality and power which is used against women trying to achieve their just and equal position in society.

The socio cultural setting of women is not favourable to them. The chasm between the values of a new social order proclaimed by the Constitution and the realities of contemporary Indian society as far as women's rights are concerned remains as great as it was at the advent of independence.

Precisely put, the status of women seen from any indicator of social situation continues to be inferior to men. The majority of women are still far from enjoying the rights and opportunities guaranteed to them by the Constitution. Society has not succeeded in framing the required norms or institutions to enable women to fulfill the multiple roles they are expected to play. The increasing incidence of dowry-deaths, prostitution and suicide indicates a further lowering of the status of women. The existence of many social practices, the persistence of women's age-old problems and issues, and the neglect of the concerns of women show a process of regression from some norms developed during the nationalist movement.

It seems as the nation marched on the path of planned development, women's plight, plunder and perversion went on increasing in most areas. Not surprising, then, that the performance of India on women's front during all these years is unimpressive. These trends go to support the contentions that the development path we followed did not necessarily produce improvement in the status of women, rather it fostered deterioration. To clinch the discussion, women suffer from inequality of class (economic situation), status (social position) and power (political condition). And, despite their numerical strength, women in India are beginning to acquire the features of a minority community.

We may now turn our attention towards the recent developments that have raised new questions on "Women Question."

The Advancement of Women

Traditionally men have defined problems of society in terms of male concerns and on the basis of androcentric biases. Hence, for long, women's concerns and, problems could not be considered worthly for study, for, it was not considered of vital importance to the well-being of mankind. Naturally, therefore, there have been very few serious studies of women. But, in the past two decades, some spectacular developments took place at the international and national levels that gave a convulsive turn to the attitude of society towards women and women's perception of their own situation that had prevailed for centuries. But for these developments, women's concern would have never found the kind of attention it has received today. Let us present briefly what these developments are and what kind of direction they gave to women's problems and concerns, knowing well that all these are matters of dispute. The most important of these developments, almost without question, is the Feminist or Women's Liberation Movement of the late 1960s and early 1970s in the United States and Europe. This movement was spearheaded exclusively by women themselves which achieved a high level of public acceptance barely within five or six years of its appearance. This soon spread throughout the globe. The vital contribution of the feminists was that they posed fundamental questions, dramatized women's demands, created new visibility of women and their specific problems and concerns, brought out a distinct 'radical feminist ideology', and succeeded in making powers-that-be to carry out substantial legislative reforms in the direction of greater equality for women. The feminist movement inspired the feminist writers committed to feminist ideals and established female sociologists to respond to women's problems. Perhaps the most impressive contribution by feminists is to be found in that large and growing area of study which has come to be known as the "Sociology of Women". Hereinafter, the feminist writers started women's studies with different values, priorities and concerns and often came forward with different answers to the same question.

It is the radical feminist that first directed attention to the home and interpersonal interactions. They viewed home and family as the source of women's oppression within all spheres of society.

The declaration of 1975 as the International Women's year and 1975-85 as the United Nations Decade for Women by the international community is perhaps the single most important white, represented a turning point. It was recalled at this juncture that "discrimination against women violates the principle of equality of rights and respect for human dignity, is an obstacle to the participation of women, on equal terms with men, in the political, social, economic and cultural life of their countries, hampers the growth of the prosperity of society and the family, and makes more difficult the full development of the potentialities of women in the service of their countries and of humanity". And, that ".... The full and complete development of country, the welfare of the world and the cause of peace require the maximum participation of women on equal terms with men in all fields". It was felt that women were speaking of the problems affecting more than half of the world's population and that "the problems of women are the problems of society as a whole". An unprecedented amount of research, programmes and policies addressed to specific problems of women have sprung up since then.

In the light of international commitment, Indian Government adopted progressive policies for women's welfare and encouraged women's studies. The Internation Women's Decade in India witnessed unprecedented efforts from various sectors — to reassess the roles of women, to enlarge the information base, to search for alternative strategies for women's equality and development, and to develop policies and programmes addressed to women's specific problems.

Another notable development in the country was the appointment of the Committee on the Status of Women in India (CSWI) by the Government in 1971 to undertake a "comprehensive examination of all the questions relating to the rights and status of women." The Committee's focus was on diagnosis of social trends and response to the principle of equality, with a view to identifying more effective strategies for its realization. The Committee submitted its report—*Towards Equality*—in 1974, that is, at the beginning of the international Women's Decade. The Committee's report was a revelation of the hitherto unknown situation of women. It brought to light myriads of problems and disturbing trends which have previously been obscured. It drew pointed attention to the absence of adequate data on women's roles, rights and opportunities in economic, political and social domains. It turned the attention of middle-class educated women towards hitherto 'invisible' woman, who is really at the bottom of the ladder, exploited as she is because of class, caste and gender. Women's studies started pouring in on their concerns and problems hereinafter. For the first time in India's post-inpendence history, scholars and policy makers found their attention focussed on a great majority of women at the lowest ring of status hierarchy. Their findings and assumptions began to confront deeply ingrained myths about the status and needs of women which were largely based on the middle and upper caste role model.

Besides or so to speak, above developments, various ambiguities and contradictions were found in the very dynamics of social change. It was discovered in different parts of the world, but more particularly in developing countries, that the process of development, itself has been responsible for certain negative repercussions on the situation of women in many contexts, and instead of improving their conditions, it has, in fact, worsened them causing further process of social disorganization. It was also noted that the data and information regarding all aspects of the situation of women was found inadquate and lacking. These revelations cautioned the scholars and policy makers towards development strategies. In India, CSWI tried to identify linkage between the demographic trends with declining work participation, illiteracy and rising migration rates among women from the poorer sections of society, and stressed that the dynamics of social change and development had adversely affected a large section of women, particularly among the poor, and had created new imbalances and disparities. In CSWI view, "Disabilities and inequalities imposed on women have to be seen in the total context of a society, where large sections of the population—male and female, adults and children-suffer under the oppression of a an exploitative system. It is not possible to remove these inequalities for women only. Any policy or movement for the emancipation and development of women has to form a part of a total movement for removal of inequalities and oppressive social institutions, if the benefits and privileges won by such action are to be shared by the entire women population and not be monopolished by a small minority."

These developments changed the orientation of people towards viewing the place of women in the development context. Instead of viewing women as *targets* of welfare policies in the social sector, they came to be viewed as *critical category* for development. This recognition is reflected in the Sixth Five-Year Plan (1980-85) which contains, for the first time in India's planning history, a chapter on 'Women and Development.' This Shift represents a reassertion of the principle of equality and a recognition that the future India cannot be built unless and until women participate effectively in the process of development. Its consequence was that women could enter many fields earlier considered to be only men's preserves. Above them all, the significant development was the recognition of women as a group adversely affected by the process of economic transformation. The Sixth Five-Year Plan emphaizes *inter alia* three strategies as essential for women's development: economic independence, educational advance, and access to health care and family planning. Thus, the shift from welfare to development and the extension of women's areas of concern to the critical area of economic development represents a new dimension hitherto not accepted.

The explosion of information about women hitherto 'invisible' to planners and analysts is another development of signal significance. CSWI pointed out the inadequacy of information and data on women. Indian Council of Social Science Research (ICSSR) organized several studies and initiated a Programme for Women's Studies. The ICSSR was followed by a growing body of researchers around the country, bringing to light a massive amount of information regarding these 'invisible' women. The Planning Commission directed the National Sample Survey (NSS) to obtain better information on women. The Census of India 1981 introduced a new category of 'marginal workers'. All this triggered the social debate on women's tissues.

An encouraging development in all these years is the growth of organized articulation of women's problem by women organizations. There has been a rapid growth in women's organizations to protest against crimes of violence against women, against the institution of dowry, against discrimination in employment and economic status and the like. While many new women's organizations sprang up, older, more established organizations also became more active. All these organizations have displayed new capacity to take up women's problems, concerns and issues at different forums-media, political parties, law, academia, the bureaucracy and other professions. On the issue of women's equality and development, they have coaleseed together. Some of the older women's organizations are All-India Women's Conference (AIWC) founded in 1926 and National Council of Women in India in 1925. Most of the new women's organizations emerged as recently as the late 1970s or the early 1980s: Manushi in 1979; Karmika in 1979, Saheli in 1981. The Janvadi Mahila Samiti (JMS) set its legal and cell in 1981 and Mahila Dakshita Samiti (MDS) graduated from a consumer movement to a more broad-based women's organization in 1977. There are very few women's organizations for rural women. One such organization is Bharatiya Grameen Mahila Sangh (BGMS) established in 1955. The National Federation of Indian Women (NFTW) was founded in 1954 and Stri Shakti Jagaran (SSJ) in 1973. Women's organizations, which have multiplied substantially during these years, have joined hands in common forums to demand improvement in laws for protection of women against rape, sexual harassment and dowry, against discrimination in employment, and against the exclusion of women's issues and concerns from the curricula of educational institutions. Typical examples of such joint forums are the Dahej Virodhi Chetana Manch, the Forum. Against Oppression of Women, the Indian Association for Women's Studies, and the National Movement for Eradication of Women's illiteracy. A significant feature of the recent women's movement is the emergence of new militant and articulate organizations of poor working women. Outstanding examples of this type of organization are the Self-Employed Women's Association in Ahmedabad and the Working Women's Association in Madras. The effort of these organizations have resulted in due recognition being given to the major role played by the poor self-employed women in the survival of their families and in contributing to the national economy.

At the office level, the National Committee of Women was constituted in September 1976 under the Chairmanship of the Prime Minister to ensure; "a fair deal for women." A Women's Welfare Development Bureau was established in the Ministry of Social Welfare to service the National Committee. Special cells for women were also established in the Ministries of Labour and Employment and Rural Development. During 1977-78, when exercises began for the Sixth Five-Year Plan, the Planning

Commission appointed the Working Group on Employment of Women. The Ministry of Agriculture and Rural Development undertook two exercises: Report of the Working Group on Development of Village Level Organizations for Rural Women; and Report of the National Committee to Review the Role and Participation of Women in Agriculture. Simultaneously, the Ministry of Education appointed a Committee to advise on Adult Education Programme for Women, Ministry of Industrial Development also appointed a Working Group on Self-Employment for Women. In 1977, the Advisory Committee on Women's Studies of the ICSSR brought a brochure, entitled, "Critical Issues on the Status of Women: Employment, Health, Education-Priorities for Action."

Next major development was the organization of national conference. During 1978-79, as preparatory action for the Mid-International Women's Decade review, Government promoted a series of state level conferences, involving various non-official organizations, researchers, women legislators and representatives of concerned departments. These culminated in the National Conference on Women and Development sponsored by the Ministry of Social Welfare in Delhi in May 1979. The First National Conference on Women's Studies was held in 1981. The Conference resulted in the formation of the Indian Association for Women's Studies whose primary objective is to promote the incorporation of women's issues into teaching and research. In 1980, a group of national women's organizations and institutions specializing research on women submitted a memorandum to the Government entitled, "Indian Women in the Eighties: Development Imperatives", asking for urgent action in the fields of employment, health, education, legislation and development of national mechanism for better attention to women's development.

Another important outcome of these conferences and consultations was the involvement of the Council of Scientific and Industrial Research (CSIR) and the Department of Science and Technology (DST) in 1980 in efforts to promote women's access to science and technology.

Varieties of movements that erupted during the early 1970s created enough awakening among women. For instance, there were many movements against price-rise and corruption, the J.P. Movement in Bihar, and the student agitation in different parts of the country. These and many other movements brought women face-to-face with problems stemming from their participation in public life sensitising them specifically to women's problems.

In the early days of independence, the radical working class and peasant women participated in the various militant movements, particularly in the Kisan Sabhas (peasant leagues) in Bihar and Bengal and between 1946-51 in the Telangana armed struggle. In the process of organization of the rural poor at the grassroots, the oppression of women was highlighted.

The demand for wage parity among the sexes was raised. Protests were made against sexual harassment by the landlords or employers. Women assumed violent postures against husbands alcoholism and wife-battering. Some talked even of the double burden of work women had to bear at home and at field. The illiterate, untouchable (Harijan) and tribal (Adivasi) women took lead in the agrarian class struggle. As women's issues began to be highlighted, women in large numbers participated in socio-economic changes. Many gave a lead, be it in Chhatra Yuva Sangharsha Vahini's struggle for land amongst the Bhuiya Harijans in Bodh Gaya or in Shramik Sangathan and Kashtakari Sangathan active among tribals in Maharashtra. There was 'Chipko' movement against the deforestation in U.P. hills by contractors and forest officials. The night patrollers of Manipur marched with torchlights, protesting against alcoholism and police atrocities.

Another strand in the process of creating awakening on women issues was the emergency experience of 1975-76. It sensitised the middle-class, Harijans, tribals, and landless men and women towards civil rights. Awareness of the democratic rights of the deprived brought with it an awareness about atrocities against women and the down trodden.

A new trend of participatory development is underway. The new organizations lay stress on the ideology of participatory development and on women's rights to equality, dignity and social justice. This has led to the emergence of a new concept of *'intermediaries'*, like educational institutions, research institutions and voluntary organizations at the state and national levels which act as support groups between women's organizations at the grassroot level and the agencies responsible for development. Recognising the valuable role that nthese intermediaries could play in extending the Government's own capacity to reach at grassroot, the Ministry of Social Welfare initiated in 1983, an experimental programme for establishing Women's Development Centres in selected women's colleges in Delhi and elsewhere.

In the process of these developments new issues have been identified that make women's equality and development a far more complex goal than had been understood before. It has been realised that women's development cannot, be one way process of benefits flowing from Government to improve women's conditions. Instead, it has to be a combination of strategies that empower women to articulate their needs and aspirations and provide opportunities to enhance their participation in the shaping of development decisions.

Retrospect

It is time now to locate the new dimensions in women's studies that have emerged due to the recent developments.

(1) Due to androcentric bias, many areas of women's concern remained 'invisible'. These include women's social history, women's perception of their own situation, their own subordination and their own resistance. They have now come to fore.

(2) The feminists argued that the barriers against women's full participation in society cannot be removed until and unless men (and society at large) share equally with women the responsibilities of homemaking and child rearing.

(3) The 'discrimination against women' was defined in broad

terms to "mean any distinction exclusion or restriction made on the basis of sex which has the effect or purpose of impairing and nullifying the recognition, employment or exercise by women irrespective of their marital status, on a basis of equality of men and women, of human rights and fundamental freedoms in the political, economic, social, cultural, civil or any other field."

(4) Attention was drawn towards the absence of adequate data on women's roles, rights and opportunities. This triggered women's studies that exploded the myths about women's status in society.

(5) It was discovered that the very dynamics of development is responsible for deterioration in the condition of women which alerted the policy makers to make changes in the development strategy.

(6) It was realized that any policy or movement aimed at emancipation of women has to form part of measures for removal of inequalities and oppression adopted for the entire women population.

(7) Instead of being viewed as targets of welfare policies, women came to be recognized as a critical cateogory for development.

(8) There was explosion of information and data on women which highlighted the plight of women and inadequacy of the efforts made towards women's emancipation.

(9) In all these years there was growth of organized articulation - several women's organizations sprang up which singularly and conjointly took the women's cause at different forums. Their *inter alia* reflected women's new capacity to take up their own issues and problems. Its impact was deep at the official level too. Varieties of women's moments sensitised the people towards women's problems.

(10) Today, the emphasis has shifted from doing things for women to work with them. This participator approach has armed women with capacity to fight for their rights.

The Existing Research Material

We seek to tread our way, through the diversity of conditions, to some understanding of the situation, constraints and contributions of rural women. We are assisted in this effort by a growing body of literature about Indian women. The magnitude of the problem is reflected in the variety of approaches and streams of researches on women in general, and rural women in particular. Keeping in view the time, trends, and concerns of studies, the researches on women may be organized into two broad heads:

Early Studies

Two steams are discernible from the early studies on women. *One stream* examines the feminie ideals in India and from that discussion it discerns the attitude towards woman and her place in society. Such studies adopt historical approach to the problem and focus on the ideals articulated in the sacred texts, such as the *Vedas,* the Dharmashastras, the Laws of Manu, the *Ramayana,* the *Mahabharata,* the *Bhagawad Gita,* and laterly, the teachings of the Buddha. The *second stream* deals with the specific problems of women and with the way attempts were made to remove them through political movements and legal reforms. The early studies remained pre-occuped with the traditional concerns of women; they did not raise new questions on the 'woman question'.

Recent Studies

Looking at the nature of the problem under investigation, recent researches may be reviewed in relation to agrarian social structure and women's problems and concerns.

Studies in Agrarian Social Structure

The research material related to agrarian social structure is very vast. However, five major strands can clearly be discerned.

The *first strand* sought the causes of growing inequality in the face of massive rural development and put forward two sets of factors responsible for it: the informational factors and the socio-economic factors. The informational factors include the differential access and exposure of the people to the "technological, motivational, educational and other kinds of information". Socio-economic factors include the differential location in the existing system of social stratification.

The *second strand* tries to analyse the pattern of economic growth and distribution of developmental benefits in villages. The genral conclusion that emerges from diverse studies is that the privileged sections in rural areas have benefited more from the development programmes, resulting in widening of the gap between the rich and the poor.

The *third strand* attempts to evaluate the specific rural development measures which include land reform. Community Development Programme, institutional growth, and Green Revolution. Various estimates and evaluations give a dismal reading of the land-reform—a programme which was initiated first and failed first. The much acclaimed Community Development Programme benefited more to the rich than the poor. The three institutions—cooperative, Village Panchayat and school—were considered vital for rural uplift. The cooperatives created more inequality. Panchayati Raj established, what Moynthan describes as the "extraordinary demi-Ray". The development funds meant for it were pocketed by, or used in serving the interest of higher groups. The institution of Panchayati Raj is dominated by the high caste and upper strata. Schools did not benefit much to the poor and low caste people. The Green Revolution launched with huge funds provided a bonanza for the rich peasants and led to pauperization and marginalization of poor women.

A *fourth strand* turned around political-economy of agriculture. The studies on the political-economy moved in three directions. One set of studies measured the extent of poverty in India. The studies have revealed that the poverty in India. The studies have revealed that the poverty is more acute in rural than in urban India.

The second set of studies focussed on the extent of penetration of capitalism in agriculture in India. This generated heated discussion among scholars. Thorner, for instance, noted that there was emergence of capitalist farming in some part of the country due to Green Revolution. Some scholars negated Thorner's findings, while others supported them. Most of the Indian debate on the development of capitalism in agriculture is related to uncritical attitude towards the orthodox Marxism—the development of an agricultural capital is taken for granted. Recently some scholars have found proletarianization and marginalisation of women due to penetration of capitalism in agriculture.

The third set of studies took up the same problem on a theoretical plane with special reference to the mode of production, involving the international aspect of the question. In the process of identification of the capitalist relations and capitalist mode of production, the distinction was made between the former and a feudal and semi-feudal mode of production. In so doing, some scholars pleaded in favour of a special concept, such as "colonial mode of production." Thus, much heat has been generated by the debate on the mode of production in Indian agriculture in spite of the fact that there is lack of adequate data base to support this or that argument. And, the debate still continues even if the question still remains to be settled whether there was feudalism in India or not.

The *fifth strand* attempts to focus on agrarian movements emerging from the changing political economy. In so doing, the roots of peasant movement and unrest have been sought. It was traced that illiterate, untouchable and tribal women have also started taking lead in the agrarian class struggle.

The studies in agrarian social structure, by and large, did not focus on women's place and role in agrarian struggle.

Recent Women's Studies

Women's studies have gone through changes in various waves of history. The *first wave* reflected in the compilation of a large number of bibliographical studies. This made women an important subject for study and brought a huge scattered literature at one place. Consequently, reviews after reviews started pouring in. This reflected diversity and volume of literature available. The emerging trend was that now studies signify a new focus moving away from historical, prescriptive, and ideal-typical accounts based on scriptural analysis to a more problem-specific and action/policy relevant research.

Then begins the *second wave* when scholars became concerned with the reassessment of roles of women in society. In that process, attention shifted to the great majority of illiterate women in rural areas and urban slum-dwellers. This made 'invisible' women visible or at least, highlighted their problems and concerns.

The *third wave* in women's studies focusses on women of a particular area, caste or tribe dealing with their specific problems rather than attempting a comprehensive macro-study. The approach was anthropological.

The *fourth wave* in women's studies is reflected in attempts towards a comprehensive theoretical overview of the problems of social change. These studies pay only scant attention on women in the process of social change.

The *fifth wave* concentrates on the role of western educated elite women as though they were trend setters among Indian women. Needless to say, a small section of elite women is not necessarily the bellwether of what is happening to women in wider society.

The *Sixth wave* is visible in the feminist analysis of women's problems. The feminist brought to the fore new dimensions of women's subordination in society. It rejected that 'biology-is-destiny' ideology and argued that sexual inequalities result from a variety of factors accessible to change. It emphasized on the reassessment of functions and roles traditionally allotted to each sex within the family and community at large. In its wisdom, men must accept shared responsibility of home and children in order to allow women's equal participation in all society's activities. Domestic work, birth control, reproduction and sexual division of labour were considered to be the causes of women's subordination in society.

Given the various waves of women's studies, it would be in order to demonstrate the specific concerns of researches in social, economic and political dimensions. In the social dimension, a large number of factors were emphasized as the cause of women's subordination and low status in society. The marriage and family found utmost attention, for, the private sphere has been considered as one of the root causes of women's problems. The focus was on both the institution *per se* and abhorrent customs that have come to be associated with it. The studies were concerned mainly with the changes taking place in the institutions of family, and marriage be of Hindus, Christians, or Muslims, in particular reference to the age at marriage, marital relationship, selection of spouse, and the family planning, among others. The abhorrent customs that attracted attention of scholars are infanticide, prostitution, *purdah,* dowry, and divorce. These studies examined the legislations made towards eradication of these evils and highlighted their shortcomings in tackling the problems.

Education of women is another popular theme since 1980 onward on which many reviews and reports have appeared. Studies directed towards the status of rural women's education—both formal and non-formal, revealed very disturbing trends. The illiteracy is more rampant among women than among men. The proportion of women enrolled at every level of education—primary, secondary, higher and professional-technical—is very small and outweighed by men in each case. The women have been prey to various constraints in pursuing their education, for, many girls act as surrogate mothers, share household responsibilities at an early age, assume other sex roles, and confront parents' apathy or reluctance resulting in drop out of many girls from schools. Interestingly, education itself is found to be aggravating the sex inequality through curriculum, textbook and lack of access. Education, as it is today, is socializing women for unknown future. While it was expected that education will give more employment to women, it is creating more unemployment among married women graduate as compared to women as a whole. Without providing any alternative, women's education was found eroding the traditional parental ties.

The health problems of women is another area which attracted attention of scholars. The main focus is on access of women to recent health programmes, their nutritional in-take, availability of the pre-natal, natal, and post-natal services, and fertility and mortality rates. The studies reported the poor health condition of women due to poor access to health services and lack of nutritional diet. More mortality was reported among women than among men.

In the *economic dimension,* three themes have attracted attention of scholars: women's employment, their participation in development, and impact of technology on them. Studies assessing women's participation in the labour force reveal that the majority of women are employed in unorganized sector and their contributions to economy go unrecognized and unpaid. Even the attitudes of husbands and in-laws are unfavourable towards women's employment. There is general tendency of segregation of work by sex in the world of work. Women are, by and large, employed in jobs which are categorized as 'women's work'. Even the employment for educated women is lacking. The studies analysing implications of employment for women in terms of role-conflict and effects of employment on personality, reveal that the majority of working women express job satisfaction.

Studies focussing on the impact of technology on women indicate that they have benefited women less as compared to men. The technological innovations have differing impact on women of different classes and castes. In many cases, women have been displaced from their traditional jobs, or thrown to jobs that are monotonus and fall in the invisible' sector of economy.

Studies dealing with the role of rural women in development conclude that women are unequal partners in development and many times development goes against their interests. Neither they are beneficiary nor agent of development. They are seldom consulted on their needs and problems.

In the *political dimension,* analysts have paid attention to the women's political participation, leadership, voting behaviour, power position, and participation in rural movements. It has been surmised that women suffer from powerlessness.

With this review exercise, it is possible to identify some broad contours of research on women and where the major focus have been. It transpires that issues have been sector-specific (women and agricultural development and modernization, industrialization, technology, educational development, law, demographic trends, etc.), area specific, group specific or issue specific (women and migration, female headed households, violence against women, sex tourism, kinship and family patterns, women in home-based production, and women in export oriented industries). Women's economic role have remained most critical area for research, analysis and data collection. This has attracted attention towards the submerged economy (hidden from view) of invisble rural women. The socio-cultural and political aspect of women's status is the other area where scholars' attention has been diverted.

An interesting trend that has surfaced is that the 'woman question' has now assumed a political, international and developmental character in place of viewing it as essentially a social and cultural phenomenon. This could be possible because women themselves are gradually getting involved with the 'politics of knowledge' by using innovative techniques of data collection, research and project development. This has been well-summed up by a feminist scholar. "Women in the citadels of academia are daily assaulting the sacred cows of learning. They are questioning the historians who have reconstructed a past devoid of women or the economist with their myopic view of labour and whose theory of growth proclaiming the magic of market place has so disastrously deluded so much of the Third World."

A close look at the concerns of researches reveals that women in India after independence confront a lot of constraints in socio-cultural, political, and economic domains. Their social situation has not improved much.

Whatever researches are, they show very little or no concentrated concern with the vital questions. viz., what are the conditions of women in rural India? What are the main constraints before them? What contributions do they make? What aspects of social structure determine their conditions, put constraints, and affect contributions? How do conditions constraints and contributions interact with one another? Not only this that the studies of the past neglect these issues, they are basically descriptive, qualitative and based on elementary quantitative data. And, all this limits their scope in so far as their predicitve value is concerned and also they cannot be utilized for making broader generalizations.

In summary, then the proceding analysis of some of the selected socio-demographic, legal, educational, economic, political and socio-cultural indicators on the situation of women reveals that even after four decades of assiduous effort women's conditions continues to be miserable and they still confront immense problems in all these domains of life. However, recent internatioal and national spectacular developments have turned the attitude of society towards women and women's perception of their own situation. Consequent upon these efforts and development, a spate of women's studies in different directions were made which *inter alia* raised new question on 'Woman Question.'

Selected Bibliography

Tawney, R.H.	The Acquistive Society (1920)
Tawney, R.H.	Equality (1938)
North, C.C.	Social Differentiation (1926)
Declareuil, J.	Rome—The Law-giver (1927)
Samuel, Dill	Roman Society in the last century of the Western Empire
Lindsay, A.D.	Religion, Science and Society in the Modern World (1943)
Ameer Ali	The Legal Position of Women in Islam (1912)
Levy, R.	Introduction to the Sociology of Islam Vols. I and II (1933)
Mac Iver, R.M.	Community—a Sociological Study (1928)
Hobhouse, L.T.	Property (1922)
Bertrand Russell	Marriage and Morals (1929)
Geoffrey Hoyland	Religion and the Family (1945)
Haynes, E.S.P. & Walker-Smith, D.	Divorse and its Problems (1935)
Holtby, Winifred	Women (1934)
Maude, Royden	Women's Partnership in the New World (1941)
Arlitt, A.H.	Family Relationships (1942)
Stern, B.J.	The Family-past and Present (1938)
Sidonie & others	The Family Marriage in Western Civilization (1936)
Calverton, C.F.	The Bankruptcy of Marriage (1931)
Nimkoff, M.F.	The Family (1934)
Falsom, J.K.	The Family and Democratic Society (1943)
Bossard, J.H.S.	Marriage and the Child (1943)
Meredith, F.	Single Women—A Catholic Interpretation (1944)

Charlotte and Emil Leitner	Your Child—Your Future (1945)
Bossard and Boll	Family Situation and Introduction to the Study of Child Behaviour (1943)
Pollock, Mrs. Deighton	The Women of Today (1929)
Ludovici, A.M.	Lysistrata or Women's Future and Future Woman (1927)
Bernard, Jessie	American Family and Behaviour (1941)
Annals	Women in the Modern World (May, 1929)
Jennings, H.S.	The Biological Basis of Human Nature
Shand, A.F.	The Foundations of Character (1920)
Fishman N.	Married Women's Bill of Rights (1943)
Gerturde Williams	Women and Work (1945)
Charlotte Luetkens	Women and an New Society (1946)
Halle, F.W.	Women in Soviet Russia (1934)
Cole, M.	Our Soviet Ally (1944)
Kirkpatrick, C.	Nazi Germany : Its Women and Family Life (1938)
Munk, E.	The Legacy of Nazism
Klineberg, O.	Race Differences (1935)
Ashley Montagu, M.F.	Man's Most Dangerous Myth (1945)
Bean, R.B.	The Races of Man (1932)
Pearl Buck & other	The Role of the Race in our Future Civilization (1943)
Benedick, Ruth	Race and Racism (1942)
Hobhouse, L.T.	Morals in Evolution (1923)
Angyal, Andras	Foundations for a Science of Personality (1941)
Ford, E.B.	The Study of Heredity
Huxlery, Haddon & Carr-Saunders	We Europeans
Huxlery Julian	Race in Europe (1939)
Flewelling, R.T.	The Survival of Western Culture (1943)

Smith, G.E. & others	Culture (1929)
Luigi Sturgo	Inner Laws of Society (1944)
Spenglar, Oswald	Decline of the West, Vols. I & II English Translation—(1945)
Radhakrishnan, S.	Eastern Religions and Western Thought (1940)
Mackay, E.	The Indus Civilization (1935)
Altekar, A.S.	Position of Women in Hindu Civilization (1938)
Valavalkar, P.H.	Hindu Social Institutions (1939)
Nehru, Shyam Kumari	Our Cause—a Symposium by Indian Women
Magnus, Hirschfeld	Women : East and West (1935)
Cousins, M.E.	Indian Womanhood Today (1941)
Natarajan, S.	Social Problems (Oxford Pamphlets on Indian Affairs No. 7)
Chattopadhyaya, Kamaladevi	Awakening of Indian Women (1939)
Mark, Abrams	Population of Great Britain (1945)
Mark, Abrams	Condition of the British People (1911-1945).

[illegible]

[illegible] this [illegible] part of [illegible] female participation through employment [illegible] per cent, while in 1961 it was 26 per cent. Between 1971 and 1981 the overall Work Participation Rate (WPR) for males declined by one point from 52.61 per cent in 1971 to 51.62 per cent in 1981. For females, WPR increased from 12.06 per cent in 1971 to 13.99 per cent in 1981. Of the total labour force of the country in 1985, only 31 per cent were females out of which 12 per cent were in agricultural labour force.

The poor women are ready to accept any form of employment however arduous and at whatever wage. The most important and the largest sector for employed women is the unorganised sector, employing 94 per cent of women workers. This sector includes landless agricultural labourers, workers in traditional village and cottage industries, migrants in the cities in domestic service, [illegible] labourers, street vendors, etc. In 1991, [illegible] per cent of women